To Judy,
I hope you enjoy the
books and all the memories

Love,
Cathy
4/12/09

just a boy from home

County Mayo, Ireland
With songs, stories and recipes

by

Catherine Bourke Chambers

authorHOUSE®

AuthorHouse™
1663 Liberty Drive, Suite 200
Bloomington, IN 47403
www.authorhouse.com
Phone: 1-800-839-8640

First published by AuthorHouse 1/8/2009

ISBN: 978-1-4343-6789-1 (sc)
ISBN: 978-1-4343-6790-7 (hc)

Library of Congress Control Number: 2008902216

Printed in the United States of America
Bloomington, Indiana

This book is printed on acid-free paper.

dedication

To Tom, my husband and loyal friend.

when an old man dies
a library is lost!

Introduction

Catherine Bourke Chambers was born in 1955 in the middle of the metropolitan city of Chicago during a time where one found many hard-working immigrants from Europe living the American dream. Cathy's father, born in 1920 was the eleventh of twelve children, and left his home in the County of Mayo with only his memories.

Bill Bourke shared this entire book from memory. It contains stories told to him by his ancestors and historical facts about the Catholic Church of his era, the stripping of the land after the South gained independence and the words to an IRA song, The Dublin Trials that his father sang and, to my knowledge, cannot be found in print. There are many more songs of Mayo, folklore, poems and expressions that otherwise could possibly be forgotten or lost if he had not agreed to sit for many hours reminiscing. So much information has died with this courageous group of men and women who survived World War II and Korea. You will enjoy reading about Patrick Shannon, a Mayo man who was a hero in World War I. Also, how his good friend Michael Fitzpatrick received his American citizenship 52 years after his untimely death in Korea.

He tells of the Irish camaraderie that was already present in Chicago upon his arrival and how he got a job being Just a Boy from Home. The singing and dancing that was found in the neighborhood pubs in Chicago as he described, "Oh, the fun we had!" But, still the innate loneliness that could be felt in a room full of people for the mother he left behind in the tiny cottage, at the end of the road, in the Village of Ballymacredmond, near the town of Ballina, in the County Mayo, Ireland.

It has taken a lifetime of trials, errors and successes to create the foundation for his family that is now continuing to flourish in the great city of Chicago in the United States of America.

IRISH SODA BREAD

4 cups sifted white flour	2 teaspoon caraway seeds (optional)
½ cup sugar	¼ cup butter or margarine
1 teaspoon salt	2 ½ cups light or dark raisins
1 teaspoon baking powder	1 1/3 cups buttermilk
1 teaspoon baking soda	1 egg unbeaten

Topping: 1 egg yolk for topping (or extra butter)

Heat oven to 375 – grease pan and lightly flour. In mixing bowl add flour, sugar, salt, baking powder, baking soda (caraway seeds if you want) and stir. Cut in butter until coarse and stir in raisins; combine buttermilk egg, and stir until flour mixture is moistened.

Turn dough onto floured surface; knead lightly until smooth and shape into ball. Place in pan and smooth top. With sharp knife make a 4" cross, ¼" deep in center top. Beat yolk lightly with fork and brush over top or cut 4 patties of butter or margarine and place on top.

Bake: 1 hour and 10 minutes or until done; remove and cool before slicing.

Don't Dad, don't! Too late, Dad has blown into his pipe creating another eruption of hot, many times glowing, tobacco ash on the kitchen floor. While balancing himself with one hand on the counter and the other holding the pipe, he tries rubbing the ashes into the light blue grout that JoAnn has just scrubbed. I'm standing at the entrance trying not to laugh out loud, but it is difficult.

"Arrahh leave it JoAnn, I'll get it in a minute," says Dad with his Irish brogue. Although after nearly 60 years of residing in Chicago, the authentic musical and rhythmical sound that he brought with him from Ireland still exists. He winks at me – as if he ever had a notion of taking a rag to the floor.

An Irishman from the west of Ireland, Bill Bourke at 87 years is beginning to talk less, look down when walking, and his once bright blue eyes that reflected love, humor, sadness, regrets are now, at times, far, far away. However, there is no doubt that my father was a man's man. And, as you read my father's biography I believe you will understand the definition of man's man from his perspective. Your word is enough; this is honorable. He was not the type of father to ask us to sit down and discuss a problem or situation as a family. However, in a round about way, his feelings and beliefs were loud and clear.

I heard many times, "Think before doing; once it's done, it's done and you can never turn back the clock."

I recall the only time my sisters Peggy, JoAnn and myself were called to the kitchen table.

"Girls, I'll say this one time, don't embarrass your mother or father." We were teenagers at this time and knew exactly what he was talking about and never forgot. As I look back now there was a certain amount of fear, but there was also respect that was brought on through fear

– And fear of what? I don't know. Dad never laid a hand on me. All he had to do was look sideways and I knew what not to do.

Dad and Mom had a life similar to many couples that were married in the 1950's. Mom stayed home until my youngest brother Billy went to school. There were five of us and we grew up during the baby boom years, quite happy with whatever we had and didn't ask for what we didn't have. There wasn't a lot of money, but we were never hungry and had a good warm roof over our heads. Mom was hired back at Hi-Low as a cashier when Billy went into first grade. She was always so generous with her check. Some went towards the weekly food bill, but the majority stayed in her purse to spend on us and referred to it as "the extras."

After a few years Mom was hired at Quigley Seminary, a high school at 79th and Western Avenue as the cashier in their cafeteria. She was able to walk there and had nearly the same schedule as our school. It was great; she was home by 3:00 P.M. everyday. After we moved further south, Mom walked to Saint Xavier University at 103rd and Lawndale and applied for the position as a cashier in their cafeteria. She was hired immediately and stayed with Saint Xavier until Dad retired in 1986.

Mom cooked and baked and canned everything that Dad brought in from the garden. I often referred to it as a mini-farm, not a garden, and it was lovely, all dug and tended by hand. There would be no rooter tiller brought into our house, only the spade and shovel. I heard it said many years ago by someone who came to visit that my father could make a shovel sing as he turned the soil and counted off the drains for planting.

We had fresh green beans, carrots, onions, lettuce, cabbage, beets, tomatoes, corn, peppers of every color and shape and I can't think of the rest. I remember that the potatoes were small, but good, and the melons were huge. Every year, Dad would bring in a basket of grapes that grew against the outer fence and Mom would make her wonderful jam. My youngest brother Bill had a friend who used to lovingly refer to Mom as Aunt Bea, from the sitcom The Andy Griffith Show. Mom's genuine kindness and welcome for everyone was innate, and it all started in the kitchen.

The kitchen was where Mom was most comfortable and this is where you would find her, but I heard Dad say many times, "God help us if Mam had to take care of the garden. We'd go hungry." Mom hated the outdoors. I could never understand why she wouldn't go out and help pull some of the vegetables, especially if Dad was working overtime. She explained very simply, "I had just turned 18 years old when I boarded the train in Ballyhaunis station (also located in County Mayo, Ireland) headed for the ship that would take me to America. I looked down at my hands and swore there would never be clay beneath my nails again," and there never was!

Things have changed since my mother died eleven years ago. We lost a mother, but Dad lost his mate and true love for over 45 years. Nothing is the same and nothing is taken for granted; he is aware of the legacy that one day he will leave. Dad can sit for hours under his overgrown oak tree in the yard or on the porch, smoking his pipe. He has his memories, his children, grandchildren and great-grandchildren around him at all times, which is an awesome pleasure for a family man of excellent health in both mind and body.

Last night Dad stayed overnight at JoAnn's house, his third daughter, and was in the middle of his ritual when I walked in: out of bed at 8:00 in the morning, makes a porridge consisting of corn flakes, raisin bran, and over-ripe banana covered with 2% milk and then places it in the refrigerator for approximately two hours so it is mushy. While waiting for the cereal's right consistency, he shaves, washes, and dresses for the day. From that point on he paces back and forth, smoking his pipe, asking where everyone is at, and what they are doing, breaking sometimes to read an article out loud from the newspaper. Naps have become essential and he takes several during the day, which prepares him for a hearty dinner. And, when Dad is on "good behavior" (not drinking) always at around 8:30 PM, he eats pie and ice cream, watches the 9:00 news, and then, off to bed.

There have been times over the past years that Dad would go on a drinking binge, and he was no spring chicken at that time. I'm sure he was close to sixty years of age and usually around this time, the men of his age preferred not to imbibe upon too much hard liquor due to health reasons. However, Dad threw the theory out the window. After retirement and especially after my mother was diagnosed with cancer, his drinking increased.

I have to mention at this point that his tolerance allowed him to drink and function for another twenty years before health issues became a matter of concern. I heard him say many times,

"I'll bury the doctor." And he did, two in fact.

He would raise his can of beer in salute, quoting a line learned in school, "Men may come and men may go, but I'll go on forever, by Robby Burns."

And a song or recitation or two perhaps would soon follow, and then the lights were turned off for the night.

Dad prided himself on the fact that he was never late for work, not one minute. Since he did not drive, his only method of transportation was the bus service. He left home in plenty of time and stood on the corner waiting at all hours of the day and night due to swing shifts. It was a long walk in and out of the railroad yard, especially on the wet and cold winter nights. So, when Peggy turned eighteen, Dad bought a new car, and Peggy of course, would drive him around. This was huge! A new Buick was purchased, with cash of course. All my father's life, items were purchased with cash, except for their home. If you couldn't pay cash, then you didn't need it.

Well, a new era was here and with it came check books, credit cards, and credit checks. Money in the bank just wasn't enough evidence to provide information of one's existence. It was unbelievable; Dad had no intentions of ever driving. His intention was to have Peggy drive him around until he decided to get a license, which doubtfully would have happened. However, due to insurance coverage, it was to Dad's benefit to have a license. So, in the same week, Dad and Mom applied for a credit card from Sears Department Store and Dad started to drive.

Eventually the need for alcohol did catch up and he had to quit completely at the age of 82. As he says, "All good things must end." I am sincerely sorry that he cannot have a beer or a shot of whiskey once in a while. He enjoyed it and at 88 years of age, I don't believe in denying anyone anything. However, Dad has chosen to quit completely. He tells everyone, "I'm on good behavior." I'm sure my mother is looking down from heaven, shaking her head and saying, "Well, it took you long enough."

On this particular day, Dad is not feeling good; he has caught a cold. And, as usual with his hand on his heart and the other holding his kidneys, he declares, "It's the worst yet, no one has had a cold as bad as this one!" Once, maybe twice a year Dad will come down with the fl u and Peggy, being the oldest, has the responsibility of taking him to the doctor. He loves it! All the attention is on him for awhile.

Medicare covers the doctor's bill, but not the medicine. This irritates him that a man of his age who has worked and paid taxes to the United States Government for all these years should have to pay for pills, and they may not even work. He says, "A good shot of Canadian Club and a man will feel good."

Peggy is the shortest in our family standing about five feet tall. Dad says that good things come in small packages. She is the foundation of our family. She always had wavy dark-brown hair, which can have a different hue these days, and large, oval blue eyes with natural long lashes. Her creamy white complexion is lovely and dimples show with her ever-ready smile. It is unanimous between my sister and brothers that as long as Peggy lives, our mother will never die.

"Dad, stop, just stop that, your liver can't take another drink," she says in front of the doctor, during a recent visit, as he is writing an order for one vitamin and one aspirin per day.

"That's a crock of you know what," he says. "Arraahh my liver is fine. For a man of my age, what do you expect?" The doctor doesn't argue with him anymore. His liver has rejuvenated and he is in good health.

The doctor answers, "Bill, I can't tell you not to drink for any specific reason, I'm just asking you not to – it makes sense at your age."

Peggy leans forward and quietly reminds him that Dad likes big pills – the bigger they are, the better they work.

As Dad has grown older, we have all acquired some sort of job or responsibility that makes life easier, not only for our father, but also for us as a family. Dad still lives in his own house and we will never take his independence away; however, it has been a constant worry for us. Well, I guess Mom was watching over and made it possible for my brother Dick to move home, and of course, Dad is quite content to have his oldest son near.

There is coming and going in the house again, doors slamming, and lights left on too long. As Dad says, "You can tell the house is lived in." It is convenient that we all live close by and can stop in and chat, as well as pick him up when he calls one of us saying, "Get me out of the house." He caught all of us more than a few times with this. At one time I used to feel so guilty, stop what I was doing and run over thinking the old man had been alone too long. Then we realized that someone may have just brought him home a few hours before, due to his wishes, and now wanted out again. But, it doesn't matter, Dad wants to be everywhere and know what's going on.

My brothers Dick and Bill maintain the house on the outside, as well as any major painting or repairs on the inside. They are close brothers and work well together. Dick is a quiet man with similar traits to Peggy. He stands five feet nine inches, blue eyes and his once full head of brown hair now shows a receding hairline with gray strands. The gray, he claims, is due to Dad. It is funny how one's role in life changes. Dick is the oldest son and named after Dad's grandfather,

father and brother. And, my brother has railroad in his blood that comes from Dad's mother's side of the family. His first and only job out of high school has been with the Santa Fe Railroad. Ever since Dick moved back home to be with Dad, the overwhelming sadness that would hit me at the door is gone.

When Dick is around in the mornings and I'm not working, we have our coffee together and do the Tribune's crossword puzzle. This particular morning Dad decides to take his bath and he is in and out with his clothes and whatever else. Dad does not like to take showers; he prefers a bath and always uses the dish washing liquid soap for bubbles. Out of the corner of my eye I watch him bend over and pull a bottle of something out of the cabinet under the sink. I do not have to check; I assume it is the liquid soap.

I am trying not to laugh out loud as Dick is explaining to me with one hand over his mouth so Dad doesn't hear.

"He wants me home at 10:30 P.M. For Christ sake Cathy, 10:30 on Friday night Dad wants me in bed so I get a good night's sleep. A good night's sleep for what, I want to know. Cathy he's giving me a curfew."

"Dick, be patient," I say, "he feels secure when you are home."

"Did you know that Dad is afraid of the dark? All day long he is turning off the lights. I'm in bed, the door is half opened so I can hear if he gets up during the night, the lights are out and Jeeesus CCChrisssst, what do you think I hear? The G.....d...... light in the hallway switched on."

I can hardly contain myself; I am bent over and laughing.

I yell from the bed, "Dad turn off that G.....d...... light. It's night. Lights are off at night!"

Dad's running around in his G.....d..... whitey tighties explaining, "It's good to leave a light on at night so you can see."

Just then Dick and I hear him yell from the bathroom,

"Dick, I'm ready to get out. Come in! Get me out!"

We glance at each other, not really understanding. Unless sick, Dad has always put himself in and out of the tub, although we insist that someone be in the house when he takes a bath in case he should slip.

"Okay Dad, get out," says Dick patiently.

Dad yells back with a laugh with a little bit of desperation in his tone, "I can't."

Dick jumps up and goes into the bathroom and bends over the tub ready to pull him out. It's the same routine, Dad holds on to his shoulder and Dick wraps his arms around him and begins to lift; only this time, he's slipping out of his grasp.

Dick tells him, "Sit back into the water".

He continues, "Jesus, Dad, you're so slippery. What soap did you use?" We could both smell a distinct odor, but could not put a name on it at that moment.

Dick pulls him out of the tub and gets soaking wet, because he could not get a good grip. Dick turns and sees the bottle of Murphy's flax soap sitting by the sink.

"Jesssusss Dad, did you use this in the tub? You smell like a clean piece of furniture. You have to take another bath to clean this shite off your skin."

"Nooooo way," says Dad, "I'm clean as a whistle and this is the way I'll smell till the next bath - out of my way."

Dick and I look at each other and continue to laugh. There are tears in our eyes and Dick scratches his head, shakes it and we go back to the kitchen table. When Dad is dressed, he explains, and he is right, the two soaps are the same color and it is our fault for buying the same colors. The bathroom scene belongs on the television program, America's Funniest Home Videos.

As adults we see humor in small things that aggravated us as children. An example is when Dad decided that the barber charged too much for cutting the boys hair. Mom wouldn't let him touch the girls, but the boys had to suffer through, the then, very modern clippers. They were terrible, pinching the skin and pulling the hair out rather than cutting it. But from that moment on, Dad refused to go to the barber and eventually mastered the art of cutting his own hair as well. The styles were short and this saved a few dollars.

Eventually Dad purchased the electric trimmer and all the attachments. Bill is the youngest and his memories of the clippers are vague, but he recalls many a balding haircut as Dad practiced with the electric trimmer. He says often, "I never thought I'd be the one using these damn electric trimmers on Dad or anyone. I hated them."

My brother Bill stands five feet nine inches with a stature similar to my father. Also, Bill is the only one that has Dad's bright blue eyes, only his are larger, and they crinkle at the corners when he laughs, just like Dad's. He has a quick and genuine smile for everyone and is the first one called to fix anything that is broken. It is hysterical when Bill arrives at the house to give him a trim.

"Dad," he says, "let's go to the barber."

"No," answers Dad with conviction, "I won't give five dollars for a simple trim around the ears that you can do and do just as well."

Bill shakes his head and laughs aloud, "Five dollars," he says, "How long have I been your personal barber? Did you ever hear of inflation?"

Dad loves it when everything in the house is clean and tidy. And this is where my sister Jo Ann comes in. Dad's house is not only clean, but every thing has its place. Jo Ann resembles the Bourke side of our family. She stands five feet five inches with short, dark wavy hair and beautiful blue eyes. JoAnn also has their quick temper that appears and disappears in two minutes, and then, life goes on as usual.

JoAnn and Dad have had a few ding-dongs over the years, especially at the end of each season when it's time to go through his wardrobe and dump the old in order to have more room in the closet for the new items. He is always giving out and following her around the house.

"JoAnn," he says, "Don't give that shirt away. It's like new. I wear it all the time."

"Dad," She answers in a sly, cute way, "Say goodbye, it's going to shirt heaven and these are going to shoe heaven and these to T-shirt heaven, etc."

Dad tells us that he can't argue with the "Queen of all nations" and, of course, Peggy and I have absolutely no pity.

Having the advantage of living close by has given our children the privilege of growing up with cousins around their own age. Our children refer to some cousins as friend, and also family. They have spent many wonderful hours with Grandpa, and the older ones, with grandma and grandpa. It means so much to them just to have the house to visit. It was here that they learned to play the card game, twenty-five and became experts on the pool table. When grandpa was in bed sick, they still went; stayed over night, and had friends meet them there so grandpa was never alone.

Once a week, Jo Ann makes a loaf of raisin bread and drops it at the house. In the afternoon Dad will boil the kettle for a cup of tea, cut a huge slice from the cake, add plenty of jam and thoroughly enjoys eating every crumb.

He says, "Cathy, no one can make bread like JoAnn." And, of course, I agree and tease him, "I know, didn't I teach her?"

Dad is looking down at the floor smiling. He won't make the mistake of mentioning JoAnn's cake for some time.

"Let's leave it on the counter and share it with anyone who stops by today."

"No, hell no," he replies fervently. "They'll eat it all and I won't have any for tomorrow."

"Dad, JoAnn will make more. It's not a big deal."

"No," he says and covers the cake with foil and puts it away.

JoAnn perfected Mom's sour-cream cake with raisins and Dad is right, it tastes just like my mother's; however, I am the queen of the rhubarb pie, which is supplied from Dad's garden. I also learned from Mom how to make the crust with lard and how to recognize the texture rather than following a recipe. In fact, as a child I don't remember Mom using measuring spoons and cups.

"Hold your hand out Cathy," she'd say. I remember her putting a spoon of baking soda onto the palm of my hand, using a knife to remove a little from all sides, and then saying, "That's the right amount for this cake."

I also acquired my mother's ability to knead bread. Last year at a neighborhood tavern called Mrs. O'Leary's Dubliner on Western Avenue, a soda bread contest was held as part of their Saint Patrick Day's celebration, and I won second prize. It was a great time to be had by all; everyone is Irish on Saint Pat's Day in Chicago.

I resemble both sides, the Rogers and the Morley's. Although, it's just in the past couple of years that JoAnn and I have noticed we are beginning to resemble each other more and more. I make dinner often and now Dad and I spend hours talking and reminiscing about his childhood and early life in Chicago. I am cherishing these hours; I know it will someday end.

Dad is not cheap; I use the word frugal. He has always made it clear that there is money to spare for a "rainy day," however, not for unnecessary luxuries such as eating at restaurants. He often reminded us, "Half pennies make pennies and pennies make shillings." I remember, many years ago before my husband and I married, we invited Dad and Mom to an elegant restaurant for some special occasion. Dad ordered a T-bone steak with all the trimmings and ate every bite. I was watching and listening for his reaction, but he said nothing.

I asked, "Was it good?"

Dad answered, "Yes, but your Mother cooks better." He later confided to Mom that it was a terrible waste of money, a pure extravagance. Mom and I ate out often over the years, but we always left a plate at home for Dad, and he was happy.

Bill Bourke's work ethic was incredible; he never missed a day's work due to illness or too much drink. If he decided to take a day off, it was by choice or necessity for his family. He always told us, "The greatest days in a man's life is when he can go to work and then come home to his family."

Faith in God, in particular the Blessed Mother, and love of family are Dad's cornerstones in life, without both he would not be complete. As a child, I can remember hearing him say, "To be a good person and to get to heaven one must believe in God and follow the golden rules." And the golden rules are the Ten Commandments from the Bible.

He says, "You can put them in any language, in any book, and call them a different religion – follow them and you'll have a good life."

The tobacco, the drink, the nostalgia for days gone by is not a burden for Peggy, Dick, JoAnn, Bill or myself. We have been given the gifts of good parents and American citizenship; we are forever grateful. Without Dad's inner stamina and desire to embark upon a better life, I would not be writing this book.

So now I ask my Father to share with us his first memories of Ireland, his family and friends, his work and life experiences, his trials and tribulations and I will attempt to retell his memoirs to the best of my ability. My father has a story that includes songs of old and tales that are older and should not be forgotten.

"Now Dad, if we write this book together, you have to tell me the truth to the best of your ability. You know this," I say, "right!"

"Arrhaa suurrrre I will. And, laughing he adds, "Remember, Cathy, don't ruin a good lie with the truth."

"Oh, my goodness," I say shaking my head and laughing. That Irish wit!

"Dad," I say, "Sit down on this comfortable chair. Here is an ashtray and candy." I'm at the computer ready, but he is filling his pipe with cherry smelling tobacco from his small, brown leather pouch and thinking.

Finally he says, "Okay, now listen carefully so I don't have to repeat myself."

the parish of knockmore

Well, goodbye to Lisaniska the cradle of my birth
Farewell to Ballinsleva hills the place for fun and mirth,
Likewise to sweet Coolcronan and its woodlands ever green
Where many the pleasant afternoon I spent with my colleen.

My heart is broke to leave the scenes of my childhood happy days
And my heart is still more broken to cross the ranging seas,
That will separate forever, me and my míle stór
That's brokenhearted after me in the Parish of Knockmore.

When I look upon the ocean I think of Lough Conn so blue
Pontoon hills and Drummin wood so charming for to view,
Bilberry and Glass Island where poteen is made galore
Which often made me sing with joy when coming from Knockmore.

Now it's first of all I recall the crystal River Moy
Where on its mossy banks I used to play when just a little boy,
My memory so oft times haunts me, that my heart is getting sore
When I think upon those pleasant times I spent in sweet Knockmore.

Goodbye to my aged mother she had no pet but me
Likewise my aged father whose head now is white grey,
My brother and my sisters, for me their hearts are sore
They are a helpless lot I'm sure in the Parish of Knockmore.

But now I'm on the ocean and I'm writing to my dear
And every line that I pen down I wet it with a tear,
It's coming from a wounded heart that ne'er knew grief before
Until I left those that I loved in the Parish of Knockmore.

In a bottle tight these lines I seal in case the ship gets drown'd
And no one left to tell this tale 'till this message it is found,
Some friendly breeze might drift its course onto an Irish shore
And who e're might find it might be so kind as to bring it to Knockmore.

Michael Duffy, Lisaniska.
April, 1893 on his way to USA.

Gaelic translations:

Lisaniska – Lis, fort; an, of; iska, water

Ballinsleva – Mountain Village

Míle stór – Thousand loves

Bill Bourke is the name, and I am a proud Mayo man. They call me Willie back home in Ireland, Erin or the Emerald Isle; they are one and my native home. The Bourkes were simple hard-working country people, adamant Catholics, used to the weather and greenery. The scenic beauty of Ireland is described in books, poetry, and paintings; however, the forty shades of green can only been seen through ones own eyes viewing the soft, rolling hills and verdant fields especially in the County Mayo.

The name Bourke can also be seen with the spellings Burke, but is derived from the same Anglo-Norman, William de Burgo. In 1179 vast areas in Connaught were granted to the de Burgo family and the name has multiplied all over the world, all stemming from this same family. However, it seems that in Mayo, de Burgo became Bourke and in Galway, Burke.

Mayo comes from the Irish word *Maigh Eo – the plain of the yew trees.* Mayo has its own unique beauty, tranquility, turmoil and history. When I was born, the landowners were wealthy, but the vast majority of Irish people themselves were poor. Oliver Cromwell is quoted, "To hell or to Connaught" which is the province including Mayo, Galway, Roscommon, Sligo and Leitrim.

The weather is always a topic since it would change so quickly due to the gusts of wind from the Atlantic Ocean. If there was no rain, my father would say, "Tis a grand day;" a little drizzle, "Tis a soft day;" or a gray and damp, windy day, "Tis desperate weather we're having!" Ireland does not often see snow, but I have seen roses still blooming in December. And our ruddy complexions were due to the clean, fresh country air and probably the dampness. There is a broad discrepancy between country and city living; both beautiful places, just different.

The country itself is old, and with age comes history that is made by people and should not be forgotten. Ireland was not always a troubled country; it prospered and flourished for a while. Then, there was a time of disheveling that brought hatred, hunger and discontentment to many. The only alternative was to leave and find new homes in foreign lands.

But now, my Mayo is thriving again; its people are building and modernizing. The Mayo men helped to build and modernize countries around the world, and now after so many years of setback, their towns are prospering and marking their place for the future with industry, literature, public officials, technology, tourism and so much more. I knew it was only a matter of time. The Mayo men will fight for their God, their family, and their land.

Ballina, Castle Bar, Foxford and Knockmore were towns nearby where I grew up. Our families intertwined as the years passed and, thank God all my memories are fond ones. I was born in a village near

22

the town of Ballina, which was founded by Lord Tyrawley in 1723 and due to its geographical position and water access, Ballina grew quickly and thrived. There was a brief setback when the French entered in 1798 determined to take over and then again with the great famine of 1847 that swept through Connaught, and not just my part of the country, but all of Ireland suffered.

There isn't an awful lot of family history to be found prior to the famine and those even less fortunate than us have no history to carry on to the next generation. However, much of this information that I am stating was given to our family from Canon John Flynn's grandfather, John Flynn who died in 1968 at the age of 102 years and it is the truth to the best of my knowledge.

There were three brothers, Jack Bourke, James Bourke and Billy Bourke. My grandfather Billy was nicknamed "the Captain." The Captain was born in the middle 1800's, a great organizer; and I suppose good at giving orders. How else could you justify the title of Captain? He was a short, slight man, hot headed and a great singer. No one in my family remembers why he had a lame step. Some suppose an injury and others possibly arthritis, but as an old man, he used walking sticks.

As a young man, "the match" was made between the two families and the Captain married Bridget King! The marriage took place in Backs Parish Church and the Captain and his new wife settled in the home place where his father and mother had lived. Now, here Cathy is where my tale begins.

They had three sons and three daughters, John Willie, Michael and Richard, Winifred, Maggie, and Catherine (Katie.) John Willie married Ellen Barrett from Carrentrila, which is about two miles from Ballina and moved to Scotland for a short time. Upon inheriting Ellen's farm, they returned to her native Carrentrila and raised three daughters. Their eldest Maisie never married, Kathleen married John Hughes in Carrentrila, and Melia married Tom Crowe from the North of Ireland, who at the time was the butler at Mount Falcon Castle. They moved to England and I have no further information.

My Uncle Michael married Maggie McHugh in Brackwansha. He married into her home place and raised six children. Celia married John Foody of Ballinahaglish, which is Gaelic for "village of the church." Bridget married Michael Brogan of Lahardane (near Pontoon) and Annie Kate married Martin Doherty in Lahardane as well. A horse fell on Michael James and left him almost a complete invalid all his life and John Willie immigrated to America and never returned. Finally, Maggie Jane married Martin Walsh, a very nice man, but much older than herself. However, they were quite comfortable. I remember him driving the donkey and cart twice a week into Ballina with the milk. After he died, Maggie Jane married a neighbor, Red Tom Walsh, another good man.

Aunt Maggie married John Langan from upper Ballymacredmond and settled in Edinburgh with three children. Aunt Winnie also went to Edinburgh to work as a young girl; however, she never married and, as far as I know, is buried there. As a child I remember well being allowed to look at the silver pocket watch that Aunt Winnie brought from Scotland and gave to my father on his wedding day. And it was my brother Pat that took the back off to look inside and broke the lovely gift.

As the story goes, another match was made through the Captain. Now when a match was made, to my knowledge without a doubt, there was a dowry made between the two families. Money would have passed hands since my mother was marrying into the home place with a few acres of land. This meant security. With a spit in the hand and a good handshake, the deal was sealed. My father, Richard, was to marry

Bridget Rodgers from the gatehouse in Shanclough. It wasn't long before marriage vows were exchanged again in Backs Parish Church in Knockmore. My parents settled in Ballymacredmond, in our thatched cottage, which still stands today and began the fourth generation.

This is where I was born, as well as, my sisters and brothers. In those days all babies were born at home, and in most cases, without the attendance of a doctor or midwife, mainly because people could not afford the expense. My sister Mary was the eldest, born on January 6, 1904, then John born February 1, 1905, Winifred Teresa (Teasie) on August 8, 1906, Bridget on January 22, 1908 but, died very young, Margaret Joanna (Maggie) on February 13, 1909, Patrick Michael (Pat) on March 18, 1910, Ellen (Nellie) June 17, 1911, Richard (Dick) June 3, 1913, Michael Joseph (Mike) October 5, 1914, Bridget (Bridgie) February 13, 1917, "miself" William (Willie) January 1, 1920, and the youngest James (Jim) on March 3, 1921. No one could foresee the changes that would take place in Ballymacredmond during my lifetime.

Ballymacredmond was a sparsely populated village on the outskirts of the Mount Falcon Estate. At the turn of the nineteenth century the railroad built a bridge over the road to our house. Thus, our village became lower Ballymacredmond since we entered under the bridge. About a half mile further down, another bridge was built allowing access to the village on the bridge, over the tracks, thus creating upper Ballymacredmond.

Bally is Gaelic for "village" mac for "son of" and the Redmond family, who at one time lived and ruled in this area as their Chieftain. It is about four miles from the town of Ballina, which can be found in the northern portion of County Mayo, located in the west of Ireland. I was baptized on January 4, 1920 in the Church of Christ the King, in the

Village of Knockmore, in the Parish of Backs, located in the Diocese of Killala and my godparents were Patrick and Bridget Rodgers.

In those days, diocesan boundaries were determined based on natural dividers. For example, the Diocese of Killala reached from Skreen, Sligo in the North and up as far as the bridge that spans the River Moy in Foxford. There were many churches within our diocese, but the Parish of Backs had the largest congregation next to the Cathedral Parish in the town of Ballina.

The people's support has followed through for many generations making our parish successful and well known today through activities as the Knockmore Gaelic Football Team, The Conn Ranger's Soccer Team, The Women's Club, Senior Citizens' Club, Parish Pastoral Council, Committee of Pioneer's Total Absentness Association, and Bingo once a week in Knockmore Hall. And the colors of saffron and blue are proudly worn by the young today representing Knockmore.

I grew up surrounded by the finest families in Mayo – in Ireland. They were more a part of my life than many family members who had already left home. There were twelve houses in both Ballymacredmonds and I can still picture in my mind, strolling and meandering back and forth, back and forth; and the talk, there was always talk going on around the village. As my father would say, "You don't miss the water till the well is dry."

Now, first there was John Flynn's, then our house, next Jack Bourke who was the son of my grandfather's brother James. Jack married a woman by the last name of O'Hara. The next house was Patrick Bourke (nicknamed Paddy O'Hara) who was Jack Bourke's son. Now, Paddy O'Hara married Mary Mangan and had the sons that I grew up with Jimmy, John and Patrick and one daughter Maisie. Paddy married a second time to Bridget O'Hara from Slievenagark, but had no children. His son John (nicknamed Dan) married Frank Devine's daughter, Eileen Barret. Patrick married Sarah Reape from upper Ballymacredmond.

There is a good story about young Patrick. As a young lad he was always called Tierney. One of the candidates at a general election, at this time, was Mr. Tierney and young Patrick used to run around the village shouting "Up Tierney, Up Tierney," and so the name stuck.

The cottages continued belonging to Frank Devine, Willie Flynn, Paddy Gallagher, Patrick King, William Bourke (no relation), Rick Barrett, The Reape Family, and the Cannon Family.

In the early nineteen twenties the Land League was trying to help the small farmer. It was known during these years that many of the rich landlords were having trouble paying their taxes to the Crown, due to the loss of man power in Ireland. Many had to resort to selling land. The land purchased would be divided amongst those farmers boarding the property, but with one stipulation. The farmer agreed to an eleven-month lease, which stated that if it did not work out, the land would be returned to the Land League. At this time another farmer would be given the same chance.

Around this same time, the Land League purchased frontage land to the Foxford Road from the Knox-Gore Family Estate and divided into three small farms. They were given to the Barretts, Reapes, and Cannons. The land that they actually owned in Ballymacredmond was divided amongst the remaining families. My father got most of the Cannon's land, approximately seven acres. Our property consisted of three or four acres before this land transfer.

Further down the road a bit was William Bourke, no relation, and his wife was Mariah Rodgers, and again, no relation to my mother. Everyone in the village called Mariah "Mom" and no more than ourselves, they had a houseful of children. There were four sons, John Willie, Paddy, Dick and Christy. And there were six daughters, Annie

Kate, Agnes, Lizzie, Lena, Bridgie, and Lily. I'd say we were the closest to this family. We grew up together, working and socializing – they were good people.

Our cottage was right across from Ketty (Catherine) and Paddy Gallagher. They had no children and were very poor. Paddy was lame as a young man. He was clearing a field that had a huge boulder and the only way to get rid of it was to dig a hole, push it in, and cover it up with dirt. There should have been two men there that day and perhaps the accident would not have happened. As Paddy pushed the rock, his leg got caught under it, and the rock rolled.

They were extremely kind to us as children. I can still see Ketty Gallagher standing at the doorway the morning I was leaving for America. When I looked back, she had a large white cloth, waving it over her head.

Patrick King, who was my father's cousin, married Kate Rodgers. She passed away young and he then married Ellen Flynn who was Willie Flynn's sister in our village. Oh, we'd have great fun with him. As a gaser I would play tricks on Paddy and the poor auld devil would fall for them all the time.

The worst one would be throwing the wet bird into the cottage. It would be a cold winter's night and the only light in the cottage was from the oil lamp. If you put your hand up under the thatch, there was always a sparrow or a wren hiding and keeping warm. I'd catch one and make sure the feathers were good and wet. Then I'd knock on the door and wait, standing off to the side. Well as soon as Paddy opened the door a small bit, I would let the bird inside and, of course, it went straight for the light and burst the glass globe. Wasn't that terrible! They couldn't get a replacement until the next day and had to travel all the way into Ballina!

We had great neighbors that helped each other through good times and bad. When my mother would use the saying "charity begins at home," she was referring to our village. They're all gone now and most of their children, but I have wonderful memories of them all.

We grew up with a simple life, not afraid of hard work and where honesty and truth were instilled into us from childhood. Attendance at Sunday mass was mandatory and there was only one way to get there, by the power from your own legs. We walked in the sun, the rain, the wind and the cold; this was part of our life.

Indeed when money was very scarce and a large family to be reared on a very small farm, my parents donated a pew to the newly refurbished church in Knockmore. I believe it cost fifteen pounds, a lot of money to a poor farmer. In those days it was the second pew to the right, if you used the main entrance, and my mother sat in it every Sunday.

It's a fact, the cottage was small, but it was home to us all. After a day at school or out in the fields, it was a welcome sight! You entered the house through the door that was between the culinary and our one main room, the kitchen. A peat fire at one end of the kitchen provided the only heat, which was always burning and God knows it was needed for the dampness. If it was cold out, my mother didn't have to look far for Jim and I; we were seated at either side of the hearth on the two little hobs or shelves where the pots were left. There was one large wooden table with six chairs and a dresser, one fairly good size window that allowed the sunlight to enter, and the large open fire kept us warm and fed. On the opposite side there was the "hag" or a small bed that was cut into the wall. Generally, this was where the old people slept. There was another door on the opposite side that led to the barn and outhouse.

The majority of homes found in the rural areas of Ireland at this time were hip roof design. They were made with thatched roof of straw from oats, case, cement and stone. The roofs would last between four and five years. These thatched roofs held the heat and were all handmade from nature's own stock. Nails! There were no nails – nor a store to go and buy them even if you had the money.

My father would call out, "Willie, yourself and Jim go up the fields and bring back plenty of sugán for the thatch." Jim and I were happy to go up the fields with the knives and spend a few hours cutting the straw and making the sugán (pronounced soo-gawn). Rain would run off the straw and not penetrate; hence thatch was used for roofs on cottages, as well as stacks of wheat, oats and barley and tied with a rope made of sugán. The anchors, called "sally rods" were made also from the Willow trees and used to hold the thatch on the roofs. The Willow branches were cut into specific lengths and bent into a "u" shape or could be twisted to make the straw fit so water would not penetrate. The sap inside hardened and the anchor held. It was not until after World War II that the thatched roofs were replaced with galvanized metal.

I remember as if it were yesterday, cutting the oats with a scythe at harvest time and then had to make sure that the seeds were separated. In order to clean the oats, my father would make a tool that resembled a whip, called a "flail." There was a sharp, circular type hook attached to the end of a strong stick and I would hit the straw over and over, shaking loose the seeds. Finally, the straw was tied into small bundles to use as thatch or to freshen the bedding. The seeds were put into a basket to dry and stored in the back kitchen area for future planting or feed for the chickens.

My father had already died when my brother John and Jack Walsh bought a thrashing machine. This was my first experience with modern farming equipment and it was amazing to witness. We didn't have much in the way of material items, but we had the necessities of food and fuel right at our back door.

Ireland's bogs maintained its people for centuries. They gave us enough turf to keep warm throughout the year and cook our food. Up around Currabaggan School there is an entire area that is bog. The Bourke's section was there, along with all the other families living around our place. When I was a child, there were no oil trucks pulling up in front of anyone's home. We utilized what God gave us. For example, England's main source of fuel was coal, other places used wood, and Ireland had its turf, or as some say, peat.

The area where I cut the turf was marked long before I was born and is still there today. There is a road that divides the area in order to make it possible to get some sort of transportation in and out to help carry the turf. In my day, we used the donkey and cart and made another level onto the crib with a few pieces of lumber. Now we could carry double the amount home.

Sometime in April, right after school, I would have to go with Dick to begin the process of cutting, drying, transporting and storing enough turf for the winter months. After my father died, Dick took over the bog and was well able for the task. He used the slán or turf spade to slice the sod and began "spitting the turf" through the decaying ground, which had been pressed down century after century.

You didn't just go to the bog and start digging. The holes were measured so that you knew what area to work in and not have a bunch of holes all over the place. When starting to cut into a new area, perhaps a six-foot by eight foot, the top layer of heather had to be trimmed. This was usually moldy and was discarded into an old hole.

The spade cut the turf in pieces measuring about six inches by fourteen inches and a hand barrow to spread it. Once a hole was dug wide and long enough and around five feet deep, it was left to fill in again over time. It was always better to have two people working the bog together – two strong backs were better than one and someone to talk to always made for a more pleasant day that also passed quicker.

31

The job was so monotonous and it didn't matter whether you felt like going. I often heard, "Make the hay while the sun shines."

The sod had to be positioned for drying. I would stand up four or five pieces, having them meet in the middle, and angle them out like a tent. We referred to this as making the "wreckels." The water could then drain out the bottom and the airflow helped to dry all four sides. Most of the time, I had to turn each piece at least once to dry the underside. You had to be careful not to break the piece of turf; the full turf burned slower than the little ones.

Drying the sod usually took about two weeks, depending upon the weather, and God knows it was always raining. But, we managed to bring home at least one cart every three or four days, and if the weather held, two loads on a Saturday. The old people would be saying, "Hurry on with the turf, sure we can'na boil prataís (potatoes) with stones."

The storage area for the turf was beside the house. Don't imagine that this was some fancy addition onto the cottage that protected the turf from the weather. It was a design handed down from generation to generation and it worked. The object was to keep the turf dry, because it would not burn wet.

The sods of turf were used as the outside walls and packed close and layered tightly against one another. You started wide at the bottom and gradually worked up into a pyramid fashion, which again allowed the rain to run off. Then, a layer of the turf mole (noul) or heather from the bog was laid on top for protection. We called this turfmore and it held the moisture preventing it from soaking down into the dried turf. Some people would build some sort of roof for protection with wood or a piece of tin, but we always used the turfmore. And every morning, enough sod was brought into the house in a basket and placed by the fire, which also helped with the drying.

Today the bog can be cut and dried by a machine. Now all the new houses have oil heating and nearly all the old ones have been converted. But, I don't care what anyone says, you can't beat the warmth and welcome of the turf fire.

the GRAND OLD RIVER MOY

Many years I've been in exile
I'd have you all to know.
I am from dear old Ballina
In the County of Mayo.
Many are my pleasant memories
That remain forevermore
Of my native home in Ireland
And the place that I adore.
Such are those treasured memories
That fill my heart with joy
Of the cool refreshing waters
Of the grand old River Moy.

You can see its grand cathedral
From the bridge at Ardnaree,
Where the fishermen net salmon
From the ridge pool to Bunree.
Many hours I've spent there fishing
When I've nothing else to do.
My fishing gear no gold could buy
'twas just an old bamboo.
I can still recall quite clearly
When I was just a boy
The cool refreshing waters
Of the grand old River Moy.

My love and I did wander
Along its banks so green
That leads along by Rehins,
Mount Falcon and Shraheen.
Gone are our parents and relations
Companions old and true
But fond memories of my childhood
I will again defuse.
I'll do the things I often did
When I was just a boy
By the cool refreshing waters
Of the grand old River Moy.

Written by: Jimmy Foody
(Jimmy's mother, Celia Bourke, was my father's aunt)

Standing outside the garden gate and looking toward the fields, they appear as a scenic painting, the majestic Ox Mountains. The Ox Mountains are on the border of Mayo and Sligo and they outline the horizon. On a fine day, the blue sky, always scattered with a few white clouds, meets with the verdant land, and the many gray stones, exuding a picturesque beauty.

It is from one of these ridges that a small trickle of water begins its descent, meeting and collaborating with other waters, and gliding gracefully as the Moy River through the town of Ballina and surrounding areas. As any great river, it is your friend and foe. The water surged over the banks in Castlebar, Foxford, Belass, Rinnaney, and Ballina ruining crops and leaving their owners homeless. And too many times, the roads around Pontoon were flooded due to the effects on Lough Conn.

It wasn't until 1960 when the Moy Drainage Scheme took control of the mighty river and dangerous flooding ceased.

The wild rushing noise from the Moy was frightening and the soft swooshing sound brought tranquility to one's mind. I fished many a day from the Pontoon Bridge in Foxford and watched the waters continue on to Killala Bay, and from there, the final journey to the Atlantic Ocean. May through September the anglers were sporting the finest salmon, and as well as trout and eel from its waters. I believe that the Moy was, and still is, one of the finest fishing rivers in Ireland, but it also brought industry.

One of the reasons Ballina and surrounding areas sustained during hard times was the River Moy. It helped our entire area prosper and brought huge recognition to Foxford when the Woolen Mills were built through the foresight and ingenuity of Mother Agnes Morrogh Bernard. She belonged to the Irish Sisters of Charity and it was with her entrepreneur ability that the mills and the surrounding towns maintained and prospered during hard times in Ireland and around the world.

It is said that as Mother Agnes Morrogh Bernard listened to the roar of the River Moy from her convent, the idea of building a mill and utilizing the river's power was materialized. The first person she contacted was Michael Davitt, Mayo's freedom fighter, and through his contacts, the mill became reality in May 1892. The blankets from this mill kept many a soldier warm during the first and second world wars that followed.

My father had the craft of making baskets. He used straw and the sally rods for reinforcement and they were utilized for all the household needs from drying the seeds for future planting or feed to holding potatoes for the dinner. Basket weaving is an art passed down, usually from father to son.

My father took each one of us, one at a time, demonstrating and instructing, but to no avail. Not one of us carried on his craft as a basket weaver. He told me, "This is a calming task. It takes one's mind off the worry of the day." It didn't work; I'd rather be fishing. I could not sit with my father and weave, but I could stand in the ridge pool and fish all day waiting for the big one to arrive. And it did!

I'd make my own rod with a stick, a piece of string, and a piece of some type of food tied to the end. I was always on the look out for a good fishing stick walking through the fields. The water would be cold, but I'd stand quiet, not a motion until a fish came by and sure enough, I'd nab it for the dinner.

When I was around twelve years of age, I was given credit for catching the largest salmon in Ballina. I was told it weighed fourteen pounds. A man offered me six pence for it, but I said no. I split the salmon, half to my brother John and the other to my mother. Let me tell you, I was famous for a while.

If you turn your back on the Ox Mountain chain, before you stands Nephin Mountain. Nephin is said to be shaped like the back of a whale and is the highest mountain in Mayo and can be seen into three surrounding counties. In Irish Nephin is *Barna Na Gaoithe,* which translates to the Gap of the Wind and referred to as "the windy gap." It was through this gap that the French soldiers entered Mayo as they attempted to take over our land.

As in the United States of America or any country, for that matter, if a person is fortunate enough to have a piece of land to sow and harvest, their family won't go hungry. For as long as I can remember, we owned one horse for saddling and plowing. In the spring, we would buy one new horse for ten or twelve pounds to help in the fields, and then sell it again in the fall to a jobber.

Jobbers were men who trained and needed horses to help exercise their racers. Usually the selling price was about the same as the cost. It wasn't economical for us to keep the second horse throughout the winter months. The feed and care cost too much.

William Bourke had a daughter, Agnes, who married William McGowan. And, it was his sister and husband who were killed on the Titanic. Now, William McGowan was a jockey for Robert Scott at Barnfield House and would usually buy back our extra horse when the harvest ended. He also sold to us Dolly, a lovely black filly. She was bred for racing, not pulling a cart. She'd rear up and stomp until finally she was free from the harness.

Dolly was bred from Martin Lightfoot and there was always competition among the jockeys. So a race was set above in Mount Falcon's racecourse. I was a gasur, perhaps eight or nine years of age. I ditched school and cut up across the fields myself and found a good hiding place where no one would see me watching. I could hardly contain myself, eventually jumping out into the open field, shouting as they ran nose to nose the entire run.

The track was marked, eight furlongs in an Irish mile, which is about one mile and a half. There are five and one half furlongs in a statue measure of an English mile. My brother Pat rode Martin Lightfoot and William McGowan, our Dolly. If there was one person watching this race, there were 200 men and women, rich and poor. I never saw such an exhibition.

I met my father and mother at the door and told them how I managed to watch the race and knew the results; we were beat! That was fine. Didn't everyone have a day out and the race was the talk of Ballina for a long, long time. It was all done for fun, but I'm sure a few shillings passed palms that day. Then life went back to its normal routine.

They weren't easy times insofar as money was concerned. We didn't have luxuries as today, but the camaraderie and the laughs that we had among ourselves cannot be replaced. We didn't have the luxuries of today and all the work to maintain a household was done under the watchful and concerned eye of my mother. She was a great lady.

I often asked myself, "How did the old people in those days raise, feed, and care for such large families in so small an area?"

And, I remember my mothers saying, "A good housekeeper is better than a big worker."

the water is wide

The water is wide
I can't cross over
And neither have
I wings to fly
Give me a boat
That can carry two
And we shall oar
My love and I.

For love is gentle
And love is kind
The sweetest flower
When first it's new
But loves grows old
And waxes cold
And fades away
Like the morning dew.

There is a ship
And she sails the sea.
She's loaded deep
As deep can be
But not as deep
As the love I'm in
I know not how
I sink or swim.

Y ou have heard the saying that opposites attract. Well, it is true in the case of my father and mother. My father was a quiet, gentle and soft-spoken man, whereas my mother was great at giving orders. No one ever said that Beesie (Bridget) Rodgers Bourke was lazy. She was born on April 23, 1876 in the gatehouse in Coolcronan, Ballina, County Mayo, but raised at the gatehouse in Shanclough about two miles to the north of Ballymacredmond. Her father, Patrick Rodgers and mother Mary Caulfield followed the railroad through this part of Mayo as it was built, finally settling in Shanclough where my mother was taught to love family, God and Mayo.

The Rodgers were originally from Balla, which is south of Ballina. My grandfather worked for the railroad and as it extended through Mayo, they moved with it. However, the position of the "gatekeeper" in the village of Shanclough which included a cottage was given to my grandparents and this is where my mother was raised.

This crossing is located on the main road toward the town of Ballina and is still there today. When a train is coming through, the gates have to be manually pulled across to stop the flow of traffic for safety and again opened when ready.

There was a train schedule and it was followed to the best of everyone's ability. However, if an accident or delay occurred, there was no way of knowing immediately. It may take several hours before the news would trickle down the line. So this meant that if someone needed to cross over, my grandfather would have to give the okay and raise the gate. In this area, this was the main crossing to the town of Ballina. On fair days, the cattle that belonged to the farmers in this district had to cross in Shanclough.

Indeed, I believed this to be a very prestigious position and spent as much time as possible with my grandparents. This job has been handed down from generation to generation, and still today a descendant of the Rodgers' family occupies the gatehouse.

My mother never had a desire to leave home. She had two brothers and two sisters. Dan immigrated to Chicago, married and never returned. Michael must have died young. I don't have any recollection of him as a child. Mariah immigrated to Chicago and also died at a young age. Her sister Kate married Patrick Bourke in Castlebar and they always remained close.

In fact, as we got older and were able to take care of ourselves, my mother would take the train to Castlebar, a lovely town about five miles away, and spend two weeks visiting with her sister Kate. This was her vacation and we all knew when the time was approaching, the big cleaning would take place in our house. She would say, "For the fear that anything will happen to me, it's all done." And, I remember as well, Aunt Kate arriving with her children during the summer and staying with us for a couple of weeks. They were Denis, Mary, Michael, Winnie, Paddy and Agnes and we had great fun together.

Beesie Rodgers kept a spotlessly clean house and maintained it through a variety of ways. She cared for 25 to 30 hens, knit socks and sweaters and fed her family with homemade bread and butter everyday with one big meal in the afternoon. However, preparing the food was not the hardest household job; it was the laundry. All the men wore two shirts for work or dress. The inside shirt was made of wool, which absorbs sweat and the outside shirt for work was cotton with no collar and had stripes. For dress, it was linen with a collar. Boiling the pots of water, washing the clothes in the tubs by hand, and then trying to get them dried was a chore.

Most of the time, the wash day was done as a community project and everyone helped each other. A big pot of water was boiled with a slice of carbolic soap and then the clothes were added. The bath basin was lifted onto two stools, and after a good boiling the clothes were put into the basin with the washboard and then, the sleeves were rolled up and the scrubbing began. The white collars and fronts got a soaking in Robin Starch and looked as good as new. The blankets were done twice a year and this is when the young children helped and they were needed. The little ones were put, with no shoes, in the large tubs and let trample and jump on the material. I remember well having to do this, and believe it or not, we looked forward to this day of play.

My mother was always discovering ways to bring extra money into our house. The eggs collected would be sold each week to an egg collector. Many a pounding of the cream I did for the butter in the churn. We had to be careful that the milking cows didn't get into the vegetable gardens. I remember well tasting the butter and knowing that the cow had eaten turnips. This had a distinct taste that spoiled the cream.

Twice a week I delivered her fresh butter, wrapped in tissue, to people in the area that did not own cows. I was given one shilling and two pennies per package, but I only brought home the shillings; I kept the pennies. This extra money purchased sugar, flour and other small necessities needed in the house.

Our diet consisted of good basic food; there were plenty of potatoes, vegetables, cabbage and bacon. It was a well-known fact that the man of the house was given an egg every day. I don't know if this always happened, but I heard it many times. It was big news around the place if a hen crowed; this was considered bad luck. The hen was killed immediately.

Mother would often say, "A whistling woman and a crowing hen wakes the devil out of his den."

I would love it when this happened. There was chicken soup for dinner and it was delicious.

We had plenty of bacon because my father raised pigs. There were no grocery stores. If you wanted bacon you had to have a sow and tend her litter, and then make sure that there were two pigs ready for slaughter every year. The meat was put into tubs with water and sea salt for curing and after several weeks, hung in pieces ready to eat.

Pigs are a lot of work. Their pens have to be cleaned twice a day, and my mother made their feed from potatoes skins, turnips and whatever else was around. And you had to be so careful about disease. You didn't wear the shoes you had on in town around their pen; germs were carried on the soles of shoes.

I believe that sewing is also an art, and my mother had it. She was a terrific dressmaker. It's a fact; the Bourkes were always well dressed and this was due to her ingenuity. I can still see my mother walking to church, her back straight and walking with her head held high, right down the middle of the road. Her graying hair was pulled into a tight bun in the back that was popular at this time. She wore a dark suit with a long skirt and jacket and a white blouse that showed a bow at the neck. This blouse was the talk of our Parish for a long time.

A package had come from America containing a man's shirt. My mother turned the collar, which made the material come up high on her neck. The bodice was cut and it buttoned down the back. Also, she cut the extra material off the bottom of the shirt and made a bow that was tied under the collar. She had the ability to make something beautiful out of nothing.

My mother had a skill of management. Today, Beesie Rodgers would be referred to as a household engineer. Thank God we never knew hunger in the way some of the Irish people suffered.

I remember well listening to my mother visiting with the neighbors. Everyone got along and took care of each other. On Friday evenings, after the day's work I would watch all the women wearing their white aprons arrive at our house. They would sit and talk for hours over a cup of tay (tea) or a suppeen (drink) of whiskey and have a smoke on the clay pipe.

Mother had what was referred to as a "weak chest." One of the remedies recommended at this time was to smoke the pipe. The doctor from our area felt that the hard pull on the clay pipe was good for the lungs and would help strengthen their capacity. As a gasur, I used to come into the kitchen a couple of times during the evening pretending to ask a question and the pipes would disappear under the aprons. The women didn't want the children to see them smoking. They had supported and helped each other over the years with ailing and dying family members, and this time of commiserating sealed the bond that could not be broken. As my brother Dick would say, "You better not put your finger in their mouth." This was their time and they were all welcome.

My mother kept her children busy. We knew our duties and did them with no complaining or we'd hear about it. I recall more than a few times when she would be on about something, my father would take the pipe from his mouth and put his finger to his lips saying, "Beesie, silence, please." And she'd be quiet - for a bit.

My father never let her out on the land. He tried his best to shield her from any hard labor and wanted life for her to be as easy as possible. God knows, there was enough to do inside the house. However, at 4:00 in the afternoon, without fail, out to the field she would go with the tea and bread to my father. I loved and respected her and not a day goes by that I don't think of her and say a little prayer to our Lady.

They were happy days going back and forth to the old people in Shanclough and listening to my grandmother tell stories about the "little people" and the "Children of Lir." I recall three prophesies: one was that there would be things flying in the air, carrying things back and forth; second, it'll come in future generations that the children will become weaker, but wiser; and finally, there won't be much difference between the summer and the winter – the rain and the cold.

I knew the train schedule and would patiently wait. I could feel the tremor coming from under the sod, touching my bare feet before the whistle was heard in a distance. I wished many times that I controlled that monstrous, all-powerful machine. I wanted to drive the locomotive, but then it was only a dream. I did dream, for hours, walking through the fields, digging the potatoes or carrying water from the well. The day would come when I would be an engineer. Railroad got into my blood and stayed with me, all the way to Chicago.

I was only a child at this time. My only adventures were within walking distance of my home and a few trips into the town of Ballina, but I knew what I wanted to achieve as a man. This dream would take hard work, determination and luck. I can hear my mother saying,

"Happiness cannot be bought for gold, even though it's a poor man's bread."

poem

Large and profitable
Are the stacks upon the ground
The butter and the cream
Do wondrously abound.

The crests on the water
And the swallows are at hand
And the cuckoo calling daily
Is note of music band.

And the bold thrush sings so bravely
His songs of the forest strand
Are at hand on the fair, fair hills
of holy Ireland.

Author: Unknown

I remember the day as well as yesterday. I was a year older than Jim and he decided to go with me to school. It was my first day. Jim was five and I six years of age. We walked a good mile and a half to reach Currabaggan School, built in 1882. It was accessible from the main road or through the fields. The short cut through the fields guaranteed that we'd be late.

It was recess on the first day and Jim said, "I want to go home." Well it didn't take much to convince me. I answered, "Me as well." We took off running. My mother made me go back the next day, but Jim stayed home for another year.

It was common then for a husband and wife to teach together in a country school. In fact many times this was a position passed down in the family. Depending upon how many children were enrolled, determined how many teachers were hired.

I never agreed with the discipline method used in schools. I often heard "Spare the rod and spoil the child." It is possible that the teachers believed that this was the only way to teach discipline. I don't know, but it is still clear in my memory the children that received beatings. What could they have done to deserve the mark of a cane or the swelling from a belt? That wouldn't happen today, not in Ireland or in the United States. Is it any wonder that so many children didn't finish school? But, let me tell you; I know plenty who left school before the age of fourteen due to the schoolmasters' tyrannical teaching methods and still succeeded.

In Ireland, it was compulsory for all children to be educated up to the age of fourteen years. The Gardai (police) would visit each school periodically to check attendance and if anyone missed too many days, a visit was made to their parents. It was the parent's responsibility to make sure that their children were in school and if they did not oblige, a fine was set and had to be paid by a certain date.

The school day began at 9:30 and ended at 3:00 p.m. We had five weeks vacation, which began the first week in August through the first week in September. This way the children would be home to help with the harvest, although now, the schools are closed for two months, July and August.

There were 85 to 90 children in Currabaggan schoolhouse at one time. The school was one big room with long tables and benches. A family would pay a couple of shillings that would cover the expense for a year's supply of ink, pen and paper. Lunch break was one half hour and we would take turns going to the well for fresh water and then, eat our piece of bread with butter. There wasn't much time for running around or playing tug-o-war with the old rope.

I recall learning the subjects of English, reading, mathematics, history, grammar, Gaelic, and having to write essays. It was here that I learned about our own Irish history; the trials and tribulations that have engulfed our small island for centuries due to man's greed for power.

Everyday there was one half hour of religious instruction, usually around 11:30, right before lunch break. Geography was also important. There were maps on the walls and you had to know where the countries were located, or else, "Hold your hand out!" demanded the master. If you pulled your hand in fast enough, he'd hit himself on the leg, but the consequences were worse. Sometimes it was easier to take the slap.

Nevertheless, I cannot say that I didn't learn. I got a few good slaps myself for not memorizing something correctly. You had to be prepared on Monday morning. There was always an essay due and some sort of recitation that had to be recited orally from memory. I can still do mental arithmetic and recite poems from memory.

It's dog's delight to bark and bite
For it is their nature too
For God has made them so
Let all your words be mild
Just like the Blessed Virgin's son
That sweet and lovely child
His soul was gentle as a lamb
And as his stature grew
Grew in fame both with man and God.
His father too
He sees his children dwell and love
And marks them for his own
Now lord of all, he reigns above
And from his heavenly thrown
He sees his children dwell
And loves and marks them for his own.

I didn't agree with the discipline methods, but these teachers had the responsibility of instructing and controlling all of us in one room. The Missus taught the two younger levels, which included their catechism and this book cost one penny. The Head Master taught all subjects to level three and up, which also included their catechism. Now, this book cost three pennies because it incorporated religious instruction, prayers, and commandments and was much more detailed. Along with all this, the Master prepared us for the sacraments of Penance, First Holy Communion, and Confirmation. This took a tremendous amount of work and effort on his part.

The Confirmation ceremony wasn't done anything at all like it is today. There were no parents or sponsors, only a Bishop, priests, the school Master and Mrs. Caulfield and us at the church. Master Caulfield sponsored the boys and Mrs. Caulfield, the girls. The year I was confirmed there were three classes and it was held on a Monday.

Our parish priests would call us over one by one and give an oral examination. If the priest was satisfied with the answers, he presented you with a ticket and that meant you could receive the sacrament of Confirmation. After everyone was finished and sitting quietly in the church, the Bishop entered and began mass. Immediately following the celebration of the mass, all students raised their right hand and made a confirmation pledge, or a promise, to abstain from all alcoholic beverages until the age of twenty-one years.

There is a funny story about a classmate of mine. He was watching and listening intently to everything the Bishop said and did. The final step that the Bishop performs during Confirmation is to put his thumb into the chrism oil and while making the sign of the cross on the forehead moves from one student to the next repeating in Latin "signo té, signo crucis" which translates to – I sign you with the sign of the cross. He then taps you on the cheek as a reminder that you are a soldier of Christ.

The lad didn't realize it was Latin and ran home to his mother saying, "Mammy, Mammy I'll drink no tay (tea) until twenty-one."

We had good clean fun. No one got hurt and we laughed, many times at the schoolmasters and at each other. We had to make our own fun and enjoy the good with the bad. As a child I was a tenor and Mrs. Caulfield often asked me to sing *Danny Boy:*

> *Oh Danny boy, the pipes the pipes are calling*
> *From glen to glen and down the mountain side*
> *The summer's gone and all the flowers are dying*
> *'Tis ye, ' tis ye must go, and I must bide.*
>
> *But come ye back when summers in the meadow*
> *Or when the valley's hushed and white with snow*
> *'Tis I'll be here in sunshine or in shadow*
> *Oh Danny boy, oh Danny boy, I love you so.*
>
> *And when ye come and all the flowers are dying*
> *If I am dead, as dead I well may be*
> *Ye'll come and find the place where I am lying*
> *And kneel and say an "Ave" there for me.*
>
> *And I shall hear though soft ye tread upon me*
> *And on my grave shall linger sweeter be*
> *Then ye shall bend and tell me that ye love me*
> *And I shall sleep in peace until ye come to me.*

There was an organ in the classroom and the schoolmaster would use a tuning fork that would start me out on the right note. Sometimes I would have to stand up in front of all the class and sing. I would be so embarrassed, but rather than get into trouble, I'd sing. I lost my tenor's voice around twelve or thirteen, but I always sang when the occasion arose, and still do today.

When May 1st arrived, off with our shoes! School was almost out for the year. This was a big day for the children and was referred to by all of us as *May Day*. We all hated wearing shoes. I suppose the grass was wet and that meant that our socks and shoes would be wet all day. During the cold days in winter many children spent the day in wet, damp clothes. There was one small peat fire in the schoolroom that provided the only heating. The seating was setup in a hierarchal manner with the older students sitting nearest the fire.

My father would buy new shoes for us every winter. Remember, we had to walk to school and back, so the shoes would get a good wearing out. In order to help prolong the life of the shoes, my father pushed in small tacks or studs around the outside of the soles. You'd be surprised at how much this helped. They were bought plenty big enough so your feet had room to grow.

There was one school year that I remember in particular when Dick, Bridgie, Nellie, Michael, Jim and I walked to Currabaggan School together. Actually, all the children from the village walked together and we'd meet up with others on the way. The girls were on time and the rest of us would be late.

I remember well Mrs. Caulfield, the schoolmaster's wife, making a visit to my mother complaining about my lack of interest. It wasn't her first time at our garden gate, and it wasn't the last time during the years that Jim and I attended the school in Currabaggan! There's no sign now of the old structure, only a large modern building with basketball nets and grounds that have been asphalted so the children can run around and play.

In Ireland the school system is different than in the United States. After leaving National School (grade school in the United States), very few had the opportunity of attending high school. High School level education was not free during my time; however, it is today. At that time, the only boys and girls who got the opportunity to attend high school were the children of the gentry or those who succeeded in obtaining a scholarship. Believe me, there were very few scholarships available.

But with all the complaining about the instructional methods in the Irish schools, many famous writers that are world-renowned came from Ireland. In the schools today the children are reading poetry by W. B. Yeats from Sligo, as well as James Joyce's infamous book Ulysses. Don't forget Samuel Beckett's literature, as well as Frederick Robert Higgins of Foxford whose poetry described Ireland to its fullest. The Book of Kells and the great Irish Monks as described by Tom Cahill in his book How The Irish Saved Civilization as they translated literature that would have been lost forever, centuries ago, if not for their perseverance.

There was also Louis Brennan, an inventor, from Castlebar. Brennan is given credit for the Brennan torpedo, mono-rail and the first helicopter. The technology that he brought to the English was priceless. These were brilliant men. But, some people don't have that ability or the capable mind to invent stories or machines. And that's good, or we would have a boring world.

All my sisters and brothers left school at the age of fourteen in order to work and I didn't hang around too much longer. Fourteen appears young in today's standards; however, when I left Currabaggan, I held the basic knowledge of reading, writing and arithmetic. I was grateful to have this much knowledge as I stood in line, waiting to go through customs in New York and watched as men and women tried to make themselves understood in many languages.

My brother Pat was working steadily and wanted me to go on and get a better education. He sent extra money to my mother from England to pay the tuition. But I refused.

"Willie," he'd say, "The pen is lighter than the shovel."

The schoolmaster hit me one too many times for things I didn't understand. I went out the door at fourteen years of age and never went back.

As I think about it now, I probably was looking for a reason to quit school. I'm sure if I really wanted to continue and finish my education, I would have. But I wasn't looking far enough ahead; only at the money that I was going to begin earning and with the hope and dream of a better life.

So it was work I wanted and work I got and never looked back until I arrived in the United States and realized that I had missed an opportunity. However, had I remained in school, my life would have been different and I am not sorry for my decision. I have a million dollar education with life experiences that cannot be learned from a book. I say with affirmation, I have no regrets.

I arrived home and said to my mother, "The master hit me and I'm not going back!"

She was sitting on the chair near the fire mending and looking up said, "Leave him as God left him, because he doesn't know any better."

Oh Come All Ye Faithful
Oh come all ye faithful
Joyful and triumphant,
Oh come ye, oh come ye to Bethlehem,
Come and behold him, born the king of angels.

(Chorus) Oh come let us adore him,
Oh come let us adore him
Oh come let us adore him,
Christ the lord.

Sing choirs of angels, sing with exultations,
Sing all ye citizens of heaven above.
Glory to God, in the highest
Ye Lord we greet thee
Born this happy morning,
Jesus, to thee be glory given
Word of the father, now in flesh appearing.

Adeste fi deles, laete triumphantes
Venite, venite in Bethlehem.
Natum videte, Regem angelorum
Venite adoremus
Venite adoremus
Venite adoremus
Dominum.

The day before Christmas vacation, Mrs. Caulfield would bring in two tins of candy. I can't say that lady wasn't good to us; she was and never forgot the candy. This was a special treat. Christmas Day was a holy day; Jesus was born on this day and each family celebrated it within their own house. Any family member that was at all able came home for this holiday. And school would be out for two weeks! But not before every child over the age of seven years received the Sacrament of Penance, as well as say a recitation or two.

> "I heard the bells on Christmas Day
> Their old familiar carols play,
> And wild and sweet their words repeat
> Of peace on earth, good-will to men!"
> --Longfellow

Christmas – the celebration of Christmas began with mass. And, you didn't go late to mass, that was a venial sin. However, there was great excitement, preparation, and anticipation for this holiday.

Market day in Ballina was on a Monday. If someone had something to sell it was done on Monday. I often watched the horse or donkey and carts leaving with the women holding onto their basket of eggs or whatever else that could be sold. But on the Monday before Christmas, you'd see nearly everyone in town buying "the Christmas," as it was referred to. They purchased things, such as currants, raisins, treacle for the Christmas cakes, and usually, a bottle of whiskey for a "droppeen of the good stuff" (a brandy or whiskey) if someone should stop to visit. And, of course, there would be plenty of tea, sugar and flour.

My father, God rest his soul, enjoyed a drop at every house in our village during that week. This was the only time I ever saw him over served (drunk.) It was a common practice during this time period, at least in our area, that the village chose one man to take up a collection for the parish priests. My grandfather was Ballymacredmond's, and when he died, my father took over the job, and when he died, my brother Dick continued until the church adopted the envelope system that we use today.

Besides Christmas my father would visit the week before Easter and right after the harvest for what was called the oats collection. He would go out in the evening to visit our neighbors with his little black book where he kept records of the donations. The name was written into the book and the amount right under. All the money collected went towards the maintenance of the priests in our Parish of Backs Church in Knockmore. The oats collection was a little extra to cover the cost of feeding and caring for the horse that the priest used for traveling.

Now, there was one more collection that was handled in a different manner. Each church had a curate or an associate pastor. It was his duty to visit every house in the parish and a donation was given and recorded. It started at the Epiphany, which is twelve days after Christmas Day on January 6 and could take weeks to complete. The villages were so spread out and traveling was not easy. The donations were tallied and divided in such a way that the Pastor received twice the amount of the curate. Even if there were two or three curates, the Pastor would receive twice the amount of the curates.

Now, the money given to the priest for a mass offering was theirs to keep. The priest is bound in church Canon law and it is a serious obligation, bound in justice that the mass be said and in a timely manner. If a priest cannot fulfill his promise to offer the mass, the full donation is then given to another priest.

Everyone in Backs Church looked his or her best on Christmas morning, and the Bourkes could hold their own. The women usually took the children to the 9:00 A.M. mass. If there were babies, one of the older children would stay home and then accompany their father to the 11:00 A.M. The women went early so they had plenty of time to start the dinner. Don't forget, everyone was walking. The men still had the cows to milk in the morning and other farming chores, but finished or not, they were at the 11:00 mass. It was worked out among ourselves in the house. It was a venial sin to be late and had to be told at the next confession. Of course, no woman entered church without a hat and no man with a hat. But, let me tell you, everyone attended mass, everyone!

There were no presents under the tree, sometimes a bit of candy or fruit to share. That was enough! We ate a good meal together and then some of us sat around the fire talking while others played cards and always the game of twenty-five. As the holy day ended, the children were up and down playing in the village and getting ready to celebrate the Day of the Wren.

St. Stephen's day, or as we call it, the Day of the Wren, on December 26 is a recognized holiday in Ireland. The banks and other businesses are closed. As children we loved this holiday and would be looking so forward to dressing up in disguises. For example, a boy would wear girl's clothing and the girl would dress as a boy. Sometimes you'd see someone wearing a mask. I suppose it was something similar to how the children dress up for Halloween here, but not as extravagant. Then we would all meet and go to the neighbors' cottages begging for a penny or whatever they would give us saying:

Give a penny to bury the "ran" (pronounced this way, but it was wren)

The 'ran the 'ran, the dróilín (Gaelic for wren.)

There is a myth or belief that the wren was involved with Judas Iscariot betraying Jesus Christ. Now, there is another poem or saying that was also popular. This one I learned when I was a littler older. A bunch of us would show up at the front door of the cottage and start chanting:

> The wren the wren
> The king of all birds
> On St. Stephen's Day
> We caught it in the furze
> Up with the kettle
> And down with the pan
> Give me a penny
> To bury the wren.

The myth that follows this particular verse says that Saint Stephen was hiding from the Roman soldiers and the wren gave him away. I don't know which one is right. They both sound good.

As I think of it now, this wasn't just a holiday for the children. The adults had a good time as well. Most of the men would have gone to the pub for a few jars and end up in our cottage. I can still see John Bourke (or Dan O'Hara) standing in the corner of the kitchen and singing *The Old Rustic Bridge by the Mill:*

> I'm thinking to night of the old rustic bridge,
> That bends o'er the murmuring stream.
> 'Twas there Maggie dear, with our hearts full of cheer,
> we strayed 'neath the moon's gentle gleam.
> 'Twas there I first met you, the light of your eyes,
> awoke in my heart a sweet thrill,
> Tho' now far away, still my thoughts fondly stray,
> To the old rustic bridge by the mill.

> (Chorus) Beneath it the stream gently rippled,
> Around it the birds loved to trill.
> Tho' now far away still my thoughts fondly stray,
> To the old rustic bridge by the mill.

> How often dear Maggie, when years passed away,
> And we plighted lovers became,
> We rambled the path to the bridge, day by day,
> The smiles of each other claim.
> But one day we parted, in pain and regret,
> Our vows then we could not fulfill,
> Oh may we soon meet and our fond love repeat
> On the old rustic bridge by the mill.

> Beneath it the stream gently rippled,
> Around it the birds loved to trill.
> Tho' now far away still my thoughts fondly stray,
> To the old rustic bridge by the mill.

> I keep in my memory our love of the past,
> With me 'tis as bright as of old,
> For deep in my heart it was planted to last,
> In absence it never grows cold.
> I think of you darling when lonely at night;
> And when all is peaceful and still,
> My heart wanders back, in a dream of delight,
> To the old rustic bridge by the mill.

This song has a beautiful and soft melody and the words are so sad, yet hopeful. There wouldn't be a sound in the room as Paddy hummed the last note.

Now the next day was another story. I remember hearing my father say to Paddy Gallagher, "I need the cure!"

"Richard," he answered, "Ye need the hair of the dog that bit ye!"

And so, another dropeen was poured.

the men of the west

When you honor in song and in story
The names of the patriot men
Whose valor has covered with glory
Full many a mountain and glen
Forget not the boys of the heather
Who rallied their bravest and best
When Ireland was broken in Wexford
And I looked for revenge to the West.

(Chorus) I give you the gallant old West, boys
Where rallied our bravest and best
When Ireland lay broken and bleeding;
Hurrah for the men of the West!

The hilltops with glory were glowing
'Twas the eve of a bright harvest day
When the ship we'd been wearily waiting
Sailed into Killala's broad bay
And over the hills went the slogan
To awaken in every breast
The fire that has never been quenched, boys
Among the true hearts of the West.
(Chorus)

Killala was ours ere the midnight
And high over Ballina town
Our banners in triumph were waving
Before the next sun had gone down
We gathered to speed the good work, boys
The true men from near and afar
And history can tell how we routed
The redcoats through old Castlebar.
(Chorus)

And pledge me the stout sons of France, boys
Bold Humbert and all his brave men
Whose tramp, like the trumpet of battle
Brought hope to the drooping again
Since Ireland has caught to her bosom
On many a mountain and hill
The gallants who fell, so they're here, boys
To cheer us to victory still.
(Chorus)

Though all the bright dreaming we cherished
Went down in disaster and woe
The spirit of old is still with us
That never would bend to the foe
And Connaught is ready whenever
The loud rolling tuck of the drum
Rings out to awaken the echoes
And tell us the morning has come.
I give you the gallant old West, boys
Where rallied our bravest and best
When Ireland lay broken and bleeding:
Hurrah for the men of the West!

August 1898
Written by William Rooney, Dublin and
a local Foxford man, J.J. Johnston.

I could hear whispering and movement in the middle of the night, but I was too young to understand what was happening until I was much older. The Irish Republican Army had a strong following in Mayo.

As it happened, I was born in 1920, after the terrible famine, the Great War, and the Easter Rebellion of 1916. The Irish men and women of Mayo left their homes and families by the thousands. As I mentioned, there were very few opportunities other than farming and then, you had to have a piece of land.

There were eleven children in my family, and realistically, only one would get the home place. There wasn't enough land to feed two families. The next option was to marry someone that would inherit their family's cottage and farm. If this didn't happen, there was no choice other than to move on.

One way to gain citizenship in countries, or at least be sure of a meal, was to join the military. Although, Ireland remained a neutral country as wars ravaged Europe, its Mayo men, and men from around the country, fought with the English, Canadian, American, Mexican, Australian, Argentina and many more armies. At this time in history, statistics showed that the majority of people living in Ireland were under the age of fifteen years and over sixty-five and the population declining. Realistically, it is impossible to build a country without the young and strong.

I believe that the Congressional Medal of Honor is the highest honor that our country, The United States of America, can bestow upon a soldier because of some heroic action on the battlefield, which often took his life. It is a fact that there have been many foreign-born recipients of this medal. I found it very interesting when I read that from 1863 to 1978 Irish/Irish American sons received 257 with the second being German-American with 126.

There was one man, Patrick Joseph Shannon from Greyfield, Kiltimagh, County Mayo, a World War I veteran who represented the fighting Irish and lived to tell his story. It was a bitter civil war for the oppressed Russians and peasants, the Reds and the Bolsheviks.

Patrick Shannon left from Liverpool, England for New York City in the United States in 1909 with a second class ticket, which cost six pounds. The days and evenings passed quickly as he played the card game of 25 with the sailors, as everyone else was seasick. It was a twenty-four hour train ride to Chicago where his brother Anthony was waiting. It wasn't long before Pat was decked out with a new shirt, suit and a stiff hat – a typical Yank.

Pat's first job was with the Gas Company earning two dollars and fifty cents a day. Before long he realized that more money could be made carrying the "hod" with an Irish contracting company named

McNulty's, which took him through many midwestern states and Canada. He had returned to Chicago in 1916 and was working steady. One morning a soldier arrived on the job site and said, "You'll join the American Army or be put on the next boat to Ireland."

Pat didn't hesitate, "I'll fight for any country I'm given a living in."

Before leaving Chicago, Pat went to visit a priest for a blessing. The priest gave him a Saint Anthony's chord, which he wore all the time inside his clothes. He told him, "If you die a soldier, you'll go to Heaven."

So off to Camp Custer as a 'rookie' and after three weeks' training, Pat was on his way back to Aldershot, England with the Coy "A" of the American Expeditionary Forces. He was trained as a machine gunner and after three weeks could name every part of the gun, as well as, put it together in three minutes. After training, they were sent to France and docked at Brest awaiting orders. It was only three short weeks when word arrived that their Battalion was picked to go to Russia.

Pat's Commanding Officer was Captain Ojar, a great fighting man, a real soldier, who always led the way and it wasn't long before they encountered the enemy. The Lewis gunner sent shock waves through our party when it jammed, but Pat wasn't long putting it right. Here he met up with another Irishman, Lieutenant Mick Foyle who arrived with twenty men to help us. I'm not sure where they came from, but they were a welcome sight.

Foyle said, "I was thinking you were in trouble."

The biggest engagement that Pat recalled taking part in was the Battle of Bistoka.

Pat said, "The Russians attacked us with huge forces thicker than any flock of crows you have ever seen."

He described the drive toward Leningrad with the Mensheviks as being too hasty. When his Battalion was within 80 miles of the city, they had advanced too far and did not have sufficient ammunition or supplies.

The saddest moment of this war for Pat was seeing three comrades lying shell-shocked in a trench unable to join a retreat. We couldn't take them with us. All we could do was put a grenade in each man's hand.

It was so cold. Horses and sleighs were used to help in the retreat. The soldiers put their blankets around their feet to prevent frostbite, but this was of little use most of the time. The fighting had shattering affects on some of the soldiers. One refrain that Pat never forgot as he and the other troops marched was:

"Oh boy, if I was ever back with Mama, I would never leave her."

After a fortnight (two weeks) of action, troops were allowed two weeks behind enemy lines, which were spent in local Russian villages. These people were trying to live normal, happy lives, surviving and doing much of the same as we do in our own country. There was a group of women using spinning wheels to make wool and linen. On one occasion Pat witnessed a wedding and at the party the musicians played with accordions, violins and flutes.

The months passed and finally the Armistice was signed in Europe and in June 1919 Pat returned to America and was discharged as a 1st class private at Camp Carter. Barely six months later Pat decided to return to his homeland and married Mary Ann Lavin from Knocknakill, Mayo Abbey, Claremoris, County Mayo on June 4, 1925. They raised twelve children, Anthony (1926), Beatrice (1927), Kathleen (1930, Annie Mae (1931), John Patrick (1933), Patrick Joseph (1934), Maura (1937), Margaret (1938), Teresa Cora (1940), Pauline (1942), Regina (1943, and Martin (1946) – all immigrated to the United States except for three sons and one daughter. Pat Shannon lived a comfortable life until he passed away on March 12, 1984 at 93 years of age.

Many an Irishman whistled and hummed this tune *Home Boys Home:*

Oh when I was a young boy
Sure I longed to see the world
To sail around the sea in ships
And see the sails unfurled.
I went to seek my fortune
On the far side of the hill
I've wandered far and wide
And of travel I've had my fill.

(Chorus) And it's home boys home
Home I'd like to be
Home for awhile in the old country
Where the oak and the ash
And the bonny rowan tree
Are all growing greener in the old country.

Well, I left my love behind me
And I sailed across the tide
I said that I'd be back again
And take her for my bride
But many years have passed and gone
And still I'm far away
I know she is a fond true love
And waiting for the day. (Chorus)

Now I've learned there's more to life
Than to wander and to roam
Happiness and peace of mind
Can best be found at home
For money can't buy happiness
And money cannot bind
So I'm going back tomorrow
To the girl I left behind. (Chorus)

Now during World War II many young lads went to England and were conscripted right at the piers or the railroad stations by a member of British Army.

They were asked, "What can you do?"

He'd answer, "I'm a farmer; I can save hay." "Well then," answered the Sergeant, "Off to Lincolnshire you'll go."

They worked hard, from daybreak until dark harvesting the food that fed many soldiers in foreign lands.

Once in a while the war came to Ireland. On this particular day it was at the Curradrish bog in the spring of 1944 when a Canadian war plane crash landed. My brother John and his oldest son Dick witnessed the landing. My nephew remembers hearing is his father saying,

"The wheels are coming down! The wheels are coming down!"

They watched as the plane glided in over the tree line of Mount Falcon, hitting ground in Tremble's field and stopped only by a wall from an old barn. If the wall hadn't been there, their house would have been flattened. There was no fire or explosion and the crew of four escaped unharmed.

Well, you can imagine the excitement. Sergeant Lynch arrived first on his motor bike and then the army followed. The men were taken to Curragh, Kildare to an interment camp and the plane was dismantled piece by piece and taken away.

However, the people of Ireland never forgot their objective. After World War II the idea of democracy was again our priority. I grew up with songs and stories of the brave men who were willing to give their lives for Ireland; for example, Michael Collins, Michael Kilroy, James Connelly, Pádraig Pearce, Kevin Barry and many more. These men, followers of the Sinn Fein Society, wanted to proclaim Ireland as a sovereign independent state and were willing to give their lives as many more before them.

And many did, especially during the six-day siege beginning on Easter Monday, April 24, 1916 on the streets in Dublin. The Sinn Feinn (Gaelic for 'ourselves alone') Society claims that it organized the revolution and the Irish National Volunteers carried it out. The people rose and marched to their death. They lost that battle, but soon they would win the war.

Now, don't confuse the IRA man of 1916 to an image of what we see and hear today on terrorism. They had the same visions as George Washington, Thomas Jefferson, and Ulysses S. Grant during the American Revolution. These were great men who fought for the independence of the United States of America and gave me the opportunity to better myself and make a decent, honest living while rearing a family. Likewise, the men fighting for a free Ireland wanted opportunities for the Irish people that could only be available as an independent country.

My father and anyone who could travel walked with Michael Collins' coffin in August 1922 as it went through Ballina station on to Foxford where mass was offered at St. Michael's Church. That September, sixteen men including Captain Tom Healy of Pontoon and John (Sean) Higgins of Foxford lost their lives in this tragic Civil War of Independence. They were laid to rest in a cemetery at Craggagh in an area referred to as Patriot's Plot.

I remember well the story of Michael Tolan's murder. He was accused of being a member of the IRA during the fight for independence. Michael was a tailor with deformed feet and was taken from the street on April 13, 1921 by the Black and Tans. The Black and Tans were a military group of men sent by England to control the political unrest in Ireland. The name represents their khaki and blackish green uniforms and was feared by everyone. I remember well this rebel song and as a young lad I listened as my brother John sang it:

It was in November as I well remember
There were heroes bold from Manchester came
It was their intention as I now will mention
To free poor Erin from a convict chain.

When Ireland heard of those men being taken
To O'Brien and Larkin he quickly flew
Saying, Kelly and Dicey my heart is breaking
We have lost our comrades, what shall we do?

Like loyal brothers they come together
Like loyal brothers they did agree
To meet the van and smash it open
And set those prisoners free.

The hills of Erin are now consecrated
No poisonous serpents there now can roam
St. Patrick banished them with his crown of glory
And the robes he wore were the shamrock green.

So now thank God their souls are in the heavens
And the angel Gabriel above them roams
Saying, you're welcome Fein's,
To your happy home.

The story goes that after Michael's arrest, he disappeared en route to the town of Galway. It was in June, late in the evening that two men, Armstrong and Lynch were out hunting foxes, when their dogs found the remains of Michael Tolan's body in the Shraheen Bog near my home. His feet had been cut off and the wrong identity placed on his body. No one guessed at the time that this man was Michael Tolan and the remains were handed over to the Poor Law authorities for burial in the strangers' plot in Ballina.

Michael's mother continually complained to the authorities about her son's whereabouts. Finally, a search was made in the jails and internment camps, but to no avail. That November the body found in Shraheen Bog was exhumed, identified and examined by three doctors who formed the opinion that death was caused by a bayonet wound and two bullets through the head.

After Ireland became independent and the truce signed, Michael Tolan's remains were again moved to a final resting place appropriate for his bravery. The funeral procession from Saint Muredach's Cathedral to Leigue was given credit as being one of the largest ever witnessed in Ballina. There were many stories during those years of Irishmen who were accused of being traitors to the Crown and "hung, drawn and quartered" in the fields.

This ballad told the story and my brother John sang it for us many times. I can only remember these few lines:

> *Michael Tolan inoffensive hero*
> *He found himself prisoner bound*
> *Without a reason or provocation*
> *His habitation they did surround*
> *In Shraheen Bog where he was concealed*
> *And you would pity his aching mother …*

Many years after, and I don't know for sure if it really did happen, someone told me that my brother John was stopped in the fields and accused by English soldiers of drowning the cattle at Mount Falcon. He was stripped and beaten, but not killed since he was only 17 years of age. I never knew whether John was involved or not and never will know. John's association with the IRA went with him to his grave.

There are many stories of how the English landlords acquired such vast amounts of land around our part of the country, as well as throughout Ireland. It is said that the first Irish Catholic settlers were sent from Northern Ireland to relocate here in Mayo because they refused to give up their Catholic faith. This may be one reason, but another was the fact that their land was confiscated. The intentions and desires of the English landlords were that the people starve and die. And as history tells it, God help us, many did die.

But remember, that it wasn't the famine that brought the Irish to this Nation; they were here before the American Revolution and fought for what we have today.

President George Washington said:

"Ireland, thou friend of my country in my country's most friendless days, much injured, much enduring land, accept this poor tribute from one who esteems thy worth, and mourns they desolation. May the God of Heaven, in His justice and mercy, grant thee more prosperous fortunes, and in His own time, cause the sun of Freedom to shed its benign radiance on the Emerald Isle

And Parke Custis, President George Washington's adopted son wrote,

"...In the War of Independence, Ireland furnished one hundred men to every single man furnished by any other nation, let America bear eternal gratitude to Irishmen."

SKIBBEREEN

O, Father dear, I oft times heard you talk of Erin's Isle
Her valleys green, her lofty scene, her mountains rude and wild
You said it was a pleasant place wherein a prince might dwell
Why have you then abandoned her, the reason to me tell?

My son, I loved our native land with energy and pride
Until blight fell on the land and sheep and cattle died
The rents and taxes were to pay, I could not them redeem
And that's the cruel reason why I left old Skibbereen.

It's well I do remember on a bleak November's day
The landlord and his agent came to drive us all away
He set my house on fire with his demon yellow spleen
And that's another reason why I left old Skibbereen.

Your mother, too, God rest her soul, lay on the snowy ground
She fainted in her anguish of the desolation round
She never rose, but went her way from life to death's long dream
And found a quiet grave, my boy, in lovely Skibbereen.

It's well I do remember the year of forty-eight
When we arose with Erin's boys to fight against our fate
I was hunted through the mountains as a traitor to the Queen
And that's another reason that I left old Skibbereen.

Oh father dear, the day will come when vengeance loud will call
And we'll arise with Erin's boys and rally one and all
I'll be the man to lead the van, beneath our flag of green
And loud and high we'll raise the cry, "Revenge for Skibbereen!"

I know that in my part of Mayo the potato famine that began in 1845 had a detrimental effect on the poor farmers. The land wasn't producing. It was of no use to these poor people; they were starving. The proposal was to leave the Catholic faith to follow their religion, and in return, their families would be given food. And of course, some had to resort to, as was said, "taking the soup." In other words they gave up their land for life.

I'm telling you the truth about this song, and without any exaggeration. *Skibbereen* was sung at every party, and at every singsong at the tavern, here or in Ireland. *Skibbereen,* a town located in the County of Cork, gives the most powerful and heart-wrenching description of what happened under the control of the landlords.

It was in Irishtown, County Mayo where the land war, and eventually referred to as the Land League, began and was led by Michael Davitt.

Davitt had witnessed his own family's eviction in 1850 in Straide and swore to help his fellow Mayoman. He spent some time in prison and discovered upon his release and return to his home in Mayo that conditions for the tenant farmer had not improved.

It seemed as though the rain didn't stop in 1879 and the potatoes failed again, which meant more starving, suffering and dying Mayomen. The story goes that a priest inherited land in Irishtown near Claremorris and decided to raise the rents and evict a certain group of tenants who were behind on payments. This angered Michael Davitt and he immediately arranged for a massive demonstration to take place in Irishtown.

On Sunday, April 20, 1879 some 13,000 men, in pouring rain, rallied to his call and, needless to say, the evictions were cancelled. It was in Irishtown that Michael Davitt realized that through organization, landlordism could be conquered. However, it was not until October of 1879 that Charles Stewart Parnell, who was nick named the "uncrowned King of Ireland" fought with Michael Davitt and founded the National Land League. There were branches formed in almost every parish in Connaught and around Ireland.

The local landlord near Ballymacredmond at the time was the Knox-Gore Family and they lived in a real mansion, Mount Falcon Castle, which was built in 1836 by Edmond Gore Perry, who married a Miss Knox Gore from Belleek. The landlord owned this large estate with the best land that could be found in the Parish of Backs. A mile or so away from the castle you would see the coach house, the house where the butlers lived, the house where the laundry was done, and so on. The stables were massive and the racecourse measured one mile and a half around with a small grandstand that still stands today. It was ideal land for harvesting or grazing cattle. I imagine the estate had more than 1,000 acres of land.

Now, this is what caused the unrest in Ballymacredmond. There were two families near the Foxford area who were allowed to rent land from Mount Falcon. They had grazing rights for their cattle on this land, whereas, the locals in Ballymacredmond did not have access or an option to rent. We were right next to the land and our cattle could not graze, and never mind the cattle, we were not supposed to walk on the property. Gates were put up. My father, Richard Bourke, believed that this was discrimination and was going to do something about it.

A secret meeting was called. Richard Nallon, Richard Langan, and James McHale were only a few of the men that supported my father when he decided to organize a cattle drive. In the dark of night they assembled and drove the cattle belonging to the two families out of the estate onto the main road. They drove them on the main road up as far as Foxford and then, let them loose. When the wandering cattle were discovered, an investigation was made. The ringleader, my father was accused and arrested and spent the next night in the jail in Ballina.

At this time there was a very eminent attorney working in Ballina, Attorney Bourke. He was no relation. His residence was Amana Estate in Church Road, Ballina. When the court case was arraigned, Attorney Bourke was called to defend the "culprits" and won the case. The judge decided in his favor and agreed that the Knox Family was discriminating against the local residences of Ballymacredmond.

As a result, the Ballymacredmond farmers were allowed grazing rights in certain areas of the estate, and of course, for a fee. However, there was one stipulation. Richard Bourke had to be responsible for the cattle in case of a breakout or any other problems. As a reward for this task, he was allowed to graze one beast of his own, free of charge. Attorney Bourke continued his legacy of justice through his granddaughter, Ireland's past President, Mrs. Mary (Bourke) Robinson.

Even though there were a few political battles won, life on the whole didn't change much. The people of Ireland were immigrating by the thousands searching for new homes, and it was no different in Ballymacredmond. John and Mary were the oldest and the house was full; it was time for them to move on. Since leaving school at the age of fourteen, John had been working for Mr. Scott, who owned a huge dairy. Mary found domestic work at Barnfield house, an equestrian estate, about a mile from our home.

However, at the age of seventeen, Mary had had enough of Ireland and wanted to go to America. Actually, it was my mother's wish that John and Mary go to America, to the city of Chicago. Her sister Mariah and brother Dan had already emigrated.

One avenue of exit that was available during this period of time was to become an indentured servant in another country. After much consternation, discussion, letters back and forth to America, and prayer, Mary alas went to Dublin to signup with a company that would place her with a family in Canada. It was everyone's intention that after the two-year service period was completed, Mary would travel by train to Chicago. One of the stipulations to be accepted as an indentured servant was to be in perfect health, physically and mentally. Mary passed the test.

My first memory as a child is going for a bike ride with Mary. She lifted me onto the handlebars of our mother's bike and off we went down the bumpy road. I still remember the wind on my face and the excitement.

"Mary, one more time," I begged.

But there was no time, the train was leaving for Dublin and it was a good walk into town. Mary and I would not see each other again for 23 years.

I was too young to understand the impact of her leaving. There was sadness in the house, but after awhile, I forgot. We were used to saying goodbye. When someone would be leaving for the continent, or the U.S.A, or America or just the other side, usually there was some sort of going away party in their home the night before. These parties became known as the "American wakes."

You'd be shaking hands with the men or kissing a lassie goodbye, saying, "We'll see you soon!" But, deep in your heart, you knew the chances were slim. I was told later that the tears fell from my father's eyes as he watched his little girleen walk down the road with her case. She turned and waved only once. I'm sure he asked himself, "Will she be better off?" Leaving home wasn't always the answer.

This was a sad time. Many a father and mother shed tears for their loss, especially around Mayo. My father and mother never saw Mary again, never met her husband or were able to hold their grandchildren. She left too young. No one really knew each other.

It is a wonderful feeling to know that the children of Ireland today have options. If they want to go home, it is possible. On the other hand, having to leave home taught the Irishman, in particular the Mayo man, how to survive. They educated themselves, their children and their children's children; their presence is from one end of the globe to the other.

As all this was going on, I was growing up – rambling through one field after another pulling a carrot or turnip from the ground and eating it as if it were an apple. But there was always a nagging fear of being captured, and then, one day the news arrived. The agreement had been signed. The South of Ireland was independent and Ballymacredmond would see more changes.

In 1932, the Irish Land Commission took over the Mount Falcon Estate. The Land Commission was a government department that arranged for the deeds of the "new land" to be returned to the Irish people. A meeting was called at the crossroads by the "Taisheach," which is Gaelic for Prime Minister who was DeValera. Representatives from the new government conducted the ceremony referred to as "the transfer of the land." Here, most of the land that belonged to the Mount Falcon Estate was divided amongst the neighboring farmers. This land had once belonged to their ancestors and now the original owner, an Irishman, would once again work and walk these fields of green.

Independence had come to the South of Ireland and enormous changes were about to take place. I could sense the excitement; tension was in the air. No one had much to say. My father had been waiting, hoping and praying for this day. He said, "Willie, this is history – and you are part of it!"

There was a celebration amongst us. As you turned off the main road and continued to the dead-end, that was our house. Over the years it became the main gathering place for everyone to meet and exchange news and everyone was there. There was singing and dancing late into the night; I can remember the women saying, "Tis a miracle, Tis too good to be true!" The rosary was said around the fire, praying for the end of the anguish, discontentment and bloodshed on both sides.

That night, at the crossroads, around the bond fire, you could hear a pin drop as my father stood up, head held high and sang. The men shouted, "Rise it, Richard, rise it!" He did, and sang The Dublin Trials with all his heart.

Every man and woman in the village shed a tear that night. Many a pint of stout was raised and hailed for our independence. But, as you know, there was a long road ahead. Ireland's infrastructure needed repair, but "When there's a will, there's a way."

When the Dublin trials are over
And this is how they got on
Before the judge and jury
They were sentenced one by one.

The murder is in the Phoenix Park
13 months gone by
Joe Grady was the first man tried
And was sentenced for to die.

But before his awful doing
He wrote a letter to his wife
Telling her what she should do
And the request that he craved
Was to be sure and mind the children
When he laid in his grave.

The crowd assembled all around the jail
And when the black flag was raised
The father and the father-in-law
At the time were standing by
And in the middle of the crowd
They both commenced to cry.

If you were to see those men cry,
Their tears would melt a stone
Trying to look over the mansion wall
With a heavy sigh and moan.

God forgive all executioners
That is all I have to say
And I hope they gain salvation
Upon the judgment day.

when irish eyes are smiling

There's a tear in your eye
And I'm wondering why
For it never should be there at all
With such power in your smile
Sure a stone you'd beguile
So there's never a teardrop should fall
When your sweet lifting laughter's
Like some fairy song
And your eyes twinkle bright as can be
You should laugh all the while
And all other times smile
And now, smile a smile for me.

(Chorus) When Irish eyes are smiling
Sure 'tis like a morn in spring.
In the lilt of Irish laughter
You can hear the angels sing.
When Irish hearts are happy
All the world seems bright and gay
And when Irish eyes are smiling
Sure, they steal your heart away.

For your smile is a part
Of the love in your heart
And it makes the sunshine more bright
Like the linnet's sweet song
Crooning all the day long
Comes your laughter and light
For the springtime of life
Is the sweetness of all
There is ne'er a real care or regret
And while springtime is ours
Throughout all of youth's hours
Let us smile each chance we get.

Faith in God and the Holy Family, Jesus, Mary, and Saint Joseph was all that many had to keep them alive. I'm not surprised that when our patron saint arrived in Mayo, he built his church on the peak of Croagh Patrick in Westport. Saint Patrick brought Christianity to us around 441 AD, and March 17th is a holy day in Ireland, not a party day. You go to mass, not the pubs! Although, I must say, I spent more time on a bar stool than sitting in a church pew celebrating our patron's holy deeds. Now, the story goes that Saint Patrick died on March 8th or March 9th. Either date could not be proven, so what we did was add the two dates together, which came to the 17th and was proclaimed a holy day.

Saint Patrick used the three-leaf shamrock that is found all over Ireland to help with his teaching of the Roman Catholic faith. It is said that he bent over and picked the shamrock to explain the holy

Trinity; that one God represents the father, the son and the Holy Spirit. Because of this, the shamrock is renowned and held in reverence by the people of Ireland.

You remember that Saint Patrick was the son of a Roman soldier, but was kidnapped as a boy and taken to Ireland as a slave. For the next six years he tended his flock of sheep and prayed until his escape to France where he began his studies in a monastery. Little did anyone ever suspect, that this young boy would return one day to inspire and guide us in our Roman Catholic faith.

What made Croagh Patrick so important, or "the Reek" as it is referred to by many? Well, I'm sure Saint Patrick must have walked the length and breadth of Ireland and then, finally arriving in Mayo, looked up from the lovely shores of Clew Bay and knew that the mountain before him was special.

Saint Patrick climbed to the top in order to look down upon this land with its lakes and rivers, hills and mountains, farmland to bog land and asked for God's graces. On the summit of this mountain Saint Patrick stayed to pray and fast for forty days. It is said that he transported the material needed by donkey up the opposite side of the mountain from where the pilgrimage is made, and I don't know why; that's what my mother told me.

Every year, hundreds! Hundreds of men, woman and children, young and old make the pilgrimage from their homes on foot. Many stopped over in the town of Ballintubber for mass in the beautiful abbey that was founded in 1216 by King Cathal O'Conor. But, Ballintubber's roots go back to Saint Patrick himself. He built a church here. Still today there are some who walk the pilgrim's path called "Tóchar Phádraig" and it is a good distance. However, I know that many people drive to the bottom of Croagh Patrick and then make the climb. Pilgrimages are made every day of the week in all sorts of weather to this sacred mountain.

I learned this recitation as a young boy:

> *Saint Patrick banned the serpent*
> *From our faunal Irish Shore*
> *I'll make them fly before I die*
> *Like the hare before the hound.*

Why do the men and women walk from as far as Athlone or put horsehair inside their clothes in order to suffer more or climb barefoot so their feet are bleeding? Some do it for penance in the hope that God will forgive them for their sins. Others are asking for a miracle or the hope of receiving a special blessing through the intercession of Saint Patrick. I don't know for sure, but I know I believe in God and through prayers and penance, I will become a better person. Even, perhaps I will be better able to handle situations that life itself brings my way.

As a gasur I watched my father and mother preparing for the walk. It was necessary to carry food and a blanket along with other necessities. Other friends and family members from the village would go as well. It was better to travel together and it took two full days.

A group would leave at day break and not return until late the next night. Of course, the children weren't allowed to go along unless they were old enough and able for the journey. I made the walk a couple of times before leaving Ireland and each time it renewed my belief with vengeance that there is a God.

There is a place about one mile and a half from our home, right on the Killala Road where it is said that Saint Patrick stopped to say mass. I remember well taking my mother and Mariah Rodgers from our village, by horse and cart, to the area.

"Willie," she said, "You promised."

"I'll hitch Dolly," I replied, wishing that I didn't have to do this. Someone was bound to go by and recognize me, out with the women, praying. It was the last place I wanted to be, but I remembered promising a few times – so, off we went.

We had to walk down a small incline away from the road where there is a stream. I can still see them, walking with their rosary beads, around and around the holy ground, praying to God for the living and the dead.

My mother, God rest her soul, told me that she was praying for her children, at home and abroad. I watched her raise her eyes up to heaven asking God to protect them in soul and body – keep their religion and be safe. I don't know how many prayers or rosaries she said, but I could hear the whisper of the Hail Mary and see her lips moving, unaware of birds flying, the misting rain, or the time passing. As if in a trance my mother prayed:

> *Hail Mary, full of grace*
> *The Lord is with ye*
> *Blessed are thou amongst women*
> *And blessed is the fruit*
> *Of thy womb Jesus.*

> *Holy Mary, Mother of God*
> *Pray for us sinners*
> *Now and at the hour of our death*
> *Amen*

The de Burgo family acclimated themselves to the Gaelic culture through language, laws, religion, celebrations, etc. and remained powerful in Connaught for several hundred years. They built numerous stone castles, monasteries and abbeys for the Dominicans, Camelites and Augustinians. In 1469 Richard De Burgo, head of the clan or "The MacWilliam," granted 200 acres of land to Burrishoole to the Dominican Order and there, their abbey was built on the north shore of Clew Bay.

One can see today from Clew Bay on the Achill Island is the castle and home of the famous pirate, Grace O'Malley or Granuaile, as well as the pirate queen. Grace O'Malley married Richard Bourke and gave birth to one son Theobald Bourke, *Tibbott-ne-Long* in 1567. This woman fought for Ireland's people and independence in the sixteenth century and led her clan and fleet of ships against Queen Elizabeth I. She is known as "The Mother of all the Irish rebellions" and loved her Connaught, its people, traditions, and freedom. Granuaile was trusted by many important clans – O'Flahertys, O'Malleys, Bourkes, O'Dowds, Conroys – and ran her fleet of ships with undisputed dominance.

As in every country, there are different scenic areas that are memorable. Well, I don't mind saying that in this part of the country, around Westport, Newport and Clew Bay, you will see the most picturesque, beautiful and breath-taking scenery. You can almost imagine, Saint Patrick standing there, with staff in hand, chasing the snakes out of Ireland.

We celebrated all the saints' days, including Saint Brigid's Day on February 1, which is the first day of spring. Saint Brigid is the patroness of cattle and dairy work and you will find her cross made from woven straw or reeds hanging over the door for protection. It was said that if you heard the lark singing on Saint Brigid's Day, there would be a good spring that year.

Saint John's Day is celebrated on June 2 with bond fires all over the countryside. This is an old ceremony celebrating the beginning of harvest season that I'm sure came from the Druids and has remained part of our Irish culture. Preparing for this fire took days of preparation. A site was chosen and all the young ones in the village and those who lived in the area would be collecting pieces of wood and sticks and piling them up. After the day's work was done, and the sun gone down, the older lads would start the fire. Whoever could spare a few pieces of turf brought them along and this helped to keep the fire going for hours. It was a great night of fun and laughing.

It was a tradition that the Brack bread be made for this night. My mother would make two loaves and put a little gold ring in each loaf before baking. Well there'd be great anticipation and excitement when the bread came out. The young boys received a piece from the one loaf and the young girls from the other. It was the belief that the boy and girl with the rings would marry. It was great fun.

BARM BRACK BREAD

(ingredients)

7 cups sifted white flour

2 tablespoons brown All Spice

1½ teaspoon salt

1 cup white sugar

2 packages of active dry yeast

3 cups warm milk and water

6 tablespoons butter

2 ½ cups raisins

¾ cup dried currants

¾ cups chopped, dried citrus peel

Combine flour, all spice, sugar, and salt into large bowl.

Dissolve yeast in ½ warm milk and water.

Add yeast and remaining liquid to remaining dry ingredients & mix thoroughly.

Knead into ball and turn out on a floured board.

Wash and grease bowl.

Knead dough until it is no longer sticky and comes away clean from board.

Return dough to greased board.

Cover and let stand in warm place until dough is double in bulk (about ½ hours)

Turn dough onto floured board and flatten.

Place butter, fruit and peel in middle and work in by squeezing and kneading until they are evenly incorporated into dough.

Return dough again to greased bowl and cover.

Let rise for about 45 minutes.

Divide into 2 parts

Shape to fit 2 pans – approximately 9 x 5 x 3

½ fill pans and cover

Leave in warm place to rise to top of pans

Wrap a play ring in parchment paper and press into middle of dough so it is covered and dough will cook around it.

Bake in preheated over 450 degrees Fahrenheit for 50 minutes

Reduce heat to 425 degrees for last 15 minutes.

Remove from pans and let cool before cutting.

We went to mass on Sunday and tried to live by the good book or our Bible. But it is human nature to become discouraged when a country sees war, hunger, diseases, natural disasters and emigration. Perhaps it was time for our Lady to renew the Christian faith and give her people in Ireland something to hold onto during times of desperation.

Again, I say it is not a surprise that our Blessed Mother, along with Saint Joseph and Saint John the Evangelist appeared at the south gable of Knock Parish Church in my Mayo. There were fifteen eyewitnesses who attest to the apparition outside the chapel in the village of Knock. The three were by the gable wall, not really standing nor floating around, but seemed elevated perhaps a couple of feet from the ground. The Virgin had her eyes raised to heaven while Saint Joseph was standing nearby. Behind Saint John was an altar, with a cross, and a lamb with adoring angels.

Pope John Paul visited the Knock Shrine in 1979 and Mother Teresa of Calcutta in June of 1993. In fact, there are more than one and a half million visitors to the shrine each year. They know that our Lady will never forsake us. I have had the privilege of kneeling to pray at this remarkable and holy shrine. I asked our Lady to intercede for my special intentions and guide me and help me to be the best I can be for myself and my family. I believe she heard me!

And while Saint Patrick and our Lady of Knock became myths around the world and people traveled from all over to witness and touch the relics left behind, few recall the legend of Father Joseph Foy as a miracle worker.

Father Foy was born in Belass, in the Parish of Knockmore in 1841 and after being ordained a Roman Catholic priest, served as a curate for a time in Killala diocese. I mind well my father telling the story of when Father Foy went on a sick call that was on the other side of the Moy River. In order to save time, he walked across the Moy estuary and, there was no doubt, because his shoes were dry arriving at the sick man's house as when he returned to his own.

And, it was said that he could put a curse on you also. The story goes that Father Foy was in the town of Ballina and upon purchasing a pair of shoes; he realized that he was sixpence short of the price. The young apprentice told the manager, but he would not give Father Foy credit. So, the apprentice told the manager to take the sixpence out of his wages. Upon leaving the store, it is said that Father Foy told the manager that his breed would not prosper, but that the day would come when people would wonder at the apprentice's wealth.

As it happens the young apprentice was James Murphy who founded Murphy Brothers in Ballina. And it was his son, James Murphy that my brother John worked for all his life and that I worked for until leaving home.

Father Foy once said that his office would be at his graveside. And this has come to pass. You can see his grave at St. Muredach's Cathedral in Ballina and watch as hundreds of visitors each year leave gifts as thanks for a favor granted. Some take a pebble from its surface as a keepsake or for good luck.

Let the bears and lions growl and fight
For it is their nature to.
Let love through all your actions run
And all your words be mild.

Live like the Blessed Virgin's son
That sweet and lovely child.
His soul was gentle as a lamb
As his stature grew
He grew in favor
Both with man and God
And his father too.

Now Lord of them all
He reigns from above
And he sees his children dwell
And marks them for his own.

(Poem recited from memory- author unknown)

Our village is a walking distance to Mount Falcon Castle, which in my time was owned by Mr. Knox, an English landlord. It was said to have about 50 rooms and the landscaping was beautiful and still is today. There is a small graveyard that can be seen from the road. I used to jump over the ditch to get in just so I could stand on the giant's grave.

It was said that Ireland once was full of giants and this was the grave of a man who stood 16 feet. There was no name on the gravestone, only the marker that was pure white now from time, but everyone knew it was the giant's grave and it remained untouched. There were other graves with headstones showing the names of the Knox family members, including thirteen smaller stones with names of their children, buried in a separate section opposite the adults.

My brother Jim, Mick Flynn, Paddy Burke and myself would enter, scared half to death, but no one would let on, or be called a sissy. We were afraid of the dead and had heard many a ghost story that would put the hair standing on the back of your neck. Ireland is an old country, with habitants long before our Lord was born, and the county of Mayo had seen its share of unjust deaths. There were too many stories not to be sure that the unsettled souls who still walked the roads or the hallways of the old castles had died too young or too soon.

My father told this story till the day he died. Crossing the fields, he heard the sound of horses in the distance. When he turned around, he saw nothing and heard nothing. He continued on for a bit, but again heard the sound of the horses' hoofs hitting the sod in a hard run.

I remember well him saying, "The sweat was out on my body as I stood there, hardly able to breathe, and watched him – a headless rider, dressed as a soldier and holding his sword in front, advancing towards battle. Following in pursuit were ten or twelve soldiers, all dressed in their uniform with swords drawn, riding hard across the field." Over the years, other neighbors witnessed the headless soldier, but no one ever identified him or recognized the military dress.

I never met any member of the Knox family, but as a child I was careful when crossing their property. They had hundreds of acres that were used for farming, cattle, and horses. Rabbits were in abundance on their property, but if anyone was caught poaching on their land, there was an awful fine to pay. This was stealing. Rabbits were used for food, as well as their skin and fur for clothing.

My mother would send me out early in the morning or sometimes late at night to bring back one or two wild rabbits. She'd say, "Willie the hares will be out, bring one home, will ye." I'd be out the door running to the area where I had been watching. Many times my friend

Christy Bourke and I were together and, let me tell you now, we never went home empty handed.

The best way to find the burrows is to stay out of sight and watch for the movement of the long grass. I learned patience here; I had no control. The rabbits would be running around in the fields, but eventually return to their homes. That night I'd make a box, prop it up with a twig and then put a bit of food well inside the box. When the rabbit entered to eat the snack, the twig fell and the rabbit was caught under the box without injury. Once I caught four at one time; it was early morning, just as the sun was rising.

I got so good at following their tracks and snaring that my mother was able to sell the skins in town for money. Once when I was twelve or thirteen and carrying a shotgun, I aimed too high and cut the head off the rabbit. It still amazes me when I think of it; my mother was able to sew it back on and get full price for the skin. And there was nothing like her rabbit stews with plenty of carrots, potatoes, onions, and turnips.

We had great fun amongst ourselves. I loved it when my older sisters and brothers were around. Around 9:00 in the evening, my mother used to ask me to sing her favorite song about, Lovely Willie. She'd say, "Willie, if you sing I won't ask you to do another thing." Every night I believed her and would sing, standing by the fireside, as everyone listened to *The Banks of Drummore..*

> One night in my ramblings, in going to a ball
> I met with lovely Willie, he was slender and tall.
> He was tall, neat and handsome in every degree
> And ardent in my bosom lies pleading for thee.
>
> There is a tree in my fair garden, lovely Willie, said she
> Where Lord Duke and Earl are awaiting for me.
> When they're all fast asleep and silent at rest
> I'll come back to my Willie, the lad I love best.

When me and my Willie were walking alone
I spied my own father, he planked a cane.
With a sharp cane and pistol he pierced my love through
And the innocent blood of my Willie he drew.

Oh father, dear father if that be your will
Innocent blood of my Willie to spill,
I'll go to strange places, strange faces to see
Where I will know no one and no one will know me.

The grave was made and my Willie lay down
They sent for the clergy to pray for his soul.
May the great God protect us on the ground where we lay
I will lie down beside him; he's my own darl'n boy.

So fare thee well father and fare thee well mother
And fare thee well brother for I have no sister.
I bid adieu to Erin where I ne're shall see more
I go to you lovely Willie, on the banks of Drummore.

We played cards, I listened to stories, and we all took turns singing our favorite song. Some of the stories that the old people would tell before going to bed did put the hair standing on the back of my neck. I remember well leaving Johnny Flynn's house near midnight.

The night was as black as coal, but it didn't matter; I knew every stone on the road without seeing anything. You couldn't see your hand in front of your face; and of course, I had to pass the hump on the road where the fairies always crossed. I can still feel the gentle breeze touching my face. I was sure they were the fairies playing around me.

Not far from Ballymacredmond there is a field with a mound of dirt with beautiful, lush green grass growing in the middle of the field and it is known as the *forgeen mora*. Supposedly there is a man buried under the mound and that is why the cattle will never eat the grass from that particular spot. It is in this field or any field in Ireland with a forgeen mora that a person can get lost cutting through at night. If you did make the mistake, there was only one way you'd find the gate or an exit. The coat would have to be removed, turned inside out, put back on, and then and only then would the person see the gate. If not, they'd be walking in a circle until daybreak.

I would be scared to death in case I would hear a fairy called the "Banshee" or see her sitting on the ditch or gates along the way. The myth says that the Banshee or Banshi goes back to the early eighth century and the name comes from the old Irish "ben sidhe," a woman of the fairy folk or fairy mound or "ban" for woman and "shee" for crying. Another translation is "Banchionte" or wailing woman. She always appears as an old woman, wrinkled with long, wild gray hair.

There have been many sightings where she has been combing her hair, or at least have a comb in her hand. The Banshee was heard often around Mayo. There were certain families that used to hear her during the night wailing and moaning. These people who tell of her are good, hard-workers that believe, as their ancestors believed, that she comes to give warning of a death in the family.

Sometimes the families were aware of an upcoming death and her appearance was expected, but many times, when she was sighted, a sudden tragedy occurred. If a comb was picked up on the road, you could be sure that the Banshee had been there, combing her hair, while wailing or moaning over an upcoming death.

There is a haunted room in a house not far from Ballymacredmond. The house belonged to a protestant family by the name of Jackson. It is said that when the sister of the new owners was on the boat to America, a man appeared to her. The poor lady lost her mind and was never right again. In the same house, the resistances complained of the noise, constant rattling and squeaking of the doors. It was hard to sleep. Finally, a local priest was asked to say a mass. This is true! As the mass was being said, stones were thrown at them.

It's hard not to believe this story as well. I heard it as a young man, long before I arrived in Chicago. A young woman from up around our way was dying during childbirth. It was a terrible winter and that night the snow was coming down hard. Someone had gone on horseback for the doctor who lived in town. Hours passed and then the knocking was heard. There were too many people in the house that verified the knocks. The door was answered three times and no one was in sight. There were no footprints in the snow leading to or away from the door, and within the hour the mother and child died.

There are ghosts in Mayo and Francie Heneghen knows for sure, according to my son-in-law Bill (Gabe) Hosty from the village of Shanvallyboct, Irishtown, County Mayo. Francie had a group of six men over one evening to play a game of twenty-five. But, there was one thing that you were not supposed to do, and that was to renege. This was considered a sin. Thomas Mitchell was present when a jug broke in the middle of the table. They didn't know where the jug came from and looked up and saw a woman dressed in black. It wouldn't have been so bad if she was in white, but black was bad luck.

Well, this broke the card game up. Anyways, it was 4:00 in the morning and time to go home. The cows needed to be milked in a couple of hours. But, no one slept. At daybreak Francie went for the priest and brought him down to the house. He sent for all the lads and they regrouped and the priest had mass right where the lady was standing. Almost immediately, the wall nearest the priest began to shake. The priest began to throw holy water and pray out loud.

"Lord have mercy on this lost soul, Lord help this soul, Lord have mercy, Lord have mercy, and God help us" over and over.

But, the wall was moving towards him. Everyone saw that the priest had broke out in a sweat and then, suddenly, he fell to the floor backwards and was laying on his back still clasping the bottle of holy water. There was barely a drop left when he spotted a shadow over him, and thinking quickly, threw the remaining few drops towards it. The water hit the shadow and it immediately disappeared. Instantly, he sprung up and said, "I won; I drove her down to where you will walk by everyday, however you will never see her or she will never bother anyone again. She's gone to her place of rest *"gathy garet" (red gate)*.

There's another good one that happened near our house. This story comes from a priest who has no reason to tell a lie to me. The mansion is outside Ballina and there were two old ladies and a brother living there at the time. The old man was ill and the family hired a nurse to take the night shift. A makeshift room had been put together on the first floor to make caring for him easier.

On this night it was known that the old man was dying. The sisters had gone upstairs to bed and the nurse sat at his bedside reading. She had lit up a cigarette, and was watching the old man who had slipped into a coma when a terrific heaving knocking echoed from the front door.

The brass knocker was used and it felt as though the house shook from the thumping. Well, the old man took hold of either side of the bed and pulled himself up, yelling, "Let her in! Let her in!" Suddenly all the birds from the surrounding forest were heard rattling their wings and soaring and fluttering by the windows. The old man, who had not said a word in days, fell back and died. His sisters went running from the room screaming. And the poor girleen who had been tending him, she took off out the door running without a good-bye and never looked back.

I haven't heard about the Banshee appearing in many years, although some believe they have heard her at night. Years ago, Ireland was unsettled with innocent people dying from the ordeals of war, poor medical attention or lack of proper nourishment. Men were murdered and died without a rightful cause; as well as, the men, women and children who suffered injustices due to poverty and lack of education. Over the years, masses have been celebrated and I am sure that has helped to put many unsettled souls to rest. Now, I hope and pray that the deceased in Ireland are all at peace.

GOOD-BYE JOHNNY DEAR

Oh good-bye Johnny dear
And when you're far away
Don't forget your dear old mother
Far across the sea.

Write a letter now and then
And send her all you can
For you'll never miss a mother's love
Till she's buried beneath the clay.

I left school for the last time, and as all my sisters and brothers, began working with the intentions of bettering myself. I don't believe I ever dreamt of being rich as those living in Ashford Castle or the likes, but I wanted to do something more than be a farmer. At this point, I knew that my brother Dick would have the home place and it was just understood that the rest of us had to find someplace else to call home. I didn't mind the idea of traveling out of Ireland and seeing other parts of world. However, I realized that before one can travel, money is needed to pay the fare.

My first job, at the age of fifteen, was with the Irish Land Commission working under Johnny Duncan. Since the land had been divided by the state amongst the local small farmers, the sod fences or ditches had to be changed. If a ditch had to be removed, it was referred to as "tramp'n the ditches." And literally, we trampled them with our bare feet and spread the sod and moved the stone to new locations. I worked from early morning till late afternoon and my wage was 10 shillings a week.

I wasn't there long when my brother John got me a job at Robert Scott's, a landowner just to the south of Ballymacredmond. He owned hundreds of acres and a large house called Barnfield, which still stands today. Mr. Scott made his money as a dairy farmer and raised and raced horses. At one time or another, my five brothers and I worked for Mr. Scott. He was a good neighbor and paid each man a fair day's wage. When I arrived at work on Monday morning, I was wearing long pants for the first time in my life.

Mr. Scott wanted the young ones to stay; running a dairy and farming took strong, young, and able-bodied men to withstand the long hours, changing weather conditions, and manual labor. I didn't have to leave right away. There was no need since extra money was coming home from America, England and Scotland and we were comfortable.

I knew my father wasn't feeling well. He was spending less time out on the land and more time resting in bed or sitting on the chair by the fire. I can remember like yesterday when I heard the news. I was walking down the road, heading toward the dairy, when a neighbor came running.

"Willie," he said breathlessly "Go home! It's your father."

I didn't know what to do. I was scared. I even thought about not going home and pretending that I never got the message. I hadn't seen anyone die before. The old people were long gone before I was born and now my father was going to die.

I was angry now, walking fast up the road to our house. The operation in Dublin hadn't been as successful as everyone believed. The memory of my father shaking hands and telling me to take care of things was vivid in my mind and the look in his eyes as he waved at the end of the road. He was going to Dublin alone for an operation that was going to make him better.

I never asked what was wrong with him, or when he was returning, but I knew he was in the hospital. Those were times when a youngster didn't ask questions – they were seen and not heard. I don't remember exactly how long my father was in Dublin, but I know he was gone for at least three months. And then the letter arrived saying, "I'm coming home." There was great excitement in our cottage, as well as in the village. Richard Bourke had been missed.

I took off running with Jim close behind toward Shanclough. We ran alongside the railroad tracks knowing exactly when the train would pass at a certain place, and I knew he'd be watching out the window, searching the fields for us. Sure enough, the train came into sight and there he was, waving his hand and smiling. I can see him as though it was yesterday. We waved and yelled and jumped and kept running until we lost sight as the engine turned toward Ballina Station.

We waited anxiously by the cottage. My mother had walked to town earlier that day and hired a taxi to drive him back to Ballymacredmond. Jack Welch lived down the road from us by Corroy factory and he owned the taxi. Well, the welcome of the world was given to Richard Bourke that day. He handed to each of us, Jim and myself, our own tin of candy. It was the only time I ever had a full tin for myself.

I remember hearing my father talking quietly to my mother late that night. He said, "I overheard the doctor saying that this operation will put years onto my life." My father lived for about another 10 years; however, he was an invalid for the last three and had to be lifted each morning from the bed, shaved and dressed.

When I arrived home the priest was sent for and my mother was sitting by his bedside. I stood at the end of the bed feeling an overwhelming sadness. Within a half hour, without a struggle or a sound, my father at the age of 64 years drew his last breath. He died as he lived, quietly. I was trying not to cry. I believed that men don't cry. But the tears were falling from my eyes and later that evening my brothers and myself carried my father's coffin to Backs Church where he would receive his final blessing.

A few of us spent the night in the church out of respect, and early the next morning mass was offered and we all prayed for the repose of the soul of Richard Bourke. We lifted the coffin onto our shoulders one more time and made our way to Ballinahaglish cemetery. Two of our neighbors had gone early in the morning and dug the grave. I helped lay my father in his final resting place. And, as the first shovel of dirt was thrown over him, I remember thinking, "Here will lay a quiet and gentle man!"

Dick had taken over the responsibilities of our land, as well as the responsibilities of the house and the people who lived inside. Jim and I were a handful and it's a good thing we were afraid of him or God only knows what kind of mischief may have occurred. We were young and needed someone to keep us in line. All my mother, or anyone for that matter had to say was, "Wait till Dick hears about this" and, without hesitation whatever we were doing, stopped.

As always, the sun rose and we had to go to work. John, Dick, Michael and myself worked in Scott's dairy. There were 47 cows that had to be milked at 7:00 in the morning and again at 3:00 in the afternoon. Here I had long days and it was seven days a week. Don't misunderstand me, it wasn't hard labor, but long hours. There were a few married men with families, but the majority of workers were young lads just passing through. They saved enough money to get their fare to England and many never returned. But I was saving my money for a Raleigh.

Every time I went to town, I walked past the bicycle store and sure enough there it was, a lovely Raleigh with solid rubber tires and a dynamo light. The light was run from the movement of the tires; the faster one could pedal, the brighter the light. I wanted that bike. Jim Helbert, God rest his soul was in town that same day.

"Jim," I said, "Will you sign for me. I'll make a payment every month."

Without hesitation, and a nod of his head, he answered, "Willie, I'll sign." I was so excited. I signed my name first and then Jim.

Outside we shook hands and I said, "Thank you, I'll never forget you for this and I won't let you down either."

Jim was friends with my brother John and had a small shop up the road. He knew that a Bourke was good on his word. The bike cost five pounds and ten shillings. I had to put down one pound and pay on it each month. This memory was vivid when I purchased me first car in Chicago.

I was riding home from town one day during the week when I stopped to talk with my cousin and friend Johnny Flynn. Now, it was his grandfather that lived right above us in Ballymacredmond so we often saw each other at school or in the village. Johnny was the oldest of thirteen children and, similar to myself, came from a modest home in Mount Falcon.

All the years we attended Currabaggan Elementary School together, Johnny was at the top of the class academically. He suffered from terrible asthma and might miss a week or more many times throughout the school year. It didn't matter a bit; the exam was given and Johnny Flynn received one hundred percent. Unlike myself, he loved school and desired to further his education. On this day, he was carrying the application that needed to be posted for a scholarship to Maynooth University in Dublin; his only chance for higher education.

"Go on, Johnny," I said and gave him the Raleigh and off he went pedaling as fast as possible on the stone road. I really wasn't paying too much attention to the time, but afterwards I realized that Johnny should have been back with the bike at least an hour or more before. The afternoon sun was setting.

I happened to walk over to the window by the fire and look down the road, and sure enough, there was Johnny and not pedaling. I went outside to meet him. I didn't have to look at the bike; his distressed face explained what happened.

"Willie, I'm sorry, so sorry. I was on my way back, pedaling too fast and didn't I lose control."

Even if I was upset, I couldn't say a word; he felt much worse than I did. The frame of the bike was damaged and from the looks of it, Johnny Flynn was lucky that he didn't have any broken bones from the fall. I took my "almost new Raleigh" back to the shop to be repaired the next day. I was working and doing fine at Barnfield and knew, with time and patience I'd own the Raleigh, and within a year, I did.

At Barnfield I had my first experience with horses and gambling at the Duneen Racetrack. My job was to get the horse to the racetrack unharmed and relaxed ready to run. Duneen was about six miles from Barnfield and the only way to get there was to walk. The horses that were running, their jockeys, trainers and helpers left early in the morning in order to arrive at the track on time.

There was such excitement all around me. Of course, when the day was over the winners were happy and the losers promised they would never gamble again. I remember how relieved I was to be able to ride the horse back to Barnfield. I was tired and disgusted, but as I look back now, it was a great day out. Well I learned a good lesson at an early age. Over the years I have gambled, but never with money that I needed.

The itch to move on was inside me. I became friendly with two other lads and we started to talk about our future. There were not too many choices. However, after two years of working for Robert Scott, I realized that there was no room for advancement.

On a Saturday morning, a total of 23 lads, including myself, boarded the train in Ballina bound for England. We were all hired, and signed on with Whimpy's, a camp that was based out of Nottinghamshire, England. John, Nellie, Bridgie, Dick, Michael, Jim and our mother all came to the station to wave good-bye.

"Jim" I said, "Use my Raleigh and take good care of it until I return."

"Willie, you know I will," Jim answered and really seemed to mean every word. But, I wasn't too sure. Jim was wild and a little reckless at times. Only time would tell.

John didn't have much to say. He held my hand as if in a vice and said nothing. He didn't have to; his handshake said it all. The girls kissed me and the lads shook hands until finally we heard the conductor say, "All aboard." I still remember how excited I was for the adventure, but how sad my mother looked with tears in her eyes as she took me by the shoulders and said, "Willie, remember where you came from."

sweet knockmore

It was at dawn on a summer's morning
From my native home I went away.
I took a notion oh to cross the ocean
To see my friends in America.

I bought my ticket at Ballina station
The sight of parting I could not tell.
My tears were falling like hail in winter
When to my comrades I bid farewell.

Then by Castlebar and Manulla junction
And through Claremorris I made my way.
But, soon the engine was gently steaming
To that lovely station called Castleray.

Where an Irish writer of splendid talent
Stood up beside me and to me did say,
"Why are you leaving your native country?
Please tell me why you are going away.

Why are you leaving your native country
That holy island we do adore
With its rocky plains and fine fertile valleys
Around by Corroy and sweet Knockmore?

Is it suppression that has sent you roaming
To distant regions beyond the seas
Where the homes of liberty, where the flags of freedom
Are proudly floating with every breeze?

I have known the landlords who have brought much sorrow
Among our people they have brought much woe.
They have crushed the home that once was happy
And sent the people from sweet Mayo.

With this remark our train was moving
And in an hour we reached Athlone.
Where I met with boys and fine hearty girls
From Meath, West Meath and grand Tyrone.

Although we are leaving for Philadelphia
Quite sad and lonely we have been.
But it is here I am and it's here I'm longing
To see the flag o're our village green.

When my friends and I arrived in Nottinghamshire, we were separated. There were different camps located all around England and Scotland with men doing all sorts of jobs. Where you were needed, is where you were sent and I ended up with a group of men building air drums. This would be the same as a landing field or runway for airplanes.

Mostly men lived at the boarding house where I was registered. You would not often see wives accompany their husbands to the camp. In the areas where the camps were set up, it was common for families to rent out extra rooms in order to make a few extra pounds. There were a few staying in this boarding house and we were treated very well for a cost of thirty shillings a week.

The room I had was small containing a cot, chair and table. I didn't need a dresser. I didn't have anything much to put in it. The food was good and there was always plenty to eat. Every day I had three meals. At breakfast there was tea with milk, bread and butter; around noon we'd all meet again and have soup with bread or a piece of meat;

and finally, around 5:00 the dinner would have plenty of potatoes, vegetables and a piece of chicken, beef, or pork.

I worked steady and within six weeks I was made foreman. My salary increased to four pound per week. This was big money. Within a few months I was able to send a bank draft or check home to my mother in the amount of twenty pounds. My brother Dick took it to every house in the village; no one had seen a check for that amount of money.

We didn't have much of a social life. You were there to work, not to be entertained. At the end of a day, everyone was tired. There wasn't any drinking or going out to dance halls. No one that I knew had the money to gamble or go out to the saloons. Work was available seven days a week, but the foreman insisted that we attend 9:00 A.M. mass on Sundays. It wasn't hard since the priest would come out to the camp.

It was a great experience for a young lad of seventeen to meet these men from different parts of Ireland, England and Scotland and listen to their stories – all with the same dream or desire that I had – to make a better life. To do this we had to leave the only home that we knew and make another one far away.

My brother Pat had been working for Whimpy's also, only at another campsite in Glasgow, Scotland. Pat wasn't a great writer, but he sent money home regularly with a short note. I remember he was away from home a long time before returning for a visit, seven or perhaps eight years. It was a happy day when I opened the letter from him.

The letter said, "I'm coming to visit you for a weekend. Meet me at the train." Now, at this time I hadn't seen Pat for a few years or more. I said this before and I say it again, "Your brother is your brother" and I was excited as I watched the train approach. I spotted him immediately as he stepped from the coach looking much the same way that I remembered. As always he wore, a dark blue suit, white shirt, tie and gray fedora, and didn't veer from this attire until the day he died. After Pat went bald, you would very seldom see him without a hat. John and I were the only two out of the six brothers that didn't go bald before the age of thirty.

He grasped my hand and squeezed my shoulder, grinning and saying, "'Tis good to see you. Are you well? Are you well, Willie?

I was well, very well indeed and happy that Pat had traveled to see me and make sure I was treated fairly. Later on in life I realized he was afraid that I would go astray and get caught up with a drinking or gambling crowd.

It's a social life that can be persuasive and, at the same time, deadly. I saw many a good lad go down whether from boredom, fear, or loneliness. These young lads were sixteen, seventeen or eighteen years old. But I had a good sense of what was right and wrong, and knew that someday I'd have to answer to the man up above.

We had a great couple of days. A few of the men knew Pat and had great respect for him; he was honest and hardworking. We spent a day in the town of Nottinghamshire watching and listening to the people and tipping a few pints. Pat took me to my first pub, and I remember the name as well as my own, *"King Billy's."*

It was here that Pat sung his favorite, *The Galtee Mountain Boys* and silenced the crowd:

I joined the flying column in 1916
In Cork with Sean Moylan, in Tipperary with Dan Breen
Arrested by Free Staters and sentenced for to die.
Farewell to Tipperary, said the Galtee mountain boy.

We went across the valleys and over the hilltops green
Where we met with Dinny Lacey, Sean Hogan and Dan Breen
Sean Moyland and his gallant men that kept the flag flying high.
Farewell to Tipperary, said the Galtee mountain boy.

We tracked the Dublin mountains, we were rebels on the run.
Though hunted night and morning, we were outlaws but freemen.
We tracked the Wicklow mountains as the sun was shining high
Farewell to Tipperary, said the Galtee mountain boy.

I bid farewell to old Clonmel that I never more will see,
And to the Galtee mountains that oft times sheltered me,
The men who fought for their liberty and who died without a sigh
May their cause be ne'er forgotten, said the Galtee mountain boy.

While sitting in a pub talking about home, the family and old friends, Pat said, "Willie, leave with me tomorrow."

I said, "Pat, what about my job here. Look at the money I'm making."

But he persisted, "You belong where I'm at, not here alone."

I wanted to go with him, but I had begun to make my own little niche in the workforce and I didn't want to go back to hard labor. I got along well with the men that I worked with every day and they liked me; I felt at ease here.

There was a different beat to my heart this day. As the train approached, I knew Pat was still hoping that I'd get on the train with him and just say, "To hell with it." But I didn't. We shook hands with the promise to see each other soon. What I never anticipated was the emptiness in my stomach and the growing need to be away from Nottinghamshire and the camp. I was lonely.

I wasn't sure how to go about quitting a job or say goodbye to the men that were my only family for nearly a year. When I look back now, I realize how wrong I handled the situation, but it was only out of ignorance, not disrespect. I packed my small handbag with all the belongings I owned, and in the middle of the night, I walked to the train station to catch the first train to Glasgow. Well, I can laugh now as I look back, but then I was a nervous wreck; I never wrote down Pat's boarding house address.

The train pulled into the Glasgow's station in the afternoon. It sounds ridiculous, but I kept looking around to see someone I knew or recognized, and of course, there was no one. Believe me; I kept saying to myself over and over again, "Why didn't I stay where I was?" Well, after a full hour of standing on the street corner watching the people hurry by, the tram or bus running up and down the streets, and listening to the Scottish accent, I finally decided to wave down the tram and ask the conductor for help. By this time, I was exhausted and hungry.

I can still see that man as clear in my mind as if it were yesterday. He was middle aged with reddish brown hair, wore a dark sweater, and had dark, but very kind brown eyes. I started trying to explain, with my own Mayo accent, how I forgot my brother's address.

"Sir," I said with tears in my eyes, "What are the chances of me finding me brother in the big city of Glasgow?"

He gave an unfeigned laugh and asked, "What's the address?"

Of course, this is where I felt embarrassed and he knew it, "I didn't write it down. I completely forgot." Sure I was a young lad and scared. I was really scared.

As my story goes on, you'll see how many good and genuine people, of all nationalities and color, I had the pleasure of coming in contact with during my lifetime. How their few minutes of contact had such an effect on making me into the man I am today.

This complete stranger took time to ask me question after question about my brother's work. Thank God Pat worked for the same company as I did or it would have taken a day or two to hunt him down. Being Irish, as the man said, "They usually stick together." He was familiar with an area where the Irish frequented a few pubs and, as it happened, it was toward the end of his route. After a few more inquiries along the road, the conductor dropped me at a corner and pointed to a boarding house.

He said, "Aye, Willie, this is close to where he's staying. The house may not be the right one, but they'll be able to give ye better information about his whereabouts. Good luck to ye, young Willie."

I was grateful; I shook the man's hand, and started to walk down the street. It was getting late now and the wind had a chill. I knocked at the door and waited. My stomach was empty and I could smell the dinner. I remember hoping that Pat would be home, and if not, saying a little prayer to our Lady that there would be a bed available and a meal. Finally, a woman wearing an apron appeared at the door and asked if she could help me.

"Good evening ma'm, I'm looking for Pat Bourke. Does he stay with you?"

"He does," she responded with a lovely smile and Scottish accent, "He's not home, but he'll be in soon," as she ushered me into the house.

"I arrived on the train from Nottinghamshire without an address. I can't believe the good fortune of finding this house."

"Ye're welcome here," the lady was just saying when suddenly the door behind me opened again and in walked Pat. Well, let me tell you that the look on his face was something I could never describe. Can you image the shock of seeing me standing in the parlor of his boarding house?

Pat took my hand and said, "Welcome, I was hoping you'd come." He never asked about my job, how I left, or why I decided; he was happy I was in Glasgow.

"Ye'll come with me in the morn'in to work."

After having a good meal, I washed up, and climbed into the small, but comfortable bed. I wouldn't let myself fall asleep until I said my prayers of thanks to our Lady for helping through this day. It was by her intercession that I was safe with Pat this night.

The cost for having the luxury of living in a boarding house was thirty shillings a week. I had my own little room and shared the bathroom facilities down the hall. Also, every morning the woman of the house had the breakfast tea with bread, butter and sometimes jam, a lunch that consisted of a couple of pieces of bread with a piece of meat (if available), and a full meal after work with plenty of potatoes and vegetables. It wasn't home, but it was an improvement from Nottinghamshire.

It was here that I tasted homemade *Orange Marmalade* for the first time. It was only served on a special occasion, and I can still remember the wonderful flavor:

(Ingredients)

8 oranges	*water*
2 lemons	*sugar*

(Preparation) Wash, dry and slice fruit very thin

Measure and add twice as much water as pulp and juice

Place in heavy cooking pan and let stand over night

Next morning put over flame, cover pan and bring to boil for 1 hour

Set aside for 24 hours

After 24 hours stir well and measure out 2 cups

Put into large enough heavy pan to produce a rolling boil

Add 2 cups of sugar - bring to boiling point and boil only 9 minutes (220 degree Fahrenheit)

Pour into hot sterilized jars and cool

Cover and refrigerate

The next morning, I met Pat and the other six boarders in the kitchen. As we ate some of lads asked me questions about Nottinghamshire, the men at the camp, and what I had done there for work. There were two Englishmen, but the rest were Irish from all parts of Ireland. Before long we were on the tram heading towards the work site. I was hired on the spot because of my brother's reputation. He was honest and hard working; there were no other qualifications necessary.

The work was different. Here we dug trenches along the coast. These trenches were created in order to hide the big ones "guns," and ammunition that protected Scotland from the German invasion. As soon as an area was concreted, a gun was installed. The camp was a good distance from our boarding house. We left early on the trolleys and had to go a good distance before arriving at the coast.

They were long days, but we had Sunday's free. So, the first Sunday in Glasgow, off we went the two of us to visit our sister Teasie in Edinburgh. I hadn't seen her in a few years and I knew she was pleased that I was with Pat. She had the welcome of the world for us and a dinner fit for a king.

Well laugh! And we did, every night, over antics from the day. I was happy here, content, growing up, becoming a man and in good company. There were pubs around us where the men working in the camps and the neighborhood residents socialized.

As it still is today, everyone had their own preferred spot to socialize. There were certain bars that the Irish frequented and found solace together talking about their homes and families. It was always a special treat to meet someone from Mayo, and often I did. It was here that I learned the song *Eileen Álannah*, which would become my favorite. Álannah is Gaelic for "Young dear one".... It has a sweet melody, and I would sing this many, many times during my lifetime:

On a primrose bank by the river side
Where flowers were sweetly springing
And crystal waters do gently glide
And birds were sweetly singing.

(Chorus)
Come home, come home Eileen come home
Come home Eileen Álannah
My weary brow is drooping now
For you Eileen Álannah.

A maiden fair did once dwell there
And sweet hearts she had many
And if you want to know her name
She was called Eileen Álannah.

Chorus
Her parents loved their own Eileen
For she was so beguiling
She had rosy cheeks and ruby lips
And they were always smiling.

But oh, but oh the joy they knew
How soon it turned to sorrow
One night late, a stranger came
And stole Eileen Álannah.

Chorus
The summer sun was sinking fast
The autumn leaves were falling
And Eileen's home was scattered fast
And the winter winds were howling.

A gentle knock came to the door
And the bolt was quickly drawn
And there lay senseless on the floor
Our own Eileen Álannah.

Come home, come home Eileen come home
Come home Eileen Álannah
My weary brow is drooping now
For you Eileen Álannah.

Perhaps a couple of months passed, or a little more, when suddenly I became ill. I owe my life to the Englishman that lived with us. I wasn't up for work so the landlady came into my room to wake me, but I wouldn't move. I told her I wasn't feeling well and would be down later for tea. When the Englishman returned from work, he stopped to see how I was and went immediately to ask the landlady to call a doctor. He recognized the symptoms of diphtheria and knew I'd die unless I received medical attention.

When the doctor entered my room all he did was look at me and phoned for an ambulance. I was taken to the hospital in Glasgow where I remained for several months. I don't recall much about the first few weeks except that the vomiting, diarrhea, shakes and delirium were constant. I was a sick young man.

The ward or part of the hospital that cared for patients with diphtheria was overcrowded and understaffed, but the nurses and everyone tried hard to make me comfortable. You have to remember; there wasn't the medicines available and knowledge that we have today.

Only a curtain separated us. The hollering out for help, the stench, the crying for loved ones, and then the silence will remain with me forever. I would say good night to a young man around my own age and during the night I would hear the curtain being pulled, mumbling of voices, and then the body being removed. I would fall asleep again only to awaken and find another strange young lad in a bed next to me. I don't know why so many died and I lived.

Let me tell you, I was lucky. The majority of the young men and women who contacted some illness far from their home, and had no one to tend their needs, usually died. Pat came all the time to see me. He made sure that I got everything that his money could buy. I was, as the saying goes, "As weak as water." Every week Pat paid the landlady to make soup. However, he had to pay extra to add a piece of meat, if available and he would bring it to me.

Teasie traveled from Edinburgh every Sunday to see me. She would replace my dirty clothes with clean ones each week and also, bring the homemade bread and jam. I still remember how happy I would be to see her come through the door. Knowing that Teasie and Pat were close by was a comforting thought. Most Sundays Teasie would have a letter from home with all the news. Our mother was anxious for me to return to Ballymacredmond.

There were some nights when I never thought I'd wakeup in the morning. But, as the saying goes, "It just wasn't my time." I guess there was something else for me to do before leaving this world. One week went into another week. I had learned not to talk to the other patients. I didn't want to know their names, where they were from, or about their families. It was too hard to forget when they died. Each man lying on a bed had parents, sisters, brothers, wives and perhaps children living so far away and they would never see each other again.

I realized one day that my body had gradually regained some of its strength. Eventually I was able to walk back and forth in the corridors and when Pat or Teasie arrived, they would take me outside if the weather permitted. You can understand now why I love the fresh air. Inhaling the fresh air lifted my spirits and made me want to get better. I wanted to get back to work. I promised God that if I ever was strong enough to pickup a shovel again, I'd never complain about going to work, and I didn't.

Finally the day arrived, Pat and myself walked out of the hospital and I never looked back. Pat hired a taxi to drive us back to the boarding house. The landlady was waiting for me and had my room ready. She had the welcome of the world for me. I was exhausted after the trip and had to go to bed. When I arrived at the dinner table that evening, I must have looked a sight. The lads were trying to cover up the shocked look on their faces. I looked emaciated.

The next morning I went to work with Pat hoping to get my old job back. But when the foreman looked at me, I could read his eyes.

"How are ye Willie? Tis good to see ye." He said extending his hand.

I smiled shaking hands and responded, "Thank you. Is it possible for me to have my old job back?" I would have taken anything at this point, but I could tell the way he glanced towards Pat that things didn't look good.

He said, "Pat your brother is too weak to work. I know what type worker he was, but now look at him; he's bone, there's no muscle."

I could feel Pat's irritation and my own desperation. I may have been away for a while, but knew the money situation wasn't good. The extra care I had took all the extra money that Pat and I had saved. Pat wanted me to go home as soon as possible, but the money for the fare was needed.

Pat looked the foreman in the eye and said, "Take my brother on - I'll do his work and mine as well."

Pat's reputation followed him again. I was rehired. And Pat was good for his word. I could only do so much and then had to rest. Pat would finish his own job and then find me and finish what I was supposed to be doing. This went on for a few weeks and then something happened that was unbelievable.

I had lost track of the war, but heard rumors that officers of the British army were showing up on the job sites and conscripting any man that was of age to fight. The Irish lads were given the option to join or be deported.

Pat had taken a fall from a horse and hurt his knee during a training session for Martin James. He had gone for the physical prior and was rejected. Every now and again if he turned his leg the wrong way, the kneecap would dislocate. A couple of us would have to turn, twist and pull his leg until the bone would snap back into place, and with a little rest, he would be back to work the next day. Eventually, when Pat was older, he went to the hospital in Castlebar for surgery. After that his kneecap stayed where it was supposed to, inside the socket.

Again, I had the pleasure of meeting and speaking with a pleasant and understanding English soldier who was the recruiter. He took one look at me and knew I would not make it in the army, and probably would be more of a "hindrance than a help."

"Can I speak with you?" He asked.

He looked me straight in the eye and I could feel there was no hatred or repugnance because I was Irish. Perhaps he had Irish ancestors, I don't recall, but he took the time to listen to my story.

He explained, "I have no choice but to take every able bodied man here for the Queen's army. It's my job and replacements are needed."

"I understand."

"Do you have a home to go to in Ireland?" the soldier asked.

"I do, my mother is there," I said respectfully.

"Then, I have a suggestion. I'm going to deport you." And with a grin, he continued,

"You will enlist in the English army today or be on your way back to Ireland in one week." He put his hand on my shoulder and added, "And from your appearance, you need to go home."

Pat was thrilled that I was going home. I was fighting the illness everyday. I could fall asleep standing up, and I swear, with my eyes opened. I'm sure it was only a matter of time before I collapsed.

Getting deported wasn't all that bad. I received a one-way ticket paid in full. But there was one major problem; I still was not strong enough to make the trip from Glasgow to Ballina. I can honestly say that I don't remember being concerned about a thing. It wasn't until many months later that I found out how Pat had managed the traveling dilemma. He called my sister Teasie, and from then on, I was in her hands. She spoke with her employer and he invited me to his home for as long as needed.

He instructed Teasie, "Go now and get him, bring him back here, take care of your brother and spare no expense."

I couldn't tell you the exact date, but it was a Saturday that Pat dressed me good and warm and called for a taxi. When we arrived at the train station, there was my sister Teasie, waiting. It was a sorrowful parting from Pat.

He kept saying, "You'll be back when you're stronger, you'll be back."

He held my hand in a tight grip and we looked into each others eyes. Without another word, my hand was released and he just turned and left. There would be many a sleepless night in the coming years that I would remember his sad and tearful eyes and wonder, "Who is taking care of you tonight, Pat?"

I must have slept because the next thing I recall is arriving in Edinburgh and having to go by taxi to the house that Teasie now had called home for well over ten years.

I never returned to Scotland.

I shall pass through here only once
Let me not defer it or neglect it
For I shall not pass this way again.

Author: Unknown

I'll take you home again kathleen

I'll take you home again Kathleen,
across the ocean wild and wide.
To where our heart has ever been
since first you were my bonny bride.
The roses all have left your cheek,
I've watched them fade away and die.
Your voice is sad when e'er you speak
and tears bedim your loving eyes.

I know you love me, Kathleen dear,
your heart was ever fond and true
I always fear when you are near,
that life holds nothing dear but you.
The smiles that once you gave to me,
I scarcely ever see them now
Though many, many times I see,
a darkening shadow on your brow.

To that dear home beyond the sea,
my Kathleen shall again return
And when thy old friends welcome thee,
thy loving heart will cease to yearn.
Where laughs the little silver stream,
beside your mother's humble cot
And brighter rays of sunshine gleam,
there all your grief will be forgot.

I'll take you home again Kathleen
To where your heart will feel no pain,
And when the fields are fresh and green,
I will take you to your home Kathleen.

My sister Teasie was the first to "cross the pond," as we often said, arriving in Edinburgh, Scotland at fifteen years of age. My mother had family there who would look after her and help with finding a job. It wasn't long before she was hired to help the cook, as well as do other little chores, in the house belonging to a wealthy barrister.

A barrister is somewhat equivalent to our lawyers in the United States. By the time I arrived, she had been working for the same family nearly ten years. Teasie would say that his wife was the essence of a lady. She acted, spoke and dressed the part at all times and, of course, expected to be treated as one also.

As the years passed, Teasie took over in the kitchen and had others helping her. Don't forget she was a young girl, fourteen or perhaps fifteen at the most when she started to work. I don't believe she had a bad experience in that house, or else, she covered it up very well. Although, I believe she was happy. The man of the house was a gentleman and respected her wishes and was good to her till the day she retired and returned to Ireland.

Although there were many a poor, young Irish and English girl at this time sent to work for the gentry and then taken advantage of night after night. I know for a fact that a young English girl of twelve years used to sit, shaking in her bed waiting for the candle to appear in the hallway. Her employer would have his way and then return his wife in the other room. These things were never discussed at home; it was a sin. Only, the saddest part of the story is, many of the young girls used to believe, or they were told, that they were the sinners.

Teasie had never married and after living with her for those few weeks I doubted that any man would ever live with her. She was too set in her ways. Don't take this the wrong way, she was a wonderful person, very religious and good to her family, but hated any sort of drink or staying out late at parties.

Every day her employer would stop into the kitchen to see how I was doing. We'd sit and talk for a while and then he'd go about his business.

Teasie told me that he often said, "Buy that lad whatever he needs."

I ate like a king and was treated like royalty. My appetite was better and my strength was returning. My naps during the day were becoming less frequent. A month of care and rest had done the world of good for me. Actually, it probably saved my life. Teasie asked for a week's vacation and booked our passage to Ballina. I was going home!

The ship that took me away, returned me, and anchored in Belfast. Teasie and I caught the noon train, which arrived in Ballina around 5:00 in the afternoon. As the train headed south through the different towns, stopping to pickup and drop off passengers, I kept thinking about what had happened. I learned through experience that the best-laid plans, well thought out ideas, even with hard work and determination, could be altered in a second.

I have said this so many times over the years, "The happiest days in a man's life is when he is working," and that is because he is able to go to work. Remember this, "When you have your health, you have it all!"

I discovered that it is not age that matures or develops a man into what he becomes, but the experiences encountered along the way. I had faced death, I had seen too many die in the hospital, and I knew humility. One day to be young and strong, at the peak of manhood, and suddenly be struck with an illness that you cannot control is devastating. Don't forget I wasn't able to feed myself, nor clean myself, and of course, the worst of all – I needed help to go to the bathroom. I had a humbling experience.

I recognized the importance of family and friends and vowed never to forget those who were good to me. I was looking forward to sitting by the fire, listening to all the news from around Ballymacredmond and America. My desire to go to any foreign country and try to better myself or find a new life was gone. I was content at home.

Mayo was near. I could smell it as the train slowly approached the Ballina station. I was once told that Mayo was like a plate with mountains around it. The flat bog lands with its heather showing lovely shades of purples and pinks, sweet Williams, rhododendrons, the daisies growing wild on the ditches; the magpies and swallows flying from one tree to the next and in the distance, of course, the people. Then I heard the conductor, "Next stop, Ballina station!" There they were on the platform, waiting; my mother, Nellie, Bridgie, John, Dick, Michael and Jim. The joy, and oh the happiness, I cannot say in words.

I was welcomed home with kisses, handshaking, and a few wallops over my thin shoulders.

Jim didn't wait a minute to break the news.

"Willie," he said, "The Raleigh is gone. I wrecked it on my way home from town."

"It doesn't matter. I'll get a new one." It didn't matter.

The look on my mother's face was enough as I stepped down from the train. I could tell that she had a shock seeing me so thin and weak and by this time, exhausted. God, Jesssuss, I was tired! Only the excitement kept me from sitting on the ground and falling asleep.

Eventually we all piled into Jack Welch's taxi and headed for Ballymacredmond. The entire village was out to welcome me home.

My mother wouldn't let me go to work right away. She had to fatten me up a bit with the hope of making me look healthier.

She would say, "Willie, you're too frail."

So I waited a few weeks and helped around the house and land. It was during these weeks that I got an update on my family. There was plenty of talk about my American relations.

Mary had made her way down from Canada to Chicago in 1923 and was met at the train station, in downtown Chicago, by our Aunt Mariah Rogers. Upon completion of her two years, the family who she worked for agreed to buy the one-way ticket to Chicago. Aunt Mariah never married and lived in Chicago on the near north side. She was thrilled with the idea of having her niece and welcomed her.

Mary's letters contained all the information about our uncle, Dan Rogers and his wife Nora and their seven children. Dan was older than my mother and left home young, which meant that none of us met him. May, their oldest daughter married, and shortly after, caught the influenza during World War I and died. They didn't have any children. Shortly after that their young son, Dan also died in a car accident.

Mickey, Jim, Ella and Teasie never married and lived with their parents. Jerry married Martha Uher and had one daughter, Dorothy.

We got the impression that the Rogers were hard workers, like ourselves. They took good care of their parents and welcomed their cousin Mary, my sister, from Canada, as well as Margaret and myself when we arrived, the greenhorns from Mayo. They're all gone now, God rest their souls and buried together in Mount Olivet Cemetery in Chicago.

Just as Mary was settling down and getting used to her surroundings in the big city, Aunt Mariah became ill with cancer and died within a few months of her diagnosis. Mary was uneasy. She didn't know where she was going to go to live or how she would survive. Her security was gone. But, through good fortune a job as a nanny became available. She was hired by a family in Oak Park and cared for their five children for approximately two years. I know that my mother never opened a letter that dollars didn't fall out.

I don't recall the circumstances, but Mary gave up this job. Maybe the children were too much. She was only a girl herself and five young ones are a responsibility. She accepted the position as a nanny for another wealthy family on the South side of Chicago, and here there were two young girls. From the letters, it was evident that Mary enjoyed it. But, trouble was brewing. It was the calm before the storm.

The man of the house where Mary was employed was a decorator. He hired a young Swedish man to help with the painting by the name of Erik Schuldt. Mary fell in love and wrote home that she was going to marry him. She made the mistake of telling that he was not a Roman Catholic and my mother lost her senses. From what I can remember, my mother wrote back to Mary ordering her not to marry this non-Catholic.

In the meantime, John and Margaret wanted to join Mary in Chicago. But again, a physical had to be passed. Margaret passed and John failed due to flat feet. Mary sponsored Margaret and sent the price of the passage and the plans were made. Margaret arrived in Chicago just in time to be maid of honor at Mary and Eric's wedding. According to Margaret's letters, Mary did not understand her mother's reaction and was deeply hurt. Mary respected her mother's wishes and never wrote home again. Now the only news was from Margaret's letters.

Margaret loved attending the Irish dances, and it wasn't long before she met a young man by the name of Con Curtin. I remember my mother telling the neighbors that Margaret was going to marry a man from Abbyfield, County Limerick, but she could never remember his name. I still laugh, as I recall how she used to explain it, "The first name is Con, but the last name – well, you hang it on the windows."

As always, time does not wait for anyone. So many changes had occurred in the lives of Richard and Bridget Bourke's children of Ballymacredmond. Another generation was beginning. Before I left for Scotland, Nellie had married Paddy McHale from up around Foxford and moved into the home place. They had one daughter, Bridie who was their pride and joy. Paddy had his land and also went to England when work was available. Their front yard overlooks Lough Conn, and with Nellie's aesthetic eye, she created a beautiful and colorful flower garden. It won prizes year after year, and well deserved. Many a happy memory I had above in their home.

The country dances were about the only place where the young people would meet and perhaps end up courting. They were on Sunday from 8:00 until midnight and it cost 4 pennies to enter. One night, into the dance walked this young handsome man visiting from England, dressed impeccably in a dark suit with a white shirt. That was it! Bridgie fell head over heels in love with Tom Bourke from Tavnaughmore, which is located above Nellie's overlooking Lough Conn. There was no talking her out of it; she would marry Tom Bourke or no one.

Out of all the Bourke's, Bridgie's story is probably the most interesting. Bridgie was the most like our mother in actions; a great worker and manager around the house. She was going to miss her terribly at home.

I remember well my mother saying, "Our Bridgie's going up the mountain."

She was afraid that Bridgie would die up there. I actually helped push her cases out the bedroom window so Mam wouldn't get upset saying goodbye. We often laughed, because Bridgie was down the next Monday and came every week to see her.

Tom and Bridgie were going to England to live. Soon after the wedding in Ballymacredmond, Bridgie had a surprise that would impact her life forever. Tom's mother was delighted to welcome her new daughter-in-law into their home. Also Tom had two sisters, Annie and Mary with special needs and they were so happy with their new sister-in-law. However, when England was mentioned, the old lady took Bridgie's hand and said,

"You didn't come in here to go out. If you go out, we'll go hungry."

Bridgie stayed and Tom went to England, sending home money and returning when possible.

They had one son, T.J. who has been raised with the same working ethics and love of family as she herself witnessed. Bridgie often said she doesn't regret a minute of her choice to remain in Ireland. However, she had some hard years in the beginning. The bog was the most difficult for her. The site was a good five miles from their cottage and it was rough terrain on foot or on the bike. She'd get there early in the morning and return home with all she could carry in a bag thrown over her shoulder. But the years passed quickly and before long, T.J. was taking care of everything.

I was young when John started courting Agnes Melvin. She was from the bottom end of the parish. They settled in Bunree, Ballina and raised five children, Paddy, Phyllis, Dick, John and Margaret. John had left Scotts and took a job with Murphy Brothers in Ballina. They opened a flourmill right beside the River Moy. It was something to witness back then. The water generated the electricity for the mill and the business prospered. This was technology and only the beginning of what was to come in the twentieth century.

Michael fell in love with Teanie Clarke who had been a kitchen girl in Mount Falcon Castle. When the land was divided, her family received their portion up around Drumrevagh, not far from Ballymacredmond. Michael moved into the home place and built up a dairy. It was unfortunate that they didn't have children. The work was seven days, but it was their way of life and they loved it.

As I said before, Dick had taken over the farm since my father had died and there really wasn't enough for two. I knew he loved caring for the land; it was part of him. So I took my mother's bike into town and asked John to get me something at Murphy Brothers. And, as fate should have it, Mrs. Murphy was looking for someone to do odd jobs around the house and care for the garden.

I was hired on the spot.

captain kelly's kitchen
[made famous by delia murphy from mayo]

Come single belle and beau, unto me pay attention
Don't ever fall in love, 'tis the devil's own invention
For once I fell in love with a maiden so bewitchin',
Miss Henrietta Bell down in Captain Kelly's kitchen.
With me toor-a-loor-a-lay, me too-a-loor-a-ladd-ie
Sing too-ra-loo-ra-lay, toor-a-loor-ladd-ie.

At the age of seventeen I was 'prenticed to a grocer
Not far from Stephen's Green where Miss Henri' used to go sir
Her manners were sublime; she set me heart a-twitchin'
And she invited me to a Hooley in the kitchen.

Now Sunday being the day when we were to have the flare-up
I dressed myself quite gay and I frizzed and oiled me hair up
The Captain had no wife and he'd gone off a-fishin'
So we kicked up the high life out of sight down in the kitchen.
(chorus)

Just as the clock struck six we sat down at the table
She handed tea and cakes and I ate what I was able
I had cakes with punch and tay till me side it got a stitch in
And the time it passed away with the courtin' in the kitchen.

With me arms around her waist she slyly hinted marriage
When through the door in haste we heard Captain Kelly's carriage
Her eyes told me full well, and they were not bewitchin'
That she wished I'd get to hell, or be somewhere from that kitchen. (chorus)

She flew up off her knees, some five feet up or higher
And over head and heels threw me slap into the fire
My new Repealer's coat that I got from Mr. Michael
With a twenty shilling note went to blazes in the kitchen.

I grieved to see me duds all smeared with smoke and ashes
When a tub of dirty suds right into me face she dashes
As I lay on the floor and the water she kept pitchin'
Till a footman broke the door and came chargin' to the kitchen. (chorus)

When the Captain came downstairs, though he seen me situation
Despite of all my prayers I was marched off to the station
For me they'd take no bail, though to get home I was itchen'
And I had to tell the tale of how I came into the kitchen.

I said she did invite me but she gave a flat denial
For assault she did indict me and meself was sent for trial
She swore I robbed the house in spite of all her screechin'
And I got six months hard for me courtin' in the kitchen. (chorus)

The industrial revolution that had exploded in England had little impact in the west of Ireland. And that's because the majority of men and women were over there working. Well, as it happened, James Murphy built a flour mill right on the Moy River. This gave a hundred jobs, as well as kept the farmer in the area busy.

My brother John was very happy working for Murphy's as he delivered the flour bags around the area. He was a well-liked and indeed, well-respected man in our town. Some of the wheat arrived by train and had to be unloaded and delivered. This was a big job. All this was done on the horse and wagon. A far cry from the semis and forklifts you see today.

James Murphy had a lovely home with a bit of land around it in Bunree. John spoke with him about a job for me. I wasn't able to do anything that took too much exertion, but I needed to get out of the house and try to get back to a more normal way of living.

I arrived at their house at 8:00 A.M. Monday morning ready for work.

"Good morning m'am," I said. "My name is Willie Bourke and I'm here to see Mr. Murphy about a job."

"Good morning to you," she said. "My husband is around back and waiting to see you."

I hurriedly answered and all but tripped backing out the door trying not to run. Mrs. Murphy was a bit older than I and lovely. She had a lovely nature about her as well. Over the years I became very fond of her and their little girl.

James Murphy was waiting and welcomed me. He was a cordial sort of fellow who never seemed impatient or intolerant. I would be their gardener and when the winter months arrived, there would be odd jobs for me at the mill.

I was told, "Bourke, if you do your work, you will always have a job."

I was hired at three pound and ten shillings a week – a lot of money in those days. My hours were 8:00 A.M. until 7:00 P.M. Monday through Friday with an hour for dinner and a half day on Saturday, 9:00 A.M. to 1:00 in the afternoon. The mill closed on Saturday at noon and did not open again until Monday at 7:00 A.M.

The vegetable garden was dug in the spring and then the seeds and plants sowed. In the autumn, I prepared the soil with my own home-made mulch for the coming year. The shrubbery had to be trimmed and the foliage piled and mixed with egg shells, tea leaves and other items thrown away. This had to settle for a certain amount of time creating a fertilizer. I would mix this into the soil in the vegetable garden area and then cover it all with some straw to help prevent erosion. Now it was ready for the next year's planting.

But the flowers were my real love and kept my interest. There were an abundance of species and colors all around. Mrs. Murphy would always walk the grounds viewing them. The garden was lovely and brought with it a quiet solitude and contentment that I don't believe could be found elsewhere in Ireland at this time.

I remember well hearing their little girl calling, "Bourke, Bourke." She would come running with beautiful blue eyes and long curling brown hair that was pulled up on the sides and tied with a colorful ribbon.

I'd yell back, "I'm here, slow down before you fall again!" Too late! Down she would go on her knees.

"Cut me some pretty flowers, Bourke, please, please," she would ask. She resembled her mother in looks, as well as good nature. I could do no wrong in either of their eyes, but they knew I was loyal and took good care of them. James Murphy did not have to worry about a thing around the house. I hated cutting the fresh flowers; they would die within a few days, but that was what she wanted.

"I'm giving them to my mother," she would announce. She always wanted flowers for her mother, but sometimes I didn't know if it was just a good reason to get out of the house, away from the housekeeper and spend time with me. Around and around, up and down the narrow paths, chattering on about school and her little friends, viewing this flower and yet another, until finally she had enough. Before taking her leave, the little girl always said, "Thank you, Bourke."

The Daisy
I am a pretty little thing
Coming early in the spring
In the meadows green I am found
Peeping just above the ground
And my stalk is yellow, flat
With a white and tallow hat.

Little children when you pass
Slightly over the green tender grass
Skip about, but do not tread
On my meek and healthy head
For you'll always hear me say
'Surely the winter is gone away.'

Mrs. Murphy and I had great conversations about the garden, the weather, the town, the Sunday night dances, and so forth. I never told this to anyone before, but there were a few times when she dressed me in her husband's suits and sent me to the dance. I looked swank!!

I remember well her finding me in the garden on a Monday morning sitting under a tree. I wasn't well. But, it wasn't from the flu; it was from too much drink the night before. She never said a word, but asked me in and poured a good drink into a crystal tumbler. It was from Mrs. Murphy that I received my first drink of Jameson whiskey, and still today, I enjoy a sip or two or three if I can get it. I had many a good drink in that house and fond memories.

The one thing I never did, for the entire time I worked as a gardener in Ireland, was water the grounds. Don't forget, the Irish winters aren't that severe so I had work around the house most days. I kept the grounds immaculate and was told that many a time. I found great satisfaction, appreciated, and enjoyed my six years in Bunree. But I was looking for something else to do.

I was home now for a couple of years and other than work, mass, and the Sunday night dances in the village of Corroy, Shraheen, Knockmore, and Currabaggan there wasn't an awful lot to do. Now, the greyhound dogs were racing on Saturdays in Foxford and this sport had become very popular around our area.

A few of the lads and myself went to the races and had a great time. Well, I took an interest in the training and developing of a racing greyhound. Not to mention the fact that some of the owners were making a purse full of money. As it happened, I took it into my head that I would buy a pup, train it myself, race it, and make a fortune.

So after leaving work on a Saturday, I began to ask around for an auld fellow by the name of Kennedy who lived outside Bunree on the way into Ballina. I was told that he had greyhounds for sale. Sure enough, in back of the cottage there was a litter to choose from. I bent over the box and picked up a six week old pup and never put her down. I paid four pounds and ten shillings for this pure bred hound. It was a beautiful spring day, and so I named my prize winning greyhound, Spring.

My mother, Bridgie, Jim, and God knows, the entire village loved Spring. I trained her earnestly for a year and a half. Every morning before work and on my day off, without fail, she got a good run. A couple of times a week I would stop at the butcher and buy a piece of steak for Spring. The red meat was good for her; it was full of vitamins. Honest to God, I swear Spring ate better than ourselves, but no one minded.

In the evenings and on Sundays, I would do practice runs and use a timer. She was fast! Then, bee jeeeessuss, she'd spot a rabbit out in the field and run after it. Well I'd be ripping mad. But I kept after her. Over and over again I'd yell "start" and she'd go and each week the time was a bit better.

Finally, I decided it was as good a time as any to enter her with the year and a half old racers above in Foxford. I had her shinning and in perfect physical shape. If I had a shilling for every time I heard, "She's a real beauty," I'd be a rich man. Well, she didn't do any good at all. All she seemed interested in was running after the rabbits in the field or playing with the children in the village.

I wasn't going to give up. I was told by another greyhound owner that she was still young enough to train. There was a school in the city of Dublin where professional trainers worked with the greyhounds, so I made arrangements for Spring and I to go. This took an awful lot out of my savings, but I figured it was a good gamble.

I picked her up the next week and went straight to the racetrack thinking this will make or break her as a runner. I'm all excited and giving the last loving pep talk and then its ready, set and go! Off she went with her hind legs pushing forward with all their might and the front paws didn't seem to touch the ground. I had a good feeling until I watched her turn right instead of left. The bastard took off out into the field after a rabbit that was scampering through the high grass near the road. Well, I decided that was it, no more. She was a pet, not a racer.

Pat came home from England for a visit and became fond of my Spring. He also saw the potential that she had and believed that a more structured training, away from me and the family would be better, and perhaps a few shillings could be made.

He told me, "Willie, I trained horses, I have experience."

I said back, "Take her, Pat, do what you can."

"Willie, I'll turn her into a champion – wait and see if I don't."

So Pat returned to Manchester with Spring. Well, after a short time of training, Pat signed Spring into a race and didn't she break her leg right there on the track before the race ever began. One of the lads had to shoot her. I was sorry that happened. I should never have let her go, but sure what's done is done. She had a good life with me, steak and a bit of brandy many a night.

I bought one more greyhound after that and felt sure that this time I'd have a winner. I ran him in a meet in Foxford and he lost. A priest approached me with an offer, which I accepted. I remember him saying, "This hound has potential, but you're not training him properly." And the priest was right. I followed him for a long time, and the greyhound won race after race, all the way to the Dublin finals.

And so, our lives went on in a very simplistic fashion in Ballymacredmond; however, my mother was seventy years by now and her health was steadily declining. I noticed she was spending more time in bed and coughing during the night. The doctor was called to the house and gave the diagnosis of asthma.

I was told it was a lung ailment and there wasn't much that could be done. She had to rest, he said, and prescribed a little white pill to take once a day. To tell you the truth, I believe my cure was the best of all. After a night in town I'd carry home a bit of brandy from the pub and she'd sip on it nice and slow and then go into a sound sleep. There was no coughing that night as I watched her sleep peacefully.

I guess the house was in need of a good woman and I wasn't making any move to settle down. As I tell this story, I still can't believe it happened. Didn't my brother Dick get himself all dressed up and walk down the road to Owen McHale's cottage. It is about one quarter of mile from our house in Corroy. He was probably 34 or 35 years of age then and was ready to settle down and so on. There was no match made. Dick asked Owen for the hand of his daughter Maggie, and Owen said yes. This was a very unusual way of handling an engagement in those days, but it worked.

The date was set and Dick met me outside.

He asked, "Will ye stand for me."

I was asked to be the best man and of course I would. There was such excitement in our house. Bridgie, Nellie, and Teasie were there doing the cooking and getting things ready for the house party that would take place after the nuptials. The day was cool and, of course a little rain had to fall for good luck, which it did later in the afternoon. It was obvious to me that there were three from our clan missing, my father, Mary and Margaret as we entered the Church of Christ the King.

The Bourkes knew how to have a wedding. It was a happy occasion. There was singing, dancing, and drinking until the early morning. Maggie McHale was a lovely girl and never said a wrong word to me. She had the door open whenever I returned for a visit and had the extra room ready. Dick made a good match for himself.

The news traveled fast when we found out that the government was building a factory right at the end of our road. I can't say for sure when construction began and ended, but I know it was in the early nineteen thirties. I do remember that it was not completed when my father died in 1936.

Corroy Factory was originally built to produce pure alcohol using potatoes, but this did not prove to be financially successful. In fact it was dangerous, I can still see the men running around in the early morning, gone mad from drinking it. The alcohol was like a poison to their mind. As soon as everyone realized how dangerous this product was and the long-term effects that this could have on the body when taken orally, it was prohibited to drink.

After that, molasses was imported from Africa and starch was used to produce glucose. This gave many a man employment for many years around our place. It was possible to farm your land and still work for a bit of extra money. However, as time passed the need for glucose became obsolete and the workers were given a severance pay. Today, with modern technology and machines the factory employs about fifteen people, mostly young girls, and manufactures plastic balls and so forth.

This factory brought jobs to our area, which in turn kept a few more families. With Maggie's help, Dick was able to keep their little farm going, as well as work full-time at the factory. This was a great financial help. It was a relief to see that they were happy and my mother was cared for.

I had been thinking about America and going to Chicago for sometime now. This was as good a time as any.

My mother only wanted what was best for me, for all of us, and she knew my options were limited in Ireland. I knew what she was thinking as I was myself. It's time to settle down and make a home. She didn't have to go into any more details.

I recall her last words, "Willie, you're running with the hares and you're hunting with the hounds."

Paddy's Green Shamrock Shore

Oh fare thee well sweet Ireland
My own dear native home.
It breaks my heart to see friends' part
For it's then that the teardrops will fall.
I'm on my way to Americay
Will I e'er see my homeland once more
For now I leave my own true love
On Paddy's green shamrock shore.

Our ship she lies at anchor now
she's standing by the quay
May fortune bright shine down each night
as we sail all across the sea
Many ships have been lost,
many lives it has cost on the journey that lies before
With a tear in my eye I'm bidding goodbye
to Paddy's green shamrock shore.

From Londonderry we did set sail
it being the fourth of May
On a sturdy ship to cover the trip
across to Americay
Fresh water then did we take in
one hundred barrels or more
For fear we'd be short before reaching port
far from the shamrock shore.

Two of our anchors we did weigh
before we left the quay
All down the river we were towed till
we came to the open sea
We saw that night the grandest sight
we ever saw before
The sun going down 'tween sea and sky
far from Paddy's green shamrock shore.

Early next morn, sea-sick and forlorn,
not one of us was free
And I myself was confined to bed
with no one to pity me
No father or mother or sister or brother
to raise my head when sore
That made me think of the family I left back
on Paddy's green shamrock shore.

So fare thee well my own true love
I think of you night and day
A place in my mind you surely will find
although I'm so far away

Though I am alone and away from my home
I'll think of good times before
Until the day I can make my way back
to Paddy's green shamrock shore.

I did not make the decision to leave Ballymacredmond quickly. I had been thinking about it for some time now, even before Dick married. However, I imagine, him bringing a wife into the home place helped to nudge my decision along. It had been a long time since I allowed myself to dream about traveling and there was no better place in the world to go than to my sisters in Chicago.

I was content where I was, but it occurred to me that things were not moving anywhere. I certainly was not going backward, but I wasn't happy with where I seemed to be going either. So it was with this mind set that I wrote to my sister Margaret and asked if she would sponsor me as an emigrant to Chicago. I could pay my own fare, but I needed the signature of someone who would meet the government's requirements for immigration.

It didn't take long for the welcome letter to arrive from the States. There were forms and so forth that had to be completed proving that there would be someone waiting for me in the United States and able to support me until I found a job. When all the documents were ready I took a deep breath and walked into the travel agent's office in Ballina to book my passage. The cost for a one-way, second class ticket was forty eight pounds.

I would leave from Ballina Station for Dublin and catch the ferry from Dublin to Southampton, England where Pat would meet me. Pat was working in London now and seemed content. He had been home for Dick's wedding and hadn't discouraged me when I told him about America.

I gave in my notice to James Murphy three weeks before my departure. Corroy Factory was hiring at the time and there was an opportunity to pickup some extra hours for more money. So I took on the work for a few weeks. Also, earlier that year I had purchased a pony for thirteen pounds and sold him for twenty three. I had bought two calves for around the same amount and sold one for another twenty three pounds and gave the other one to Dick. I was ready now, and in the spring of 1948, I left for the United States.

It was daybreak before I went to bed, but still I was restless. This feeling would go away once I said my good-byes and was on the road. The house was sad that morning; we all tried to act as though it was just another day, which helped to keep our minds from thinking about the inevitable. And then, it was time, the tears were in my eyes as in my mothers and Dick. I promised I'd be home in a year's time and I truly believed it.

I looked back at the end of the road. It was heart breaking. My mother at the gable with the rosary beads and there was Ketty Gallagher with a white sheet, waving it back and forth. Everyone was out to wave me good-bye. These were tough people and used to saying good-bye. I stood for a minute taking a last look at my beloved Ballymacredmond. Time stands still for no one and when I return, there would be changes. These cottage doorways now filled with the presence of the women I grew up with and learned to love, may not be alive. I had to implant this vision in my mind forever – and I did.

Ballina station was crowded. There were younger men and women than myself leaving today and I am sure without the security that I felt. I had family waiting for me on the other side. It was time. I knew John didn't want me to go. He had been like a father to me and I would miss him as a son misses his father. He took my hand and held it in his strong grasp, not saying a word, just staring and blinking back the tears. We never said a word to each other, there was no need. Oh, there was plenty of hand shaking and slapping on the back until finally the last call, "All aboard."

Jim picked up my bag and walked with me. I grabbed it and jumped on with a hasty last farewell. I hurried to a window seat and stared. There they were, my brothers, standing together and I knew as soon as the train pulled out they would head straight to the pub to have a drink on me. They would order pints, raise their glasses together and say, "To Willie." I didn't have time to dwell on my departure for very long. I was sitting in a car with friendly people, full of laughter, joking, story telling and a song that will stay with me forever, *Paddy's Green Shamrock Shore:*

> *From Derry quay we sailed away*
> *On the 23rd of May*
> *We were taken on board by a pleasant crew*
> *Bound for Americay*
> *Fresh water there we did take on*
> *Five thousand gallons or more*
> *In case we'd run short going to New York*
> *Far away from the Shamrock shore.*

So fare thee well, sweet Lisa dear
And likewise Derry town
And twice farewell to my comrades bold
Who still dwell on that sainted ground
If ever fortune will favour me
And I do have money in store
I will come back and wed the sweet lassie I left
On Paddy's Green Shamrock Shore.

We sailed three days, we were all seasick
And no one on board was free
We were all confined unto our bunks
With no one to pity poor me
No fond mother's ear, no father's kind words
To comfort my sore head
This made me think more of the wee girl I left
On Paddy's Green Shamrock Shore.

We safely reached the other side
In fifteen and twenty days
We were taken as passengers by a man
and led round in six different ways
So each of us drunk a parting glass
In case that we never meet more
And we bade farewell to old Ireland
On Paddy's Green Shamrock Shore.

Dublin was a busy city. I suppose similar to many cities around the world at that time; people everywhere, traffic jams, and pollution. I was relieved that I didn't have to spend the night here alone. There were four of us that seemed to hang together during the train ride to Dublin. One lad was remaining in Dublin to work in his uncle's grocery store while the other three, as well as many more from that train would be continuing on to England. By the time we got to a nearby pub and ordered ourselves a pint, it was time to go again. The bus was leaving for the port, and so with handshakes, smiles, and many "good lucks" we parted. Before I realized it, I was on the ferry and headed for Southampton's port and the *Queen Mary.*

I was getting tired; actually I was very tired as I stood by the rails looking at the rough ocean water. The wind would "cut the face off" you that day. I found a chair under an awning and away from the direct wind and there I remained. I recall the children playing around me and a group of women talking and laughing at a nearby table. A few times the porters came around asking if I needed anything. I must have dosed, because the boat was pulling into Southampton's port before I realized it; and there was Pat!

I could pick him out of a hundred men and women standing on the dock. Pat was no more than five feet, five inches, but the breath of his shoulders appeared the same. Pat had been working for a building construction company for some time now and seemed content. He carried the hod, which has been obsolete for many years now.

The hod was a sort of tote bag where the bricks were placed in, thrown over the shoulder, carried up the ladder to be unloaded at the top where the bricklayers were waiting and down the ladder to be filled again. The strength of a man to be able to do this all day was phenomenal, but I could tell that Pat had aged and this hard work and rough life was showing.

"Willie," he said, "Cé caoi bfuil tú?" (How are you?)

I grabbed his outstretched hand smiling; I was happy to see him and said, "I'm well, Pat."

His hands were hard and callused. In fact, still today, they were the hardest and strongest pair of hands I ever felt. It didn't take us long to find a pub and order a pint. It was a quite place where we could talk. I gave him the news from home and, other than me going to America, everything and everyone was well. I had been traveling now for a day and a half and a bed with a good meal was what I needed.

We stood looking at each other, not knowing what to say. America was a long way and not many returned to their native land. Our sisters

Mary and Margaret hadn't come back yet for a visit and I knew Pat was thinking that this could be the last time we would see each other. I realized this also.

"Willie," he said with his heart in his eyes, "I'll come for you if you need me."

"I'll work for awhile, Pat and then I'll be home for a visit. Wait and see. We'll be together soon," I answered trying to be optimistic.

Not another word passed between us. I knew it was time to go. I held his hand and put my other arm around his shoulders. For a split second, Pat put his head on my shoulder, but quickly moved away, with a soft "slán" (good-bye), turned and left. I lost him in the crowd.

I had no idea what sort of a sailor I would be, but I did not anticipate the storm the Queen Mary would encounter almost immediately after setting course. There were people everywhere; people were looking for each other, children crying, and the personnel on board were trying to get us all to our rooms. Finally a young man directed me and I entered my cabin with a small bed, toilette area, and a chair. There were hooks on the wall to hang my clothes. I remember that I was exhausted and instead of wandering around with curiosity and excitement, I fell asleep.

The next four days are all together in my memory. There was no morning, afternoon or night. I had the most awful case of seasickness that anyone ever experienced. The rolling waves under me were no worse than the movement in my stomach. I heaved, gagged, and spit every ounce of fluid that was in my body. I believe the first cup of tea I had was when we were pulling into New York harbor.

I was never so happy to see land. I was on deck as the Statute of Liberty appeared, and in the horizon, the United States of America. What a journey! Let me tell you, after the experience of coming, I was in no hurry to return. I couldn't wait to get my feet on American soil. This was the land of opportunity and, with Gods help, I would succeed.

There were smiles on all our faces. It was hard to distinguish between the happy, relieved, and apprehensive; but they were all smiling. I couldn't tell you the name of one person on deck, but I am sure everyone had a destination with family or friend awaiting their arrival. Our destinies were in those hands that awaited us.

This realization did not come that morning, but several months later as I pondered my fortune found not in money or materialistic items, but through family and their new found friends. They had paved the road for me and many more immigrants during the twentieth century.

It was March 12, 1948; a cloudy overcast day with a cold breeze coming off the Atlantic and New York Harbor was bustling with activity. Finally, my turn arrived to board the ferry that would take me to dry land. I could hardly wait for the steady ground to be beneath my legs. I was very aware as my one foot touched American ground for the first time.

"Follow the signs for immigration," said a man in a blue uniform. I will never forget those words; they were spoken with an American accent. The man seemed to carry out the "o" sound much longer – fooloooh and so forth. It was unusual, but understandable.

As I tell this story now, the sight of these immigrants trying to express themselves will remain heavy in my heart till the day I die. What an awful and frightening experience to be in a new country and not be able to communicate. This is a situation where a man feels helpless.

It didn't take long before my papers were stamped and I continued down the walkway to a huge room where Ann Bourke from Ballymacredmond was waiting. Nan, as I called her, had left Ireland nearly ten years before, around the time I returned from Scotland and hadn't made a trip home. I recognized her immediately. She was a lovely girl in looks and personality.

We had grown up together and I knew she was happy to see someone from home. There was plenty to catch up on. Many changes had occurred since she left as a young girl, but my brother's marriage was the topic. No one thought Dick would ever marry.

Well for the next two days I went around New York City to see all the beautiful buildings and sites. I had a hamburger and french fries for the first time and a cold beer. It took a couple of swallows to get used to the taste, but I overcame it quickly, thank God. I loved everything!

There were many Irishmen in the pub that we visited the first evening. It was a great night. The Irish emigrants had not lost their love of song and story and I partook in the folly of the night singing another favorite *"Galway Bay."*

If you ever go across the sea to Ireland
It maybe at the closing of your day
You will sit and watch the moon rise over Claddagh
And see the sun go down on Galway Bay.

Just to hear again the ripple of the trout stream
The women in the meadows making hay
And to sit beside a turf fire in the cabin
And watch the barefoot gossoons as they play.

For the breezes flowing o'er the seas from Ireland
Are perfumed from the heather as they blow
And the women in the uplands digging praties
Speak a language that the strangers do not know.

For the strangers came and tried to teach us their way
They scorned us for being what we are
But they might as well go chasing after moonbeams
Or light a penny candle from a star.

And if ever there is going to be a life hereafter
And somehow I am sure there's going to be
I will ask my God to let me make my heaven
In that dear land across the Irish Sea.

Nan walked with me to the train depot and waited on the platform until the train pulled out. There were tears in her eyes from a different type of lonesomeness.

"You'll be alright, Nan," I said trying to comfort her a little before leaving.

"Sure, I will Willie," She answered and then added something that I never forgot.

"If only we could have our Ireland over here!"

"Nan," I said and put my arms around her small frame, "Most of Ireland is here."

"Willie," she said, "Have a good life." I kissed her one more time and walked away.

I gave one last wave from the step of the car before boarding. The car was full and I tried to get a window to wave and call out one more time, but it was too late. The train was pulling out so quickly and there were so many people. My last glimpse of Nan is standing on the platform and that was the last time our paths would meet.

I had a berth where I rested, but I couldn't sleep; my mind was racing. Mile after mile I had watched pass through the window. Their winter was just coming to an end and it had been a cold one with plenty of snow. The trees were still bare and the ground hard and no flowers anywhere. I remember seeing the evergreens that never lost their shape or color. There was a chill in the air, but the sky was crystal clear blue. This was my fourth day in the United States of America, and still no rain, no mist, only snow.

I was becoming excited and apprehensive; I was a long way from home. It is hard to explain, but I felt good about this change. I realized that there were not too many chances in life and I would have to make the best of this opportunity. Anyway, it wasn't like I could turn around tomorrow and go back. Not that I ever intended to, but there still was no option, I didn't have the money.

I knew without being told we were nearing Chicago. The people on the train were becoming restless and then, before I realized it the conductor came through each car announcing, "Chicago, Union Station." I said to myself – final destination. I glanced at my watch, exactly sixteen hours. I was tired, but in far better shape descending onto the train's platform than I was disembarking at the port only a few days before. I always liked the feeling of solid ground beneath my feet and I still do today.

Someone once asked me, "What did you like best about New York?"

I couldn't give an answer; everything was so out of the ordinary and there was so much more to see. However, the one thing that remains in my mind today was how quickly the people were moving – everyone was rushing somewhere. I never witnessed anything like that; men, women and children of all ages walking as fast as they could move their feet.

I knew I was in "America the Beautiful!"

> *Oh beautiful for spacious skies*
> *For amber waves of grain*
> *For purple mountain majesties*
> *Above the fruited plain*
> *America! America!*
> *God shed his grace on thee*
> *And crowned thy good with brotherhood*
> *From sea to shining sea!*
>
> *O beautiful for pilgrim's feet*
> *Whose stern impassioned stress*
> *A thoroughfare of freedom beat*
> *Across the wilderness*
> *America! America!*
> *God mend thine every flaw*
> *Confirm thy soul in self control*
> *Thy liberty in law!*

take me home to mayo

Take me home to Mayo
Across the Irish sea
Home to dear old Mayo
Where once I roamed so free.
Take me home to Mayo
And let my body lie
Home at last in Mayo
Beneath the Irish sky.

My name is Michael Gaughan
From Ballina I came
I saw my people sufferin'
And swore to break their chains.
I took the boat to England
Prepared to fight or die
Far away from my Mayo
Beneath an Irish sky.

My body cold and hungry
In Parkhurst Jail I lie
For the loving of my country
On hunger strike I'll die.
I have just one last longing
I pray you'll not deny
Take my body home to Mayo
Beneath the Irish sky.

So, take me home to Mayo
Across the Irish sea
Home to dear old Mayo
Where once I roamed so free.
Take me home to Mayo
And let my body lie
Home at last in Mayo
Beneath an Irish sky.

I didn't have to look far for my sister Margaret. She hadn't changed a bit, although it had been nine years since we met. As I approached, I realized that there were three other women standing near. My God, one had to be my sister Mary.

Tears were in the eyes of this strange lady as she put her arms around me and said, "Willie, you're a man now." The voice was Mary's. I remembered. "I never thought I'd see you again." The tall, quiet man standing to the side was Mary's husband Erik Schuldt. Honest to God he could have been from Ireland with his ruddy completion. I liked him immediately. He was a gentleman.

Then, Margaret had her arms around me and I felt a wave of relief. The elderly lady with a round, pleasant face and welcoming smile was my aunt, Nora Rogers, nee Walsh, and her two daughters who were born in Chicago, Ella and Teasie Rogers. "You're welcome, Willie, you're welcome Willie as the flowers in May" over and over and all I could say was thank you, and it's good to be here with you, and I thank you again for your kindness for having me, and all that.

I also discovered that the spelling of my mother's name Rodgers was now Rogers. This was not an uncommon occurrence with immigrants during this era. Spelling mistakes were made at the port of entry, as well as places of employment. Unless you were able to communicate the correct spelling, your name changed. Also, Eric's surname became Schultz.

After the dinner, Con Curtin and myself took a walk up to Pat Barrett's, a corner saloon where a man could have a quiet drink or two. "Saloon" was my first new word in Chicago. If you are going to live in America, one has to talk like an American. So from now on I was not only in a tavern, bar or pub, I was drinking in a saloon. Budweiser was probably the most common alcoholic beverage on draft at this time. However, Pabst Blue Ribbon and Schlitz were available as well. A glass of draft at this time was .15 cents, a bottle .25 cents, and a shot of whiskey .25 cents. I always loved the ambiance of a tavern. After entering and finding two open bar stools, I looked around, not at the décor, but the faces of these hard working immigrants.

A tavern sometimes gets a bad reputation because of the drink, the smoke, and at times the disrespectful language, as well as, verbal and physical fights. These are small inconveniences that have to be kept in proper perspective. There is more to this place of business. Once you frequent the same place several times and, of course, pay your way, one establishes a kinship with the owners, as well as other customers.

Many times, this was the only place where a man could go, other than the small rented room above someone's kitchen. Oh, there'd be arguments at times over political issues and so forth, but on the whole, within a few hours the world problems would be solved and then, home we would go for the dinner and a good sleep.

Con and Margaret Curtin gave me a place to live until the day I married and I was well taken care of. Their three bedroom bungalow was located in Saint Sabina Parish near 79th and Throop Street on the southwest side of Chicago. Everything was close by. There was a bakery, pharmacy, butcher, grocery store within walking distance and the neighbors were friendly and welcoming to all. But, it took getting used to in a different way. The openness that one finds in the country, the solitude, calmness and serenity was gone. Now, instead of the rooster crowing or the mooing of the cow, I woke to the slamming of car doors, screeching of brakes, or the shrilling scream of an alarm clock.

I was so impressed by the magnitude of everything I saw; the cars, trucks, streetcars, roads, houses, everything was bigger than big. Some of the apartment complexes that were built held thirty separate living areas. Many of these buildings were on corners, which provided more parking for tenants on the street. Of course, people didn't have the cars they have today. Then you would see a row of houses, similar in structure and color down the block, front porches facing each other. Our neighborhood, as it was referred to as, was clean and well maintained.

I laughed when I saw a sprinkler on the lawn. However, after surviving my first sweltering Chicago summer with temperatures reaching well into the nineties, I would let the water from the sprinkler wet me. The modern conveniences were in every house, such as the full bathroom, hot and cold running water from a tap (faucet). The indoor plumbing was intriguing and a wonderful convenience. In the kitchens there were gas ovens with the range on top for pots and an ice box, usually in a corner or out on the back porch. It was extraordinary how the milk, butter and other foods could be kept cold during these hot months with a block of ice, which was delivered when needed.

The homes were lovely and warm in the winter with very little dampness due to the oil heat. I had felt dampness; in fact I knew what it was like to be soaking wet and very cold, but I never expected the extreme cold that I experienced in Chicago that first year. If I thought it ridiculous to dig a dungeon below the house, I soon learned to appreciate it.

One learned quickly how to dress for the Chicago weather. I still say, having enjoyed the speed and convenience of traveling by airplane and lived through this age of computers, that electricity was the greatest invention. Every room had a least one electric light and some worked with a switch on the wall – up for on and down for off. All this I found fascinating.

I believe I arrived on a Thursday and that first Saturday I met a man who would be my good friend until the day he died. Jim Fahey, a friend of Con and Margaret, stopped in to introduce his nephew, Jim Lyons who had arrived a month or so before me. Jim was about my size, dark hair and a sense of humor that one can only be born with. We were best buddies from then on. Our wives became friends, we shared good and bad times and our children are still friends today.

"Willie, we'll go together to the dance at Flynn's Hall on Sunday," he said.

Of course we went and many more Sundays after that were spent together.

Within a few days I had met so many relations and their friends that I stopped trying to remember names and who belonged to whom. I was invited to dinner at my Aunt Nora's house. Remember now that Dan Rogers, her husband, was my mother's brother, but had died some years previous. Here I met Ella and Teasie's brothers, Jim, Mickey and Jerry, and many more friends and neighbors.

The dinner was ready and we all had a feast. It was a fine *beef stew:*

Cut up a piece of chuck beef into 1 ½ - 2" pieces

Cut a ¼ pound of butter into large frying pan and melt

Put 2 cups of flour into a paper or plastic bag

Add portions of meat and shake until all have been lightly covered.

Place meat in hot pan and add salt and pepper – to taste

Turn pieces until brown – no need to cook the meat

When browned, put meat in large Dutch oven or heavy pot

Add enough cold water to cover the meat and put on lid.

Cook slowly over medium heat and stir occasionally

Bring to simmer – at least 1 ½ hours

Add onions, fresh carrots diced, fresh green beans, tomatoes (peeled)

Cook until meat is tender and carrots are soft. Depending upon the amount of meat and vegetables used, the time will differ.

Stir occasionally and the flour from the meat should thicken the gravy. Add more water if necessary. Make sure there is enough gravy for dipping your bread.

Boil a pot of potatoes separate – skins on or off.

Note: You can add a small amount of celery and other
        vegetables, but be careful not to overpower the
        original flavor.

After the dinner, the girls got themselves ready and we went on the streetcar to Flynn's Hall at 63rd and Kedzie. Well I'm telling you now; I thought I was at a pub in Ballina with only one difference; the brogues or accents represented Ireland from coast to coast. The "craic was mighty" until the early hours of the morning. And by craic, I mean good conversation with plenty of Irish wit.

The music, the dance, the laughter were in every establishment. But, sometimes, the distant look in someone's eye, an inflection of sadness perhaps would be heard in the tone of voice, and always, when "home" was mentioned, it was Ireland they meant. For a brief time, I would feel a longing or desire to be somewhere else, but it would pass. There were too many people around talking and laughing. It didn't take long before my spirit soared again.

Flynn's Hall was quite large. It held a couple of hundred people comfortably and was packed every Sunday night. This was an era for the old time waltzes, the quick step, the fox trot, and the floor was full. The band would play some of the old traditional kailie music with the reel, a good jig, the stack of barley and sometime during the evening the lines were made for the Siege of Ennis.

Everybody was here for a good time and a good time was had by all. We were friends, all of us together bound by one commonality – we had no mothers or fathers to go home to and many didn't have a sister or brother, aunt or uncle. As an old man said, "Most of the Irish are related – It's like buying a bonham (baby pig) from the same litter."

I was old enough and wise enough at this point to know how fortunate I was to have Margaret. She was busy raising four children and Con worked a steady job as an electrician on the railroad. Their oldest son Dick was about twelve years old when I arrived and then there were John, Donna and Michael. They were great kids.

Well let me tell you, I wasn't in Chicago long when I found out about a sickness called the "mumps." All the kids came down with it and so did I. The glands on both sides of my throat were as big as golf balls, and there was a pain in my throat that I never felt before. I didn't know what was wrong, but ended up in bed for nearly a week under my sister Margaret's care, and thank God recovered.

Mary's two children, Dick and Barbara, were young adults by the time I arrived. They were nice young people and made me feel so welcome. I found out that Mary had packed K-rations for Johnson and Johnson during the war years, however at the time of my arrival she was employed by a hotel and enjoyed her work, the people she associated with, and Chicago.

It's a shame that I wasn't able to spend more time with Mary. I suppose we were both busy. The time passed quickly, but we did see each other at weddings and wakes and so forth. However, it was with Mary that I ate my first "sandwich." Previously if I wanted bread, I ate bread with butter or jam or perhaps without any spread. If I wanted meat, I ate meat – all separate. Now everything is put together between two slices of bread and you pick it up with your hands and hope that nothing falls out. I thought this was the greatest invention and always enjoyed what was called the *Denver Sandwich:*

(Ingredients)

1 egg sliced tomatoes   *3 slices of toast*
chopped onion and green pepper   *mayonnaise*
American cheese

Scramble the egg in butter and put on 1st slice of toast spread the top of the 2nd slice with mayonnaise and cover with tomatoes and sprinkle with onion and green pepper 3rd slice of toast spread with mayonnaise and cover with cheese.

Put sandwich together and place under the broiler flame until cheese is melted.

the old bog road

My feet are here on Broadway
This blessed harvest morn
But oh the ache that's in me
For the spot where I was born.
My weary hands are blistered
From toil in cold and heat
But oh to swing a scythe today through
A field of Irish wheat.
If I'd the chance to wander back
Or own a kings abode
I'd sooner see the hawthorn tree
On the old bog road.

My mother died last springtime
When Erin's fields were green
Her neighbors said her waking
Was the largest ever seen
There were snowdrops and primroses
All piled beside her bed
And Fern's church was crowded
As her funeral mass was said
But here was I on Broadway
Building brick by load
As they carried out her coffin
Down the old bog road.

Now life's a weary puzzle
Past finding out by man
I take the day for what it's worth
And do the best I can.
I'll go my way and earn my pay
And smoke my pipe alone
If no one cares a rush for me
What needs to make a moan
O God be with you Ireland
And the old bog road.

Monday morning arrived and I was on the streetcar early. Jim Rogers had set up an interview for my first job with a trucking company at 27th and Ashland. All I was doing was unloading crate after crate of different foods. It was fine; the lads were fun to be with and the pay decent, but the hours were crazy. I started at 4:30 in the morning and never knew when I would finish. I remember well meeting an old man at the bus stop and he'd say the same thing every morning, "The man who invented work should have stayed and done it."

I was getting into a regiment; a more structured work schedule than I ever remembered. There was very little leisure time, but I was working and that was good. In the spring of 1948 there were plenty of men out of work or without a steady paying job. Let me tell you, I wasn't the only man standing at the bus stop at 3:45 in the morning.

I wasn't on the job two weeks when the sky opened up and a downpour of rain from the heavens soaked me at the bus stop. Well, I did what I thought everyone there was doing. I went back home. Margaret heard the door opening and was out of the room asking, "What happened? Why are you back?"

I was wiping my face with a dish towel and told her, "Will you look out the window – It's raining from the heavens." I sat on a chair and was getting ready to unlace my shoes.

"What are you doing?" she asked, trying to whisper.

"No one can work in this weather," I said.

I remember well her laughing as she told me, "Willie, you're in America now! In Chicago we work in the rain, snow, sun – it doesn't matter. Everyone dresses for the weather and never misses a day of work because of it."

I couldn't believe it! In Ireland on a bad day like that we would be by the fire in the home place, warm and dry. I couldn't argue. Connie was up and getting ready for work now. So I put on the raincoat she gave me and out the door again to the bus stop. Everyone enjoyed that story about the greenhorn for a long time.

I was on this job for about six weeks when one day a driver that I had become friendly with told me the news.

"Bill," he said, "I heard from a reliable source that the fruit company on 14th and Ashland is looking for a cooper."

"How's the pay," I asked.

He answered with a smile, "Well, I know it's better than what you are getting here."

Of course I had to ask, "What exactly does a cooper do at a fruit company?"

Again he answered, "Can you use a hammer?"

"I can," I answered with a nod of my head.

I can still hear the old timer telling me as a lad, "Willie, swing with the full length of the hammer." That's what puts the power behind the tool.

He continued, "Then you can hammer in the few nails around the pieces of wood to make a crate that will hold the fruit. You see them here being repaired by a few men. It's the same thing. Of course you can do it. Go and get the job."

"I will," I said.

He gave me the "thumbs up" sign and said, "Good luck."

I never said a word to anyone, but as soon as break time was called, I walked away quickly and caught a streetcar headed north. The time was going to be close. I was on 27th and Halsted and I had to get to 14th Street, complete the application and get back again in 30 minutes. Incredibly, I did it! I got the call the next day to start on the following Monday. I was so thrilled. I remember well the hours were from 8:00 in the morning until 4:30 in the afternoon with a half hour lunch, weekends free and I earned $10.00 per day. I was living right.

Whenever possible I spent the weekends with Aunt Nora and after a good feed on Saturday, Jim and myself would catch the streetcar to Dan Curran's saloon, next stop The Harp and Shamrock at 53rd and not far away a quick hello in Erin's Isle. Later in the evening, the young crowd that could get transportation by streetcar, taxi, or a ride, made it to McGinty's Tavern at 74th and Cottage Grove.

I was acclimating myself into the American culture with no trouble at all, and the radio was one of the many benefits that I reaped as a new immigrant. I listened to all the famous singers of the time, Bing Crosby, Frank Sinatra, Nat King Cole, The Everly Brothers and, of course, Elvis Presley. The big bands, such as Jimmy and Tommy Dorsey, Glenn Miller, and Guy Lombardo were still going strong, but in the background, every now and then, rock 'n' roll. But to tell you the truth, I never thought that rock 'n' roll music would have made such an impact on the future of music, not only in the United States of America, but around the world.

There were so many of the Irish girls, eighteen and nineteen years of age working for wealthy families in the big houses beside Lake Michigan, who would make it to McGinty's on a Saturday night. The bar area was in the front and then a dance hall in the back. In the summer, the owner opened the doors and we would dance and sing until the police would be called and send us on our way. There is nothing but good memories for me from these places.

I was learning my way around the neighborhood and making new friends. More and more people were calling me "Bill," which is the common nickname for William here. I was writing home regularly and was able to send a bit of cash in every letter. I knew my mother would like this. And with that her letters were arriving every couple of weeks or so with the news from around our place. She was lonesome for me and I was for her. Right from the start I opened a savings account that would pay for my first trip home. Every paycheck, without exception, I put money into it.

There was a work ethic here amongst us and it became contagious, but still, I was restless. I had too much idle time on my hands and I wanted to work, to do better. After six months with the fruit company, and realizing there was no where else to go except repairing crates, I started asking around again. As it happened the Gas Company was hiring, and again on my lunch I filled out an application in their main office at 122 South Michigan Avenue, which is not there today. I didn't have to wait long to find out I was hired.

At this time, the gas company was installing underground pipes and making connections throughout the city. It wasn't the manual labor that bothered me. I could use the shovel and dig a hole as well as any man. It was being in the hole that I couldn't stand. I'll never forget it.

I had been digging for six weeks and the boss put me down in this hole to dig some more. I had had enough. I threw the shovel to the side and walked away and never looked back. A man can force himself to do many things, but there are limitations, and I guess I found mine. However, quitting a job without having another one lined up was not acceptable, but I did it and had to live with it.

In the meantime, I had already decided to try and further my education. Kelly High School at 6238 South Stewart, and I believe it still stands today, offered courses for emigrants. I enrolled in an English course that turned out to be, believe it or not, very basic. The school had setup this program for the non-English speaking immigrants and those who spoke English, but perhaps could not read. As the instructor explained, I was one of the fortunate ones to have had some schooling. But I continued to attend until my work schedule changed. It wasn't all that easy and it was somewhere to go on an evening.

I had made enough contacts myself by now that I knew I could go into the fire or police departments. They both carried a big Irish population, but I didn't think I could do either. It is funny how life takes its little turns and twists before finally a man comes up with a plan that works. I had been jumping on and off streetcars since the day I arrived and they really intrigued me. I decided I wanted to be a motorman with the Chicago Transit Authority and drive the "Green Hornets."

There was one route to follow, and only one, so that the electric current would keep the bus moving. I didn't have to worry about getting lost around the city. I knew from seeing the same drivers every day at the same time, the routes did not change. So who did I tell? I sat down at home, at the kitchen table with my brother-in-law, Connie

Curtin, who had become my good friend and remained so until the day he died.

Connie's cousin had a contact and I was sent to pickup a letter of recommendation. I was told where and when to go and who to see. The man handed me an envelope to take with and I knew it contained my future. If a picture can tell a thousand words, I am sure my face showed all the emotions of relief and happiness as I shook the man's hand and left. It wasn't until I got to the bus stop that I pulled the envelope out of my pocket and sprawled across the front was written, "Just a boy from home."

I patiently waited outside the office at 7:45 A.M. to be called for the interview. It wasn't long when I heard my name. I stood up and walked to the lady holding the door open. I'm telling you now I was sweating and my heart was beating so hard and so fast that I was sure she could see the thump, thump, thump against my shirt. But I was put at ease almost immediately by this pleasant, middle aged, Irish American with a quick smile and a good sense of humor. We shook hands and when I handed the letter of recommendation, he smiled and asked me to sit down.

We talked about my family and what relations I had here in Chicago and he told me a little about his own family. When it came down to business, though, it was straight forward. Honesty was the main character trait that the company needed in their employees. The street cars, as I knew them, were changing. The conductor's job was being eliminated completely leaving the motor man to drive the vehicle, take the fare and make change.

He asked, "Can you do this?"

"I can."

"There is no drinking tolerated. Do you understand?"

"I do. I have no problem with that."

"You must be on time. The street cars run twenty four hours a day, seven days a week. If you are late, then the man you are to replace will be late going home. Do you have a problem arriving for work on time?"

"I don't. If I have been late for work, it was due to a circumstance that I had no control over."

I remember well the last important issue we talked about, which was how to deal with the public.

He gave the scenario, "If a man or woman boarded and refused to pay, what would I do?"

I said, "I would tell the person the price of the ride and if you can't pay, then you have to leave."

"Let's say," he continued looking me in the eye, "If a customer paid their fare, but once the street car began to move became ignorant, belligerent and loud-mouthed, what would you do then?"

"Well, I tell you what I'd do, and I've seen a few of these antics already. I'll stop the street car and walk to the person, nice and easy and say 'get off.' And, if the person refused, I'd send for the police."

He agreed with me completely and we continued to discuss the issue of working with the public and all the types that you meet daily. I knew what he was looking for. Would I be patient or throw a punch? Would I call the police or try to take control of the situation myself? I believed then, and I still believe that for the one miserable troublemaker you meet, there are a hundred pleasant, good-natured people around, and that's what I told the man.

He continued, "Bill, the expectations are clear, if there is a problem with stealing, drinking, punctuality, or not showing respect to the customers, you'll lose your job. Do you understand?"

"I do understand," I said.

"Well then, you're hired and I welcome you." We stood up together, shook hands again, walked to the door and he asked his secretary to give me all the paperwork to complete at home and return as soon as possible.

I asked, "Can I stay and give it all to you now?"

Of course it was okay with them, "Stay as long as you want," I was told.

I was thinking if I had any questions, I could get them answered right away and not waste another day going back and forth.

I was hired by the Chicago Transit Authority within a week and began training as a motorman. I found out that before the Chicago Transit Authority was created, the Chicago Surface Lines controlled the city's streetcars and purchased the Green Hornets in 1945. The name was given by Chicagoans because of their color, which was a green and creamy white. They were very modern looking and had a smoother ride compared to any other streetcar around. Not only was their appearance more modern, but the acceleration was much better.

I had to carry a gadget around my waist that was created for holding coins. Eventually, I could put the coins in the quarter, dime, nickel or penny slots without looking and give correct change while driving. Passengers entered through the two front doors and usually exited through the three rear doors or the single middle door. The rear doors were nicknamed "blinkers" because they opened to the side of the doorway and resembled a blinking eyelid. This was a good system that kept the passengers loading and unloading rather quickly.

I was comfortable sitting in the driver's seat almost from the beginning. My run was Archer Avenue from Pulaski Road to State Street. I'd head north on State and turn around on Clark Street or Roosevelt Road. Chicago was truly a city that never slept. Men and woman were coming and going to work at all hours of the night and day.

The shifts took some getting used to, but the money was worth the inconvenience. Many times I had a four-hour shift in the morning during rush hour and again another four-hour shift in the evening rush hour. It was during these hours when the traffic was congested that the Green Hornet would run into trouble. If someone accidentally veered from the electric line or the cable detached from the electric lines, the streetcar stopped. It was hard as well when other vehicles would cut in front of the streetcar to turn or park; the driver could not go around. Of course, this meant that all the succeeding streetcars were lined up – just waiting.

Another problem was the rain, especially where viaducts were located. It was inevitable that the viaducts would flood after a bit of rain and again, because of the electric motor being so low to the ground, the streetcar could not go through deep water. There were tracks for re-routing, but it was always difficult and very time consuming.

I was still working for the CTA on May 25, 1950 when the worst streetcar disaster occurred in Chicago at 63rd and State Street. It was raining, the viaduct was flooded and the streetcar proceeded through hitting head on with a truck carrying a gasoline tank. This was a terrible tragedy which killed 33 passengers. The investigators discovered that the steel bar that was put across the windows for what was originally thought to be a safety factor, prevented people from climbing out and the fire and smoke engulfed the streetcar.

This job was seven days a week, twenty four hours a day. I signed up for the extra-board, which meant you had to wait for other men to call off or the boss to put on extra streetcars. I wasn't going anywhere in particular anyway, so I used to sit around playing cards or a few games of pool hoping to be called. Sometimes I did and sometimes I didn't. The bosses were good to the men with families. They always tried to get them out first, and rightly so, they had children to feed.

I got to know everyone and they all knew that Bourke was reliable. The company could put all the spotters they wanted on my streetcar, I never took one penny that I didn't work for. I got good at recognizing the swindler and threw him off, but the deprived had a different look and I always turned my head and let them take the ride. There weren't too many, but enough that I still recall the voice that held the sound of pleading and a face with the look of desperation.

There were many Irish immigrants during these years that had never traveled outside their own town until leaving for America and had no experience with other nationalities, races, religions, etc. I had some knowledge of what prejudice meant while working in England and being Irish. But, then I also witnessed many, many times how the working man had the same common goal and could get along and help each other.

Now, I'm not sitting here pretending that I have not been narrow-minded at certain times in my life, because I have, but not to any one group of people of color, race, or religion; it was due to their immoral acts that I rejected them. I have to say that when I arrived in Chicago and began working, the Irish were no longer the lower class people. I felt that we were accepted as a hard working class of people, most of us with hardly any education, but we were willing to work. Only once, on 79th Street over East by the lake did I see a sign in the window showing, "If Irish Need Not Apply!" However, there were many old timers still around at that time who dealt with narrow-mindedness and ignorance.

I caught on quickly to the neighborhoods. The white people lived in one area of the city, the Asians in another and the Blacks in another. And then those areas were separated again. The Irish took over one church, while the Italians dominated another parish, and so forth. But this was the United States of America and I was told in a very clear way that everyone was to be treated equally. After a person paid their fare, if a seat was available, then it was theirs – man, woman or child.

Well, let me tell you, I wasn't six months working when I had my first run in with a white man who thought he could change the rules on my streetcar. I soon showed him who had the power. I never remembered seeing this man before, but even after all these years, I could point him out on the street today.

He paid his fare and was walking toward the rear when I heard him say, "Get up! I want to sit there! Get to the back of the car!"

I didn't react for a second or two. I couldn't believe my ears. I turned around quickly, spotted the black woman who had got on at State Street, and realized he was demanding that she leave her seat. Well, the hair was standing on the back of my neck. I could feel the blood rushing to the top of my head. I pulled the switch and came to a halt and stood up; I was angry.

"Who are you talking to," I asked.

He answered, "Ya know who I'm talk'n to!"

"Well, you'll talk to me now and not this woman," I shouted back.

The woman was staring at me and made a move as if to leave her seat, but I beckoned her not to go. She looked straight ahead, not saying a word, and there was dead silence on the streetcar.

I said in a very clear voice, "You'll find another seat or out you go! This woman has as much a right to that seat as you do," I added in a loud voice, "And don't forget that."

He stood glaring at me for a few more seconds and eventually walked towards the back and sat down. I kept my eye on him until he left and then I sighed with relief as I watched him exit through the back door. I didn't look for trouble, but I had learned to handle myself over the years with arrogant bastards, and I don't believe that fellow expected the reaction he received.

I was with the streetcars now for a good three months and was happy. The weeks were going by quickly. I still missed my mother and my home, but I discovered, as many other immigrants, that work was the best medicine for the mind. When you are busy, the time isn't there to think, so I worked every hour I could.

I arrived home to my sister Margaret one afternoon and of all the things that one might imagine, I never thought I would hear the terrible news she had from home. My mother was dead!

I sat staring at Margaret, and finally asked, "How do you know?"

"Willie," she answered with a tearful voice, "here's the telegram."

I didn't have to read it. I knew it was true and she was dead. Still today as I talk with you I have a feeling of dread that makes one sick, nauseated. I tried not to cry, but I couldn't help it, the tears ran down my cheeks. I cried at the table, at the saloon, walking to work, driving the streetcar and always in bed when I was alone. The nights were the hardest and the longest.

There was an unexplainable hurting pain, such a void, and a great loss. Also, I suppose there was a certain amount of guilt. I promised her I'd be back and we would see each other again. I was gone from home eleven months. Never, in my wildest dreams, had I imagined that my mother would not be waiting for me when I returned.

I realized later that Margaret had phoned Mary at work and asked her to come home early. She wanted Mary there when the news was told. They both dreaded having to break the news knowing I would not take it well. I had a little money saved for myself, but not enough to go home. Mary said right from the start that she would give me the money to go back, but I said no.

It would cost double or more to fly and the time was still against me. Ireland is six hours ahead of Chicago, which meant that her body was already in the church and the burial was scheduled for the next morning. I really saw no purpose in going. It wasn't as if she was sick in bed and needed to be cared for. That would have been another story. No, she was gone, gone forever. I could do nothing in Ireland, and so, I decided to remain in Chicago and go on with my plans. I knew this was the right decision and that my mother would have agreed.

Now another chapter of my life was about to take place.

my wild irish rose

If you listen I'll sing you a sweet little song
Of a flower that's now dropped and dead
'twas given to me by a girl that I know
Since we've met, faith, I've known no repose
She is dearer by far than the world's brightest star
And I call her my wild Irish Rose.

My wild Irish Rose, the sweetest flower that grows
You may search everywhere,
But none can compare
With my wild Irish Rose.
My wild Irish Rose, the dearest flower that grows
And some day for my sake,
She may let me take
The bloom for my wild Irish Rose.

Kitty Morley sat with her legs crossed, hands around her new brown purse and staring, without seeing or blinking out the window of the train that had just left Ballyhaunis station. Her long awaited adventure was commencing! She had been waiting for a ticket since Mary left that same year in February. The coat she was wearing arrived in the post a couple of months ago. There was one good coat to travel in and she would mail it back home for the next immigrant.

It was hard to understand why her parents wouldn't let her go with Mary; they were sisters, just two years in the difference. But Tom Morley was adamant, "No daughter of mine will leave this house before eighteen years of age." All the talking and reasoning in the world would not change his mind. And so, the notion of leaving home became an obsession as the days, then weeks and months past.

It felt odd sitting alone and not knowing exactly what to expect or what to do. "Keep asking questions," her mother had said or another suggestion, "follow the crowd." Well, it didn't matter anymore; what happens will happen. Kitty was eighteen years old as of August 9 and her journey to America, to the great city of Chicago, located within a state called Illinois began on this cold, clouding, drizzling, miserable day of November 12, 1948.

Catherine, nicknamed Kitty, was all of five feet in height weighing about nine and one half stone, which is one hundred and thirty five pounds. It wasn't good to be too thin. This was a good sturdy weight that showed good health and physical strength. She had the unusual hair color of blonde, not common in this area with large, bright and expressive blue eyes, fair skin and rosy cheeks. But the loving nature that she exuded when in her presence is what made Kitty unique to her family and friends. It was innate, this ability to make everyone feel special and at ease while in her company.

Kitty loved her home, not necessarily the small two-room thatched cottage that her mother, father and five other siblings lived in, as well as Granny who had to be ninety years of age now, but the love and security that was found inside these four walls. There was no arguing or problems with the drink that some families had to endure. As her mother said many times, "Alcohol is the ruination of many a home." However, the Morley's difficulty stemmed from the ever-present issue of money. There never seemed to be enough to do anything extra. But no one was ever hungry and the cottage was warm from the turf provided from the bog located right outside their front door.

Ballyhaunis, located at the eastern end of Mayo, wasn't considered a big town, but it wasn't too small either. On our side of the town you would find, Tulranhan, Logboy, Brickens, and Bekan (pronounced Bacon). The town prospered because of the cattle and sheep fairs that were held throughout the year. It wasn't uncommon to see a poor farmer walking with his calves or lambs over his shoulders to sell. Also, there were boxes of chickens, hens and eggs to sell to the local traders. Going to the fair was an important day and big money would be exchanged.

A story goes that a man was standing with an old mule and along comes another farmer ready to strike a deal.

"How much for the sleep'n beast?" He asked.

"Well I don't know," says the owner, "How much will ye offer?"

"Twenty pounds I'll give."

Highly insulted the owner retorts, "Well I wouldn't wake him up for thirty."

And of course, after the men finished with their negotiating and a price was fixed, it had to be sealed with a pint at the pub.

It is confirmed that a family was living in this area by the name of D'Angulo who settled around the thirteenth century. However, at some point this property was exchanged with the Nolan family and they resided in the Tulrahan Estate. The Nolan family was Catholic and generous to the Church. Winifred Nolan Beirne, sister of Edmund John gave the site for Saint Mary's Church in Logboy to be built, as well as funded the majority of its construction costs. However, the site of Logboy Church is low-lying and is surrounded by bog and marsh and when built, it was not accessible for all the people in the district.

The church that was used prior to Saint Mary's was in Tulrahan in the town of Carrownedin, which was very close to Tulrahan Castle. This site was more convenient especially for those families located in the southwest end of the parish. Today there is only a depression in the ground where sand was quarried. There were walls until 1888, but they were used to build the new school. If you look carefully at the field of grass, you can see the path used from the main road and it is referred to as "Bodhrin an Aifrinn (church road.)"

Saint Mary's was completed in 1836 or 1837 using the stones from Cleary's Quarry. Although, it's known that some stones had to be transported by horse and cart from the Knock Crockery in Rosscommon about thirty miles away. All of these stones had to be cut by hammer and chisel; there were no angle grinders.

There are three churches in Bekan Parish, Saint Mary's Church, Logboy, Saint Theresa of The Little Flower Church, Ballinvilla, and Saint Margaret Mary Alico, Bekan. No one could really say where the name "Logboy" originated, however there is a folklore that has followed. There is a tee in the road that leads to Saint Mary's Church where the young ones used to meet in the evenings. As a pastime logs were cut and the young lads would fight, joust or play other games; hence the name "Logboy."

The countryside is passing quickly now and Kitty wonders when the train will cross the border of Mayo. She heard one of the other passengers say, "We're out of Mayo, it won't be long until we arrive at Cobh, County Cork." No one ever said that, "I'm leaving from the city of Cobh in the County of Cork - it was always said, "I'm leaving from the Cobh of Cork."

Kitty felt the small loaf of bread, wrapped in paper and tied with string in her pocket. It may not be necessary, but in one of Mary's letters she said, "Don't go without Mam's seasick bread." It was the "miracle" medicine on board the ship with Mary.

Recipe

2 cups of oatmeal

Soak in water until soft

Add a sprinkle of salt

Drain water and mix with a small amount of flour until consistency is firm

Shape into pancake and pan fry in lard.

When Mary was on her ship, she had said nothing about the bread and really didn't believe that it would help the terrible lurching up and down of a stomach. They were a couple of days out, with Atlantic waves' rolling, when one of lads she met asked, "Mary, do you have any of that oatmeal bread for the stomach?" It was still packed in her bag. Mary saved the day!

More memories about home continue in a torrent. Ballyhaunis had a history of poverty and sorrow for the poor Irish tenant farmer and when Patrick Nolan-Farrell and his family left, he put a bailiff, Luke Dillon, in charge. As local folklore says, this Luke Dillon kept a keen eye on the estate and controlled the one water pump; it was twenty feet deep, right outside the backdoor. None of the tenants that lived in the area were allowed to go near this pump for any reason. This meant that many tenant families had to walk one mile to the nearest water well. During the famine years and before the Land League, Dillon found pleasure evicting and burning the cottages of those tenants that could not pay their rent. These were hard years and as the old people would say, "Let the harm of the day go with them."

It is a fact that in November of 1881, Luke Dillon was shot to death on the road near the Estate and his killer never discovered. There was no love lost; everyone felt relief. However, it would not be until 1907 when the Land League took possession over the Logboy Estate that the tenant farmers began to work their own land with a new beginning of independence.

During the early years, while the Land Commission was establishing itself throughout Mayo, a plan was created to plant top-class trees, such as oak, beech, ash, sycamore, spruce and others on acres and acres of the Logboy Estate. These trees became the property of the Land Commission and it was prohibited to go near this area for grazing, and one would never cut down a tree. There was a penalty; it was strictly forbidden.

In 1937 the Commission divided this wooded area between the bordering farmers, but still controlled it for many years. The Commission was specific with its instructions and sectioned off each piece with wooded stakes and five rows of bull wire (not barbed wire). It was then the responsibility of each farmer to make the land "fit for grazing." However, if the farmer needed to cut down a tree, the Commission was notified and permission granted with the understanding that another young tree would be replanted – it was a law, a tree for a tree.

After the striping, Tom Morley was given land up around the village of Kildarra. It was in this area that Kildara Church existed and not far away is St. Brigid's well. This old church is mentioned in the Edwardian Taxation in 1306, acknowledged again in 1584 and in 1951. All that remained of the church at this time was a small portion of the walls, perhaps three or four feet of stones; however, the foundation was discovered some years ago.

The Morley's attended mass at Saint Mary's Church in Logboy, which was about a mile and a half from home and as Granny would say, "A good stretch of the legs." They attended Tulrahan School after it was built, and as the auld man would say, "Just up the field." This school was run as the majority of country schools in Ireland at the time. The head master was strict, the students were disciplined, and the consequences at times harsh.

Many years previous, a match was made between Michael Morley of Redhill and Catherine Moran of Carrickacat. Catherine married into the home place and it was there that my father Tom and his two brothers John and Luke were born. Their father Michael died at a young age leaving Catherine to raise her children alone.

However, the years passed quickly and before she realized it, Tom was the only one home. John married into the home place of Maggie O'Donnell, and Luke at a young age went to England for work. He wasn't in England very long when word came that he was leaving for San Francisco, California and had signed on for the job of "earthing." It was there that he met Maura Moran from Clare Island, married and remained there until his death, never returning to Ireland.

Men were needed to build up this new country and many came from Ireland. They had to be strong, strong mentally and physically in order to endure the rigors of construction, as well as the disease that came from the dirt. They helped dig the new roads, waterways, foundations for homes and all the other things needed to sustain a growing population. Earthing became a popular occupation for many immigrants; no education was needed, only a strong back. By the time I arrived in the United States, earthing was almost obsolete while landscaping was becoming very popular.

Now, Tailor Loftus lived right beside Saint Mary's Church, as was said, "A stone's throw away." When you came out his door, the church was there with its gray walls, stained-glass windows and regal front doors with a capacity of holding easily one hundred parishioners. Tom Morley had ordered a dark blue suit and on this particular night, it would be the last fitting. The suit was finished and he would be in soon to pick it up. It was his first new suit and he wore it well. The material was beautiful wool and the lining in the jacket would give extra warmth and protection from the strong winds.

Tom bade his farewell and with his suit wrapped in heavy brown paper and tied with string, began his walk home to Redhill. It was a surprise when he recognized the Ruane family with their newly baptized son, David coming out of the Church. It was very common at this time for babies to be baptized during the week in the afternoon.

Tom knew of the baby's godmother, Maggie Hosty, but had never met her. She was a lovely young girl who smiled often.

"Tom, that should be your wedding suit," said John Willie Ruane, the child's father.

Tom or Maggie did not realize that their destiny had been made. Within a couple of months the match was made to the daughter of John and Mary (Ruane) Hosty from the village of Carrickacat, a few miles away. The courtship didn't last long; Tom Morley and Maggie Hosty were married in St. Mary's Church in Logboy and they married with a love that only continued to grow as time passed. The love that they had for each other was given to their children with the genuine kindness that was exemplified through simple gestures.

Maggie was welcomed by Tom's mother, Catherine, and the village of Redhill with open arms. Maggie often said, "How could we manage without the help of the old ones?" Catherine and Maggie worked together to make a good solid home. Often Maggie would go to the fields to help her husband while his mother stayed around the cottage minding the children, knitting, tending the foul, and preparing the dinner for us, as well as boiling the pot of spuds for the sow.

Before the year was out, the next generation of Morley's began with twins, Mary and Catherine. However, Catherine died after a few weeks, which was not expected since she was the bigger of the two. Catherine (Kitty) was next. It was not uncommon to name the next child after a baby that had previously died. Then Michael was born, fourth Bridget (Della), and finally another set of twins John and Margaret.

The village was full of life during these years. Just up the road lived Maggie Mahon who was married to Denny Morley (no relation) and daughter, Nellie; up a bit further were the Murphys and past the turn a good bit, the Brennans. There wasn't a lot of money, but no one was ever hungry or lacked love and attention. They had worries, not common today in Ireland, and that was the fear of their children leaving and never returning.

In one letter Mary wrote not to worry about traveling alone; there were plenty of girls my age, all headed for America from every part of Ireland and traveling alone. She said it was fascinating to hear them talk with their accents and I was to make conversation with them. She explained, "Get friendly, so that if you need help then you will have someone to call."

Silently I decided that when I got settled in Chicago, I would acquaint myself with more people and hopefully have a wonderful social life. I heard that there was a great night life, music and dancing everywhere you go. And money was of no concern – sure didn't I hear that it grew on trees. At that moment, I looked down at my hands and swore to myself that I would never have clay beneath my nails again. I love my family and I love my home, but I'll never miss the farm work, which would be the only life that I would ever have in the county of Mayo.

Oh the fun we always had in the McGee house. There were four girls, Mary, Theresa, Mena, and Phyllis, and often Mary and I would cross the bog to visit in the evening.

Mammy would warn us going out, "Be home before 10:00."

With or without whoever was home, the rosary began at 10:00 P.M. The chairs were pulled close around the fire and Mammy would begin with the Act of Contrition. Coming home late from McGee's wasn't an excuse to miss the rosary. The door was locked and we'd knock and knock until Daddy would finally hear us and open it.

"Your mother will be talking to the two of ye in the morning." Back to bed he'd go and into bed quietly we'd go, and then of course

Mary and I would be the first ones up in the morning ready to help with all the chores.

Saying goodbye to my mother and father was a terrible experience. Reunions are wonderful, but the leaving is something else. I've heard of visitors from America who would get up before dawn and walk to the station in order not to have to go through the goodbyes. I always thought, "How silly!" But now I understand.

Kitty remembered all too well the tears in her father's eyes when Mary left, and now they overflowed, showing a thin line of water on his weather-beaten face. He was saying good-bye to another daughter. He whispered in my ear, "I'll miss my little girl." And I know he was telling the truth. My father never raised his voice or his hand to any of his children and gave us everything to the best of his ability.

I'm Granny's name sake and that meant something special in our house. Many a time she made an excuse for me so I didn't have to work on the land with the rest of the family. Granny would say to my mother, "I can't do it without Kitty's help." Mam would shake her head and walk away. I knew Granny would be lonely when I left as I would be for her, everyday, for a very long time.

"Go to Mary," Granny said, "It will be better when the two of you are together." She made it as easy as possible to leave, and in her heart she realized, I would be happier, more content in Chicago.

Often as a child Granny and I would be alone and tears would appear in her eyes. I asked, "Why are you so sad today Granny?"

She would wipe the tear and say, "It is twenty two years and seven months since your granddad passed." Always, always she knew the exact length of time since her only love went to heaven. And because of this strong faith, she did not fear death; one day they would be reunited.

When it came time to kiss goodbye, I couldn't talk. She took my face gently between her worn hands and said, "Be brave and be careful."

I wasn't brave and I didn't know what I had to be careful about, not yet.

Mary resembled the Morley side of the family with her black, wavy, thick hair and expressive brown eyes that enhanced her small nose, high cheekbones and lovely smile. Perhaps being the oldest in the family and having the burden of responsibility that goes with that, Mary exuded determination and willingly accepted it as she bade her good-byes, crying, and boarded this same train.

Austin Murphy, from Redhill, was a few years older than Mary and had already immigrated and attained citizenship in New York. During his visit home she mentioned how much she wanted to go to the states and be with her family in Chicago. Austin agreed to sponsor and loan the money for her passage. Mary turned twenty one years of age as World War II ended and the ports opened once again for immigration.

Tom Lyons, the travel agent, located on Main Street in Ballyhaunis made the arrangements for Mary along with nine other friends to travel together from Ballyhaunis on February 14, 1948 to Cobh, Cork where the S.S. Washington was ready to pull anchor on February 15. A good neighbor and longtime friend of the family, Harry O'Riley booked a hotel room in Cobh for them all to stay that night. It would be a long eight-day journey before arriving in New York Harbor on February 21.

What wonderful memories the Morleys have of the O'Riley family. We were always welcome and often frequented their home for an evening of singing and dancing. They had a little shop that sold necessities and sweets and it was the only house that I knew of that had a piano. Mary, Harry's sister, played the piano, Harry the fiddle, and Herb was musical as well. It was here that we learned to appreciate traditional Gaelic music.

Harry used to say, "Ye're the best dressed girleens."

Granny had bleached the bag or sack that the flour came in to pure white. She cut off the name brand and sewed lace on the bottom that would show under our skirts. It was made from nothing but love, and we wore them proudly to the dances in Cloonfad..

There was no way to arrive at the dance in Cloonfad except to walk. If we went across the field, which was shorter, our shoes were ruined or if we walked the roads, time was wasted. To solve this dilemma, we would wear rubber boots or wellingtons and Daddy carried our shoes. When the dance was over, we took the roads home.

Three taxis were booked from Ballyhaunis to Cobh and everyone met at Tom Lyons' early. There were Mary Morley, Ed and Mary Ellen Beesty, Mike Morris and Helen Hopkins bound for Chicago; Tom Ruane and Mike Robinson, New York; Ann Higgins, New Jersey; Yank Connolly, Canada and Mary Madden who was Ann Ganley's niece headed for the state of Washington. It truly felt like a funeral. For sure, many of these parents, brothers, sisters, friends and sweethearts would never see each other again. It was another "American Wake."

During the war years Mary asked Mam if she could go to England to work and make a few pounds for traveling expenses, but the answer was "no." Mam's two sisters were married and settled in Chicago with children and if she were to leave Ireland, the destination would be America without question. And you didn't question!

Our mother was a small woman with blue eyes that sparkled when she laughed and easily filled with tears of joy or sadness. She was quick to give a smile, but just as quick to turn a stern face that portrayed firmness when needed to keep a house with a family running smoothly.

Her hair was gray and pulled back into a bun, but her skin was as fresh as someone ten years younger.

There were no instructions on how to act. In her eyes and mind, the rearing years were over, and without a word it was understood what acceptable or unacceptable behavior was. However, it was made very clear, "When writing home, put your Daddy's name first."

I can still see her standing on the platform waving her small hand and the tears running down her face. How many daughters had already left and never returned. She looked so afraid for me that my heart was breaking.

I kept saying, "I will be okay; I'll be fine; I'm old enough to take care of myself." But the fear for the unspoken future could be seen in her face and heard in my voice. Later, I realized that I would never really know my mother as an adult. This is one of the many tragedies of emigration.

So why can't I stop these silly tears from running down my face? I'm so happy to be on my way to America. Rest Kitty, close your eyes and rest and think about your family that is waiting in Chicago. Can you imagine what it must have been like for Mary to arrive not knowing anyone? I am lucky to know that she is waiting for me.

"Kitty," Mary wrote, "There is someone from every county in Ireland and, oh my goodness, the fun and laughter we had everyday. The time flew by and before I realized it, I was aboard the largest ship that I could ever imagine."

One person from the group came up with a great idea of exchanging room numbers so that they would not get separated. There were two people to a berth and most had roommates they had never met.

The agreement was made that all would meet for breakfast every morning and this was also a good way to make sure everything was okay. And, of course, plans for the day could be made. However, that first morning Mary Madden was missing. For some odd reason, she had not given her room number and, as it happened, no one set eyes on her for the entire trip. The ship had docked when someone pointed to a thin woman in the distance. Mary Madden had been deathly sick and was almost unrecognizable. Everyone felt terrible.

In Mary's letter she tried to give a vivid picture of what to expect upon arrival in New York Harbor. She explained that there would be hundreds of men and women swarming on the dock and the noise and confusion will be overwhelming, but don't be scared. Mary was fortunate, almost immediately she spotted Austin, hands in pockets, and smiling. What a relief! But there were many who didn't have to look through the crowds; no one would be meeting them.

Austin and his wife said, "Mary, our house is your house for as long as you want to stay." Mary felt welcome and knew their hospitality was genuine, but was anxious to get to her final destination. So after a wonderful and restful vacation, they parted at the train station on March 2.

Mary boarded the train thanking God for her good fortune and ready to undertake the sixteen hour ride to the Midwest of the United States. It was cold and damp with plenty of snow still on the ground. The train was full to capacity with passengers, but all strangers.

on the shores of amerikay

I'm bidding farewell to the land of my youth
And the homes I love so well
And the mountains so grand in my own native land
I'm bidding them all farewell
With an aching heart I'll bid them adieu
For tomorrow I sail far away
O'er the raging foam, for to seek a home
On the shores of Amerikay.

It's not for the want of employment I'm going
It's not for the love of fame
That fortune bright, may shine over me
And give me a glorious name.
It's not for the want of employment I'm going
O'er the weary and stormy sea
But to seek a home for my own true love
On the shores of Amerikay.

And when I am bidding my last farewell
The tears like rain will blind
To think of my friends in my native land
And the home I am leaving behind
But if I'm to die on a foreign land
And be buried so far, far away
No fond mother's tear will be shed o'er my grave
On the shores of Amerikay.

Kitty will never forget, for as long as she would live the immense vastness of the ocean liner that brought her to America. It was almost impossible to comprehend something that size, floating on water and moving at such a speed that in four days the Statue of Liberty was in sight. But Kitty's voyage was not as eventful as her sister's. The moment the ship pulled anchor and began to gain speed, she felt her stomach do a turn. From that moment, sea-sickness became a reality.

John Murphy, Austin's brother, was scanning the crowded dock in New York Harbor. He remembered Kitty vaguely as a little girl, but hadn't seen her in many years. When Austin asked him to sponsor and lend the fare to one of the Morley's, he was happy to oblige, and now, here he is looking for an eighteen year old blonde with a rusty, brownish colored coat.

There was Kitty standing to the side, looking anxious, scanning the crowd of faces, a small carrying bag and holding tight to a little purse that probably held a small amount of money. She was suddenly aware of a young man approaching from the side. She had been anticipating this moment for a long time and hoped that it would not be difficult to recognize John. She continued to stare, not allowing herself to breath, hoping and praying silently that this man was John Murphy. It was and the feeling cannot be described. The apprehension was gone and replaced with an absolute relief.

"Kitty Morley," He asked with a pleasant smile and quickly accepted her extended hand in a welcoming grasp.

"It's good to see a girleen from home and you're welcome to the

U.S.A. and my home," he said. She noticed he had not picked up any American accent, the Mayo brogue was still quite apparent.

The car was lovely and big and there were no holes in the road, rather potholes as I learned later to refer to them, and no fear of a puncture in a tire. There were so many cars; all shapes, sizes and colors and the lorries or trucks, the streetcars, the trains, everything was big and moved fast. Where was everyone going? The buildings were huge – everything appeared massive in size and the sight was endless. Kitty absorbed all this with awe and knew immediately that city life was so, so different.

As Mary said, the welcome of the world was waiting for me. The kettle was down and the cups on the table before I had my coat off. The next two days were like a dream, meeting Austin, his family and many more. We talked about the neighbors and the terrible, sad news in Carrickacat.

My Uncle Johnny Hosty (my mother's brother) married Mary Caulfield in the home place and she died last year in childbirth. A snow storm hit Mayo; the worst storm that anyone could remember. It took hours to get the doctor from town. Uncle Johnny went by horse, but by the time they arrived back, Mary and the unborn child had died. The sadness was overwhelming to witness; the five other small children, Jim, Jack, Maureen, Kit and Della all crying for their mother and their father in a daze of disbelief. It would make you question God's goodness and wonder at the reasoning of it all.

My mother's older sister Delia fell in love with a man by the name of Jim Ganley. A fine young man that everyone loved; however his mother, a widow, was against it and made it very plain to everyone. From birth Delia had a bad hip, which caused a limp, and so the old lady did not think she was good enough for her son. However, Jim was to have the home place, which meant they had to stay. He built a small addition onto the back of the cottage and there they lived comfortably together.

Delia was a dressmaker and worked from their little room, earning enough extra money for them to survive on. After the birth of their first daughter Bridie, everything seemed to be going well. And, as the neighbors said, "You couldn't be alive if you didn't feel the love."

But good fortune did not stay with them for long. Delia gave birth to their second daughter, Mary on Christmas Eve and died New Year's Eve from what was said, blood poisoning. It was said, "Jim Ganley would bring a tear to a stone." Everyone tried to help, to talk to him, to feed him since he was a diabetic, but his will to live was gone. Neighbors would see him, day after day, sitting on an old wall or ditch looking across to the cemetery. It was not a surprise when news spread that he died, a short time after Delia, literally from a broken heart. The parish priest said, "They married for love and will be buried for eternity together."

Jim's sister, Ann came home from New York to look after Mary and later married in Ireland. Bridie went to Carrickacat to be raised and if

Maggie Hosty had a dream of immigrating to Chicago, it ended at this time. She took care of Bridie and when she married, Bridie also went to Redhill where she lived until immigrating to Chicago and a few years later her sister Mary followed, never to be separated again.

There was one brother Michael Hosty that moved to Manchester, England and married an English woman. He lived through the chaos of World War II and the loss of a son in a foreign country. One of his letters stated, "There are cousins fighting on the same side in this war, and the shame is, they don't know each other." He never returned to Ireland.

Kitty told the story of her sister Mary's frightening experience after leaving New York. She sent a letter to Aunt Nora stating that she would be arriving on March 3rd in Union Station at 7:00 A.M. But, a snow storm in Chicago slowed all mail deliveries and the letter was not received until nearly a week after her arrival. Thank God there were travelers' aides available at the station to guide people in these situations.

A call was placed to Aunt Nora, who in turn called Bridie Ganley, who had arrived ten years previous. Her husband, Jack Coyle had a car, but had already left for work. Then, Aunt Nora called her son Jim who worked nights as a manager of the Cosmo Theatre at 80th and Halsted. He left straight away for Bridie, who would recognize Mary, and with no more trouble, returned with another Irish cousin to his mother's door by noon.

As a precaution a phone call was made from John Murphy's house giving Mary all the information about Kitty's final journey to Chicago rather than a letter. It had been a wonderful and exciting week for the young eighteen year old who had never been anywhere, except her home town. However, no more than Mary Morley, after saying good night, it was crying that put her to sleep. The days passed, and once again, it was time to leave. As she waved good-bye from her seat aboard the train, her heart was pounding.

Aunt Nora, standing at the front door smiling could have been her own mother. Maggie was smaller in stature, but the kindly face and eyes were the same.

"Kitty," she said, wrapping her arm around her, "you're a thousand times welcome." And there was no doubt. It was wonderful meeting family that you heard mentioned since a child and being able to put a face with a name. Aunt Nora had immigrated to Chicago and married John Fennell from County Clare. They had four sons, Tom, John Leo, Jim, Joe and three daughters, Kay, Mary, and Helen.

Aunt Kate married her childhood sweetheart, Michael McDonald who was raised less than one mile from Redhill in the Village of Curnacarta, Tulrahan. It was the McDonald family that owned The Forge. The country blacksmith was the farmer's friend, especially in the spring. Here the horse shoe was made with the glowing iron that was taken from the blazing fire with tongs. The iron was soft while hot and then hammered on the anvil turning it every which way until the shoe fit the animal.

It was at this forge that the ploughs were fixed, harrow pins sharpened, handles put back onto the spades and other hand tools, kettles and pots were repaired, and if you needed a calf to be castrated, the blacksmith did it. This was the place to go to spend an hour or two in good company listening to a good yarn or two. When you needed a gate, horse cart, donkey cart or a wheel, well you'd find it at the forge. Mike's brother, Jack stayed in the home place but never married and worked the forge until his death, and then the old forge closed. The need for a forge wasn't as great anymore; cars and tractors were replacing the horse.

This site is now the home place where Gerry and Maureen Godfrey's house resides. Gerry, a native of Curnacarta returned after working many years in England with his wife and two daughters, Geraldine and Sinéad. Numerous horse shoes ranging in sizes that would fit the smallest mule to the largest working horses were found while digging the foundation of their new house, and tossed into a pile with no value.

However, it wasn't long before the Godfreys' realized that the McDonald Family was still alive in America and very interested in their ancestors' old forge. The first time Maureen asked a visiting relative if he would like one as a souvenir, the value of the discarded old horse shoes became irreplaceable. To be able to take into one's own hands something that perhaps his own grandfather had touched brought tears to the young man's eyes. The last shoe was given out several years ago, but still visitors come and take pictures of the land where their ancestors' once worked the anvil. There are many pictures of The Forge circulating in the United States, as well as many old horse shoes.

Mike's brother Owen who lived close to Tulrahan School could be heard all around the area playing the accordion in the fine weather. He'd sit in a chair outside the door and play every tune he knew and perhaps twice. Often children would be seen sitting on the Tulrahan graveyard wall in the evenings listening to one melody after another.

Why did Mike McDonald leave the forge and his home? Well, as we all knew and recognized at the time, the business could only support one man's family. It was time to immigrate. Kate Hosty, his childhood sweetheart, was waiting for him in Chicago. It wasn't long before they married and began their new life, never having the opportunity to return to their native Mayo. They had two sons Johnny and Jim and three daughters, Mary, Helen, and Kay.

Aunt Mary married Tom Kelly in Chicago and had one son, Tom. She was a young girl when she left home and still young when she died from a flu epidemic that swept through the city of Chicago in 1918.

Uncle Jim also immigrated to Chicago, married Helen Barlow and had one son, Jim and two daughters Mary Therese and Helen Francis. When a letter arrived in Redhill on August 15, 1947, Maggie Morley sat quietly by the hearth and cried. Jim had died and what hope there was to ever see her brother now was gone forever.

"How are all the Mannions of Derryhog?" Mary asked and my mind quickly returned to the present. Patrick and Mary Ann Mannion's children, Dominic, Mary, Margaret, Luke and Teresa grew up with the Morleys.

"Kitty, do you remember Mammy sending you to Derryhog to help with the cleaning for the Stations," Asked Mary, smiling?

Having the "Stations" was an honor and each family within a certain area took their turn. The neighbors arrived in the evenings to say the rosary and the priest would visit as well. The house is whitewashed, the inside and outside are spotlessly clean, and the children must act as angels. And after prayers, tea is served with sandwiches and there is plenty of homemade raisin bread, treacle, and soda bread for everyone.

"Well I do," said Kitty, "And all the children down with the measles. The next day, I didn't know what was wrong with me. I just wanted to go home."

"I remember well," answered Mary smiling, "Mary Ann didn't want you to go home and infect our house, but you wouldn't stay. I can still see you wrapped in Pat's black coat, sitting on the back of the bike, arms wrapped around his waist, and your face red as a beet."

Aunt Nora asked, "Did anyone else get them?"

"No, thank God" answered Mary, "It was really unbelievable when you think about it. We were all together; there was no other place to go and I was in the same bed with Kitty."

Kitty and Mary Mannion were best friends and as always, when staying in at their home, they ate and slept together, and talked into the wee hours of the morning. Kitty told her about her dream to go to America, to the land of opportunity, where a woman's job was not just in the home; money could be earned, there were jobs. They would always stay together and remain best friends. But, what is good for one isn't always good for the other.

Mary was an excellent seamstress. She could knit, embroider, and sew anything with a needle and thread, and she wanted to be a nun. Mary was adamant with her decision of becoming a nun and serving God for the rest of her life, so she chose the Cloisters. The Cloisters are a secluded Order with guidelines more rigid regarding contact with family and friends. Your family, friends and earthly material items are secondary to the life of prayer and devotion to our Lord.

In Mary's lifetime many changes occurred in the Catholic Church regarding the lifestyle of Sisters and her Order was also relaxed. Everything was for the better. However, it would not be until June of 1976 that Kitty walked into the Convent's visitor's room and there was Mary, her veil framing her small and lovely face, smiling and blinking away the tears of joy. During this visit a glass partition was still setup, which in later years was discarded. It didn't matter to Kitty; they had a wonderful visit, but sadly never saw each other again.

The conversation at Fennell's went on until midnight, reminiscing, laughing and crying about home and eating the finest *Apple Pie* I had ever tasted.

Crust ingredients:

3 cups of sifted white flour   *½ cup of cold milk*

1 cup of lard (Crisco)   *½ teaspoon of salt*

Put flour in large mixing bowl with lard and use two butter knives to cut in lard until it has a mealy texture. Add in cold milk slowly, constantly stirring.

Place flour on table in order to knead. Separate into two even pieces and work with the piece that will be the bottom crust of the pie. Shake more flour on table area and with a rolling pin begin to flatten dough, turning it over and adding more flour to surface when necessary – make sure the dough does not stick to the surface.

Have pie dish ready!

(This pastry crust recipe is for one large pie or two smaller ones.)

Filling

6-7 tablespoons of flour   *1 ½ cups of sugar*

1 teaspoon of cinnamon (increase to taste)

Mix together

Peel 6 or 7 large green apples.

(Hard, sour apples are better)

Slice thin into large mixing bowl

Add above mixture and mix thoroughly.

Fill pie dish with apples and mixture

(don't be stingy, they reduce down)

2 tablespoons of butter – sliced on top of apples.

Cover with pastry and squeeze ends together. You can double over ends so as not to waste the good pastry – there should be plenty of apple filling to eat with it.

Put a little cold milk into a cup, and with a brush, dab on pastry. This gives it a flakey, lighter texture. Use a fork to make 5 or 6 holes on top of crust.

Preheat oven: 350 degrees
Cook for 1 hour and 10 minutes
(Use your own judgment about covering the edge of the crust with a parchment paper or aluminum foil. This will prevent the edges from getting too brown.)

No one realized that when the lights went out and the doors were closed for the night, Kitty cried night after night. When would she ever feel the security that can only be found in one's own home with family and friends from childhood? What had she done? There was no return ticket, now, "She must lie in the bed she made."

If you're irish come into the parlor

In sweet Limerick town, they say
Lived a chap named Patrick John Molloy.
Once he sailed to U.S.A.
His luck in foreign parts he thought he'd try.
Now he's made his name, and is a wealthy man,
He put a bit away for a rainy day;
So if you gaze upon
The house of Patrick John,
You'll find a notice that goes on to say:
If you're Irish come into the parlor,
There's a welcome here for you;
If your name is Timothy, Pat or John
So long as you come from Ireland
There's a welcome on the mat,
If you come from the Mountains of Mourne
Or Killarney's lakes so blue,
We'll sing you a song and we'll make a fuss,
Whoever you are you are one of us,
If you're Irish, this is the place for you!

There was always excitement at Aunt Nora's. Her sons were coming home from the army around this same time, Helen was getting married, grandchildren were running around the house and the welcome was there for everyone.

Most of the Irish girls arriving in Chicago during this time had no training and took on house keeping jobs. Mary Morley's first job wasn't good; she hated it. She was paid $20.00 a week and the woman wanted her to do everything, but mostly, they were not nice people. But she stayed until another offer came. The day ended and 7:00 p.m. and the tears of loneliness began as the bedroom door closed behind her. How different life would have been if someone had offered her a return ticket.

But as always, someone from up above in heaven was watching over and giving guidance. An old employer of Helen McDonald and

Mary Ganley at 5488 South Everett called for a recommendation, and Mary was hired. Here she had Thursdays and Sundays off, light house keeping, cooked meals, and more or less watched the grandmother who also lived there. The lady of the house shopped and gave her a menu and the laundry went out to a cleaners.

Kitty loved Chicago. Oh, but the food was glorious, especially the bakeries! It wasn't easy to walk past one without stopping in to buy a cookie or fruit tart. Also, the roasted potatoes with roast beef or a pork roast and gravy were delicious. But every now and then, the longing for a boiled dinner with a piece of boiling bacon and cabbage had to be satisfied. And what do you do with leftover cabbage?

colcannon

Boil a pot of potatoes – when soft, drain and mash
In another saucepan heat milk and plenty of butter
(Use any leftover potatoes that have been peeled and boiled reheat with milk and butter)
Add milk and butter to potatoes and beat until fluffy

Chop up the cooked cabbage into small bits
Add a finely chopped onion
Place cabbage and onion in frying pan with plenty of butter
Continue stirring while heating
Combine together
Salt and Pepper to taste
(And don't be stingy with the butter)

And you couldn't eat Colcannon without humming *The Little Skillet Pot:*

Did you ever eat colcannon made with lovely pickled cream?
With the flour and scallions blended like a picture in a dream?
Did you ever make a hole on top to hold the creamy flake –
Of the creamy flavory butter that my mother used to make?

Yes you did so you did, so did she and so did I
And the more I think about it sure the nearer I'm to cry.
Oh but weren't they the happy days when troubles we knew not?
And our mothers made colcannon in the little skillet pot.

Did you ever go a-courting as the evening sun went down
And the moon began a-peeping from behind the hill or mound
As you wandered down the boreen where the leprechaun was seen
And you whispered loving phrases to your little fair colleen?

Kitty was hired as a nanny by the Thornton family in Hyde Park.
She had every Thursday off and every other weekend. The boy was
fifteen, and wasn't herself only eighteen, but it didn't matter, they had
a fabulous relationship. Her duties were simple, but Kitty took them
seriously. She got him up for school and made sure he ate. And after
school, he did homework first, and then there was free time. However,
many times the family must have noticed her swollen eyes because they
always spoke kindly, which comforted this young girl so far from her
mother and father.

She heard the shouting from the bottom of the stairwell, "Kitty
come down!"

It was Christmas time already. How quickly these five weeks
had gone by since she was hired. The aroma of evergreen filled the
stairwell as she ran down. The red, gold, and green ribbons and all the
decorations of every size and shape made up her first Christmas tree
and it stood in the corner of the sitting room with people talking and
laughing exhilarated with the Christmas spirit.

"Kitty, this is for you and Merry Christmas."

"Kitty, Merry Christmas from all of us."

"Kitty, Merry Christmas and best wishes to you and your family."

The tears began to well up in her lovely blue eyes, but quickly disappeared with the excitement, the laughing, the talking and the genuine tenderness extended during a time that should call families together. Not in Kitty's wildest dreams did she image opening such beautifully wrapped Christmas presents. She held her first bottle of perfume, her first broche, and wore her first silk nightgown with lovely blue flowers to bed that night. Kitty didn't forget to thank God before falling asleep.

Always on Kitty's free weekends she would take the streetcar to either Aunt Kate or Aunt Nora's house, and stay there until Sunday night. She was content and felt comfortable with work and her new relations, and so, as Kitty turned nineteen years of age she contemplated the past year with gratitude.

Kitty had just arrived at Aunt Kate's house on this Thursday afternoon, thrilled at having a long weekend ahead. Her employers were out of town and she did not have to return until Sunday night. Not long before, the mother of the man she worked for had moved in with them; however, there was a private nurse who tended to her needs. Once in awhile she had been asked to sit with her while they were out for dinner, and it was no trouble. However, no one expected the poor old lady to die that day.

The phone call came from the lady of the house asking Kitty to go back. The body had been removed, but they wanted someone home to take messages and so forth.

She told Kitty to call someone to stay with her, if she was afraid. Well, of course she was scared to death and begged Mary to come spend the night with her.

The house was quiet and a little eerie as they she sat in the kitchen having a cup of tea and a piece of fresh Apple Sauce cake that the cook had left out.

(Ingredients)

1 cup unsweetened apple sauce	*1 teaspoon cinnamon*
2 cups sifted flour	*1 teaspoon soda*
½ cup butter	*½ teaspoon nutmeg*
¼ teaspoon salt	*1 cup raisins (chopped)*
1 cup sugar	*¼ teaspoon clove*

(preparation)

Cream butter and add sugar gradually

Then add applesauce and beat until smooth.

Now add dry ingredients sifted together.

Beat well.

Fold in raisins.

Pour into loaf cake pan, greased and floured

Preheat oven to 325 degrees Fahrenheit, and bake for at least 1 hour.

Mary wasn't afraid at all. She told Kitty, "You don't have to be afraid of the dead, only the living." Well that was good sound advice, but Kitty decided she was far too confident and came up with a brilliant idea to really give her a fright. Running up the stairs quickly, Kitty pulled a sheet out of the linen closet and threw it over herself. She was having trouble not laughing out loud. It was going to be so funny. Mary was far too self-assured and positive that there were no ghosts.

You can just imagine Mary, waiting patiently, thinking about nothing in particular. As the minutes passed and then a couple more, suddenly she realized that Kitty was gone far too long. Mary was almost at the end of the hallway that ended at the main entrance when she spotted a white, flowing movement rounding the corner of the stairs that headed right at her. Oh the Lord God Almighty, be jesssus, anyone could hear the two a mile away with the screeching and goings on.

Those first two years went by quickly and the young boy Kitty had been caring for graduated from high school and was going away to university. Kitty had matured a great deal and was ready for the next step. It was time to move on, become a little more independent. Mary Ganley Leehy, Kitty's cousin, worked at the Hi-Low Grocery Store and on this particular day, she stopped in to pick up a few items and say hello. Well, was it God watching over her or just luck as she turned down an aisle and walked straight into Mrs. Rooney, the owner? She was bluntly asked,

"Are you looking for a job?"

"Yes," answered Kitty.

"Well," continued this well-dressed, but not too showy elderly lady, "Would you like to work here for me?"

"I'd love to."

The very next day, Kitty was behind the cold cut meat and cheese counter looking pallid and somber. The smells from the different meats were nauseating. It wasn't easy, but she kept at it, and before long was promoted to checker. Now, this job was great, especially for someone who enjoyed meeting and talking with people. And this is where she stayed until her first child was born.

In the meantime, Mary Morley had left her housemaid job, got a room that had a hot plate and a toaster and attended McCormick College at 63rd and Woodlawn for secretarial training. She realized that through education, a job with more pay and weekends off would be available.

However, it wasn't easy and the days were long. School began at 8:00 and ended at 11:30 A.M. From there, Mary walked to the "el" train station depot, caught the next one out headed for downtown Chicago. She arrived at the restaurant in time for the lunch hour and stayed through dinner. As a full-time waitress, the restaurant paid for one meal. She purchased a sweet roll the night before and brought it home for the morning.

This school offered a one-year course of typing and comptometers, which is a type of adding machine. Upon completion, Mary interviewed for her first job in the accounting department of Goldblatt's where she remained one year. Illinois Bell, the phone company in Chicago and surrounding areas, was hiring. Mary applied, was hired immediately and before the year ended, became an American citizen. Illinois Bell paid for her day off to go downtown to be sworn in. She asked a new friend Sarah Mazolla, who became a life-long friend, to be her sponsor.

Mary and Kitty moved into a bigger apartment at 78th and Green. It wasn't that easy to get apartments during these years that were furnished and especially affordable. This one had a back porch where you could sit out, especially on the hot evenings; the one big room had a pullout couch where Mary slept and Kitty in the Murphy's bed that pulled down from the wall. There was a small kitchen with a refrigerator built into the wall and a tiny stove with a table and four chairs, and best of all, their own bathroom.

The sisters were working steady and sending money home with every letter, which was greatly appreciated. Of course, every week a few dollars was put into a savings account. Shortly after Mary had arrived and saved a bit of money, Aunt Nora said, "Every woman needs one good black dress that can be worn anywhere." So, off she went and purchased a lovely black dress with a high neck and long sleeves.

It cost $75.00, which was a lot of money in those days to spend on a dress. The same suggestion was made to Kitty, and within a couple of months purchased a lovely black dress with a V-neck and a thin belt that clasped in the front.

Both Mary and Kitty were elegant in their new dresses and at Aunt Nora's suggestions, went to a professional photographer to have their picture taken and send them home. It was a gift that was appreciated more than any amount of money. They placed it on the mantle in the sitting room for all to admire. It was said, "Fine feathers make fine birds."

a mother's love

An Irish boy was leaving
Leaving his native home,
Crossing the broad Atlantic,
Once more he wished to roam,
And as he was leaving his mother,
While standing on the quay,
He threw his arms around her waist
And this to her did say.

A mother's love is a blessing
no matter where you roam.
Keep her while she's living,
you'll miss her when she's gone.
Love her as in childhood
when feeble, old and grey
for you'll never miss a mother's love
till she's buried beneath the clay.

And as the years grow onward,
I'll settle down in life,
And I'll choose a nice young colleen,
And take her for my wife.
And as the kids grow older,
They'll play around my knee
And I'll teach them the very same lesson
That my mother taught to me.

A mother's love is a blessing
no matter where you roam.
Keep her while she's living,
You'll miss her when she's gone.
Love her as in childhood,
When feeble, old and grey,
For you'll never miss a mother's love
'til she's buried beneath the clay.

When we left home, all of us hoped to see the old people again. So, when a parent or family member died, all of us mourned together. Out of respect, I made up my mind that I would not go to the bars or dances for a few weeks. However, the weeks went into months and I was getting more and more depressed.

As I think about it now, it was all of six months since her death, and I was just sitting at Margaret's kitchen table when Jim and his steady girlfriend Hannah Landers from County Wexford (and later his wife) arrived. It was a Sunday, and I wasn't due back at work until Monday morning. I had no choice; they insisted that I go with them to Marquette Park to see the geese around the pond and the flower garden.

Jim said, "Get the hell out of the house, walk around, and get some fresh air. I agreed. I believe now that it was all their compassion that broke this burden of guilt that weighed me down. I knew Jim was right. I needed to get out, so off we went and who do you think we met in the park? It was Kitty Morley. Jim, Hannah, Kitty and myself began to talk about home and that was all it took for me to breakdown. I went to the nearest tree, sat on the ground beneath it, and cried.

No one knew what to do. I remember it was dusk and Jim said in a stern voice, "Bill, enough or you'll end up in the hospital or back home, and then what?"

What he said had an impact. I knew I was going nowhere and had to straighten myself out, and I had to do it now. I didn't go to the dance that night, but I was out the following weekend, surrounded by my "old friends," these old friends who now I knew for about one year.

On Sunday there was a dance at Marquette Hall located at 69th and Western Avenue and I knew from Jim, who got his information from Hannah that Kitty Morley would be there. I needed to talk to her and give a better explanation about my actions at the park on the previous Sunday. I decided to move on again with my life and I had a good feeling about this Morley girl.

Many times I would show up at Flynn's Hall around midnight, still in uniform. I'd put my uniform cap behind the bar and open my shirt collar. It was against the streetcar rules for motormen to be in a tavern wearing their uniform. However, if I took the time to go home and change, the dance would be over by the time I returned, so sometimes I carried a dress shirt and made the best of it.

It was near midnight by the time I arrived, and as soon as I walked in I spotted her blonde hair. Our first dance was to *The Walls of Limerick*, a lyrical set and Kitty was a great dancer, light on her feet and could do all the sets. Before the night ended, everyone was on the floor for *The Wild Colonial Boy:*

There was a wild colonial boy, Jack Duggan was his name
He was born and raised in Ireland, in a place called Castlemaine
He was his father's only son, his mother's pride and joy
And dearly did his parents love The Wild Colonial Boy.

At the early age of sixteen years he left his native home
And to Australia's sunny shores he was inclined to roam
He robbed the rich; he helped the poor and shot James McAvoy
A terror to Australia was The Wild Colonial Boy.
One morning on the prairie as Jack he rode along
A listening to the mocking bird a singing a cheerful song
Out stepped a band of troopers, Kelly, Davis and Fitzroy
They all set out to capture him, The Wild Colonial Boy.

"Surrender now, Jack Duggan, for you see you're three to one
Surrender in the Queen's high name for you're a plundering son."
Jack drew two pistols from his belt and proudly waved them high
"I'll fight but not surrender," said The Wild Colonial Boy.

He fired a shot at Kelly which brought him to the ground
But turning 'round to Davis he received a fatal wound
A bullet pierced his proud young heart from the pistol of Fitzroy
And that was how they captured him, The Wild Colonial Boy.

There were a group of girls at the dance that arrived together on the streetcar and intended to go back together. Hannah was at 55th and Blackstone, Mary McAndrew worked in the big house next to Kitty, Mae Fitzpatrick and Kathleen McAndrew were within walking distance and Nora Hartnet lived the furtherest away.

Kitty loved getting letters from home and hearing all the news. Mae often told the story when the two were taking an evening walk and Kitty, out of no where blurted out, "Oh, didn't I forget to tell you, we had a foaling at home!" She was so exited. She always had an innocence that complimented her sincerity.

Kathleen McAndrew was great for telling jokes. No matter how "down in the dumps" you were feeling, Kathleen would make you laugh. This one night Kathleen, Mae and Kitty were taking a walk. It was late and a dark night, not a star in the sky.

Kathleen said to Kitty, "Did you know Santa Claus had no children?"

"No," answered a bewildered Kitty, "I never thought about it."

"Well," Kathleen said quickly, "He couldn't because he put IT into a stocking."

You could hear the three laughing on the next block. Kitty decided she wanted to rest and somehow thought that this very neat and trimmed hedge that they were passing was a bench. Before either friend could say a word, down she went, crushing the twigs and making a right catastrophe of the hedges. But, the laugh was worth all the scratches and cuts.

After that, a good cup of tea was needed with a piece of *Whole Wheat Bread:*

(Ingredients)

2 cups of white sifted flour	*1 cup of a dry bran or wheat*
¾ cup of sugar	*3 tablespoons of margarine or butter*
½ teaspoon baking powder	*½ teaspoon salt*
½ teaspoon baking soda	*1 egg*

Add 1 cup buttermilk to dry bran or wheat (Allow bran or wheat to become soft.)
In large bowl combine dry ingredients
Add margarine or butter, and egg
Mix into dry ingredients until coarse
Add buttermilk mixture and mix
Place on floured surface and kneed until you have a firm ball.

Butter and flour baking pan
Place in pan – push down softly on top, but
do not flatten cake to the edge of pan.

Make a cross with a sharp knife
About ¼ inch deep.
Place a patty of butter in each quartered section.

Preheat oven to 350 degrees Fahrenheit
Cooking time: 1 hour 10 minutes
Check the middle before taking out - Make sure it is dry.

With youth comes a certain amount of fearlessness and I suppose recklessness, and many times this ends in tragedy. There was one taxi ride that didn't end up all that funny for Kitty. I had asked to take her home and hired the regular Yellow Taxi from the area. The four of us squeezed into the backseat, Jim, Hannah, Kitty and myself, all full of laughter and talk. The girls never drank at the dances, but Jim and I had had a few jars of the good stuff. The driver was coming up to a street light that was about to turn red when, Jim, just teasing put his finger on the nape of the driver's neck and said,

"Keep going or I'll shoot!"

Well, the poor man gunned the accelerator and as the taxi raced through the intersection, we were hit broadside by another car. Kitty was hurt the worst. She ended up in the hospital for three days with a concussion and stitches, but thank God no broken bones. Well, needless to say, that ended the nonsense with the taxi drivers.

Talk about feeling guilty! Terrible we felt for the trouble we caused, but it was a lesson well learned and never happened again. I didn't have a clue what to take to the hospital when I went to see her. There was no question about it; I had to go and I had to find some sort of special gift. Sure enough, I spotted the loveliest pair of slippers through the display window of a shop on 63rd street.

As I walked through the corridors, I recognized the odors that only a hospital can have from the disinfectants, the foods and, if possible, I believed that I could smell the medicines. This was the first time I had entered a hospital since my own stay in Scotland. It was better to be the visitor!

There she was, sitting in a chair looking out the window, alone. "Hello Kitty," I said, "How are ye keep'in?" As I kissed her, I laid the box wrapped in brown paper on her lap.

As soon as she spotted me there was a smile on her face. "I'm fine now," she said. "And, I'm going home to Aunt Nora's tomorrow. It will be good to have a real cup of tea. The water never seems hot enough."

"That's good, that's good," was all I said. She knew well that I felt out of place, like a right bollox. Herself and Hannah, and all the other girls would have a good laugh over this in the years to come. And we all did – for many years.

I said my good-bye and told her I would be calling. She said nothing as we parted, but as the old saying goes, silence gives consent.

the boys from the county mayo

Far away from the land of the shamrock and heather
In search of a living as exiles we roam
And whenever we chance to assemble together
We think of the land where we once had a home.

Those homes are destroyed and our homes confiscated
The hand of the tyrant brought plunder and woe
The fires are now quenched and our hearts desolated
In our once happy homes in the County Mayo.

Long years have now passed since with hearts full of sorrow
This land of the shamrock we left far behind
But how we'd like to go back there tomorrow
To the scene of our youth, which we still bear in mind.

The days of our childhood, it's now we recall them
They cling to our visions wherever we go
And the friends of our youth we will never forget them
They too are exiles from the County Mayo.

From historic Killala, from Swinford to Calla
Ballyhaunis and Westport and Old Castlebar
Kiltimagh and Claremorris, Belmullet and Erris
Kilkelly and Knock that's famed near and far
Balla, Ballinrobe, Ballina and Bohola
Keeloges and Foxford a few miles below
Newport and Cong with old Straide and Manulla
Charlestown too, in the County Mayo.

Then on with the cause 'till our aim is accomplished,
Those who would fault us are cowardly and mean,
So stand in the fight 'till the tyrant is vanquished
Expelled from our dear little island of green.
With the foes of our land we have fought a long battle,
Soon they will get their last death-dealing blow.
When old Nick has received them, their brains he will rattle,
For the wrongs they have done to the County Mayo.

From Galway to Dublin, from Derry to Kerry,
New York and 'Frisco and Boston also,
In Pittsburg, Chicago, Detroit and Toronto,
There are stout-hearted men from the County Mayo.

Now boys, pull together in all sorts of weather
Don't show the white feather, wherever you go,
Act each as a brother and help one another
Like true hearted men from the County Mayo.

Upon arriving in Chicago, I applied for my social security number, and registered for the draft. After two years, it was necessary to "declare intention," which meant that the government was basically asking, "Are you going to become a citizen?" After three more years I could ask for the paper work to actually apply for American citizenship. Then, it was almost another year before everything went through the process and I was notified to appear at City Hall to be sworn in and take the oath.

I was given a study guide that contained historical information about the United States' conception and present government proceedings. I had to be able to recite the Pledge of Allegiance and know what the red, white and blue stars and stripes in our flag represented. Another requirement was to have a sponsor; an American citizen and I asked Con Curtin. I was in a cold sweat when the man called me to his desk;

I did not make one mistake and walked away with a feeling that I could never justly describe.

There were two other ways in which to obtain citizenship that I was aware of at this time. It was possible to become a citizen by marrying one and then, it was just a matter of going through the process. And the final way was to serve in the armed forces and if you were fortunate enough to return, automatic citizenship was granted. It the late 1950's and early 1951 it seemed as though the young Irishmen were just off the boat a couple of months when they were drafted and sent to Korea.

Mike Fitzpatrick was a great friend of mine. He was the second oldest of five and at the age of eighteen left his home in the village of Coppagh, which is located on the Mayo Abbey side of Claremorris in May of 1947. Mike was only five years old when their mother died. He and his sister Mae, or Mary, were left in the home place with their father, while their two brothers and sister were raised by family that lived close.

Work was plentiful at this time in Whiting, Indiana where Standard Oil and the steel mills were operating and employed hundreds of men and women. Many an Irishman worked at these locations before their doors were shut and this is where Mike got his first job. It wasn't long before he was able to send for his sister Mae.

On December 24, 1947 Mae was en route with twenty three other Irishmen and women on a merchant marine ship that had been used to transport soldiers during World War II. The fare was twenty six pounds and the ship had little comforts to offer during the stormy crossing. A friend met Mae at the port in New York and they spent a few days together during the holiday season.

She only spent the couple of days because Mike was waiting and anxious to have his sister with him. The B & O train that carried her brother to Chicago and many life-long friends pulled into the station at 63rd Street on December 31, 1947. In New York Mae had sent a telegram to her aunt and uncle, Anne and Bill Kane. They didn't have any children and were glad to have Mae stay with them until she found work. Mae stood on the platform, staring and praying and still no one approached who looked as if they were searching for a young Irish immigrant.

A young American couple finally asked where she was going. She showed the address that was written in a letter and the man said,

"It's not out of our way."

With a grateful "yes" Mae grabbed her bag and followed them to the street where taxis were lined up one after another. The couple took Mae's fifty cents, but it was worth it; at least she was that much closer to her relations. When the taxi pulled away, Mae looked at this huge building and wondered, with amazement, why her aunt and uncle would want to live in a house so big; after all, it was only the two of them.

She stood for a good while not knowing where to enter when an old lady came out the door and asked who she was looking for. The lady brought her into the hallway and told her to press the button. Her aunt opened the door of their apartment on the third floor and couldn't believe that Mae had arrived. Apparently the telegram was never received.

After work on Fridays, Mike would catch the bus from the depot in Hammond, Indiana and it would take him all the way to 63rd and South Park in Chicago, which was referred to as "White City." He traveled around the same time every weekend so he would meet the same people waiting for his transfer bus. All the Irish that worked at the Mills used this route to get to and from the south side of Chicago. Washington Park was a walking distance from the bus depot and many a Gaelic football game was played there on a Sunday morning.

All the Kane's were musical and one of Mike's cousins taught him how to play the piano accordion. Well, it didn't take long before Fitzpatrick could play anything he heard. McGinty's Pub hired him for Saturday night entertainment and all the crowd from home would be there.

Mike was so happy when his sister Mae arrived; the evidence was in his smile as she was introduced to everyone. Kitty found Mae a job with the Magner family, who lived down the street from the Thortons. Kathleen McAndrew was hired by Mr. Magner's brother who lived across the street. All the families were Catholic, which made the girls' families happy in Ireland.

The months passed quickly. I would have enough of the snow and cold weather when suddenly the weather changed and it was spring, and then the heat was enough when the leaves on the trees would begin to change, and the cool weather was back again. The Korean War was the talk and to tell the truth, there were many of us, myself included, that wasn't sure where Korea was at on the map. Well, as more of our friends were drafted, we soon found out.

It was a cold, bleak November's day in 1950 when the news arrived to the South side of Chicago; Mike Fitzpatrick was drafted into the Army. He loved this country and was very willing to put his time in as a soldier to fight for its beliefs. When his time was served, I remember well Mike saying, "I'll return an American citizen." A big party was planned by his family in Whiting and we all went. Some of us had cars at this time, and if you didn't get a ride, you took the streetcar.

What a night! We talked and laughed, and as the night went on, we settled down and had what was referred to as the "sing-song." Everyone that knew a song and could carry a tune sang their favorite and Mike sang his, *Noreen Bawn:*

There's a glen in old Tir Conaill
There's a cottage in the glen
Where once dwelled an Irish colleen
Who inspired the hearts of men
She was handsome, hail and hearty
Fair and graceful as the dawn
And the neighbors loved that widow's
Lovely daughter, Noreen Bawn.

Till one day there came a letter
With her passage paid to go
To that land of the Missouri
Where the Mississippi flows
So, she said good-bye to Erin
And next morning at the dawn
The poor widow brokenhearted.
Parted with her Noreen Bawn.

Many years the mother waited
Till one morning at the door
Came a gentle hearted woman
Costly were the clothes she wore
Saying "Mother don't you know me?
Sure I've only got a cold."
But her cheeks were flushed and scarlet
And a tragic tale they told.

There's a churchyard in Tir Conaill
Where the flowers wildly wave
There's a gray-haired mother kneeling
O'er the green and lonely grave
Oh my Noreen she is saying,
"I'm so lonely since you've gone,
Twas the curse of emigration
Laid you here, my Noreen Bawn."

Now I couldn't tell you what the weather was like on September 12, 1951 when the news spread among us that Mike was killed or missing in action. Mae was working in an office now and had her own apartment. A younger brother, Jim had arrived in 1949 and hung around with us as well. Needless to say, Jim and Mae's hearts were broken; all our hearts felt the loss.

Other than a telegram that went to the home of a family member, the only other way to know if a man had been killed or missing in action, was to read it in the newspaper. The Chicago Tribune, a prominent newspaper in Chicago then and now, made sure that the names were listed. Mae spoke with the editor and requested that Mike's name be withheld until more information was received.

However, "This is news," she was told.

Now the world knew that Mike Fitzpatrick was dead. I suppose it was denial, God help us; Mae was sure that it was a mistake and he was a prisoner or held in some hospital half way around the world. However, all these fantasies were destroyed when the telegram arrived in June 1952 stating that Mike was coming home in a casket.

Where was home? Was Mike on his way to Ireland, Indiana or Chicago? Mae had to talk to someone. The 5th Army headquarters, which was located at 54th and Lake Shore Drive, would answer her questions. Mae had her first experience with bureaucracy. Upon entering a pleasant man listened to her tale and sent her to the 5th floor. Another man listened to her story and said she had to go to the 3rd floor and then back to the 5th floor.

It was exhausting and the tears couldn't be stopped. Eventually, she went back to where she started, at the main door. He must have felt sorry for her and made a call to Arlington Cemetery, the home of the Unknown Soldier. Mae was determined that Mike would be buried in Chicago. Finally, the answer came that Mike's body was en route to Ireland and there was only one way to get him back. She had to have instructions ready when the ship docked that she would claim his body in Chicago.

The only way to contact Ireland was to use the old pay telephone and it was a tedious, time consuming job. Every penny, nickel, dime and quarter had to be put into the coin dispenser one at a time. Then, Mae went to Western Union and had to pay for a message that went to the Army stating her intention to claim the body, as well as pay for the reply, which cost one week's wages. A reply arrived, but it was not correct and she had to do the same thing over again. Her brother's body was in transit by ship to Ireland and it would be weeks before more information arrived. It was so disheartening.

Mae hurried home from work everyday, expecting to find the telegram waiting. Finally, out of desperation, she asked her landlady who was from Czechoslovakia,

"Has a telegram come for me?"

The landlady never said a word, walked to a table and took the letter from a drawer and handed it to Mae with an odd expression on her face.

As it happened, somehow the landlady thought that Mae was going to move away, so she hid the telegram not understanding the significance of its contents. What a mix up, right from the start!

Mike's remains were in transit by train to Union Station in downtown Chicago. Mae's next visit was to the undertaker, Mr. Kenny and he offered to go with her to meet the train. Kenny Funeral Home was located at 54th and Halsted and he was known for helping and guiding the Irish immigrants when a death occurred and was especially helpful and kind to Mae at this time. They went together in the hearse that would carry the casket back to the funeral home for the wake. There was one soldier accompanying her brother.

She asked, "Will there be a military honor guard at his funeral?

The answer was no.

And then, "At least will taps be played at the cemetery?"

The answer again was "No."

Mae asked, "Why?"

The serviceman answered, "He wasn't an American citizen when he died."

Later Mae telephoned the Army headquarters to find out about any medals that Mike should be awarded, especially the Purple Heart. The man on the other end of telephone told her about a pawn shop that she could go to and buy one. This was something that Mae could not let go of; it was so disrespectful and not American.

Mike had been trained as a Medic, shipped to Korea in May and killed on the frontlines. He had told Mae in one of his letters that now she could call him "Doc."

The Irish Community came out in full force. Remember what I said, 'We were a long way from our parents and Mayo. There was a two-night wake and mass at Visitation Parish. Mike's last letter to his sister gives an example of his humor and how he made the best of what he had to do and didn't complain. Mae received this letter on August 16, just two days before Mike was listed as missing in action.

> *"Dear Mae,*
>
> *Just a few lines to say hello. I don't know if I should write this letter or not but it's something to kill time. The Lord only knows when I will get to mail it. I have about nine letters in my pack and no place to mail them. As soon as I get to some mail box I will drop them all in. We are completely cut off from civilization. Well Mae we departed Japan on June 1st from Sasebo. It's about one hundred miles from Korea. We got to Pusan the following morning. We didn't even get to stay in Japan one week. While we were there we were restricted to our area. We got*

to see quite a bit of Japan. It took us about thirty-six hours from Tokyo to Sasebo.

I thought I was going to see something when I got to Pusan, but it's no more or no better than a filthy sewer. We got a train from Pusan and traveled up the east coast. I never did find out what place it was. We left there again by truck and moved on about fifty miles to Wangu. I don't know how long we will be left here. It's not a bad place. We had our first country bath since we left the old sod. There is a kind of a creek or a river right beside me. It feels good for a change. We had to take a bath today. I was never as black or as dirty before in all my life than I was last night. The roads are newly made roads and they are made from dirt. By the time we got to Wangu we were white from dust. We had to take our clothes off and go out and dust them.

We sleep in big tents. About thirty guys to each tent. Our beds are one blanket, rain coat and the bare ground. The weather is pretty tough. I got so sun burnt today. It has been raining quite a bit this last while. Anyhow this is supposed to be the rainy season in Korea. Well, Mae we have seen some of the things after the war. Mostly all the houses are completely demolished. Nothing left but a pile of burnt cinders. It's pretty easy for a Korean house because they are no more than four posts stuck in the ground and a kind of grass or straw roof. It's a pitiful sight.

Well Mae we are assigned to the second Division and 23 Inf. Regt. Right and the second Division is in the reserve. I don't know how long that will last but some guys say it might be in the reserve for several weeks and maybe only one day. It's hard to tell. The darn army changes its mind so often you can't believe a thing till it actually happens.

Did you get any mail from John Culligan. I was going to write to him but I thought he might be in the same boat as myself, no permanent address. I will mail this as soon as I get my permanent address and not till then. From the time I mail a letter till I get a response it will take at least thirty days. So when I write don't just leave it till tomorrow to mail it. Answer it right now and don't forget. I better bring this to an end and see if we got any movies tonight. By the way we get movies here. Our theatre is a white sheet hanging on a few high posts at the bottom of a hill. We get a lot of big logs to sit on. The only thing we lack here is news. We don't hear a darn thing.

Well Mae I will call this off for now, hoping it finds you and hoping to hear from you soon. Bye bye and good luck and good wishes from your loving brother Mike.

PS We are just after moving. I don't know where we are at but we are mighty close to the real thing. I'll write again as soon as I find out where I am at."

Let me tell you, Mike Fitzpatrick received a grand send off and he has never been forgotten. He died too young, but a hero.

I pledge allegiance

To the flag

Of the United States of America

And to the Republic

For which it stands

One nation, under God

Indivisible

With liberty

And justice for all.

the cottage by the lee

Tis well I know that often folks keep wondering
When in my eyes a far off look they see
What it can be the cause of all my dreaming
What is this dream so very dear to me.

And truth to tell 'tis often I go roaming
In dreams along the road of memory
To where my heart will find its consolation
Within that lovely cottage by the lee.

My home sweet home that I so fondly cherish
The dear ones they mean everything to me
In all this world if there can be a heaven
I sure it's in that cottage by the lee.

Tis grand to stand outside that cottage doorway
And gaze across the corn fields rich and gold
To hear the stream go rippling by the meadow
Or watch the shepherd call to his fold.

From down the lane that winds behind the garden
The blackbird greets the smiling summer morn
And as his music echoes o'er the valley
You smile and bless the day that you were born.

Yes that's my dream, my lovely dream of homeland,
And though I thought a rover I could be
It's soon I found I left my dear behind me
Within that lovely cottage by the lee.

It was after the holidays in 1952, just over four years since I arrived when my cousin Jim Rogers told me that the Santa Fe Railroad's Corwith Yards were hiring; they were looking for a switchman. The Atchison, Topeka and Santa Fe Railway (abbreviated Santa Fe) was initiated by Mr. Cyrus K. Holliday in 1859. The first tracks reached the Kansas/Colorado state line in 1873 and connected to Pueblo, Colorado in 1876 and during my time the Santa Fe tracks extend through Arizona, California, Colorado, Illinois, Iowa, Kansas, Louisiana, Missouri, Nebraska, New Mexico, Oklahoma and Texas.

It was the Chinese immigrants that built the railroads through the United States' prairie and cut through the mountains. They worked like slaves and, from what I understand, were treated no better. They used dynamite to level the hills or cut through a rock, and if a tunnel needed to be checked, a Chinaman was sent in first. If he did not return, that only meant that the oxygen level was insufficient. Usually a canary bird was used, but at this time in America's history, an immigrant's life would do. I remember an old man telling me that there was a Chinaman's skull beneath every spike on the line.

The Corwith Yards was considered a switching yard; built in 1887 and at one time was the world's largest railway yard. All railroads converged here. It is a landmark in Chicago's history of railroad freight transportation delivered into the Midwest and out. I arrived at the Corwith office at 9:00 A.M., located at 3611 West 38th Street, which is the Brighton Park neighborhood and occupies nearly a square mile of land. This line was the last stop, the dead end for the live stock, grains, fruits and vegetables coming from the west and backed up almost to the legendary, Chicago Stock Yards.

I asked the young lady at the receptionist desk for an application, and this is when one has to believe that God does have a plan and timing is everything; one day before or one day later and I would have missed an opportunity that would never have come my way again.

"Say mister, there is a nicer job than this going. Here's the fireman's application."

What the hell is a fireman on the railroad? I asked myself.

I guess the young lady noticed my bewilderment and offered a little more information,

"With this job you're on the engine and the job has an extra board for overtime."

That's all I needed to hear. Now, believe me I wasn't too particular about what job I got, I just wanted, as the saying goes, "To get my foot in the door" and then I could apply for other positions as available. A switchman's responsibility was to turn the switch which would allow the train to move into a particular track and this, of course was all outside work. So, needless to say I never filled out the application for that job.

I smiled from ear to ear as I handed the lovely lady the completed fireman's application and obviously said all the right things. I was called the next morning for an interview and hired, however it would be six weeks before training would begin. I gave in my notice at the CTA and off to the travel agent to book a trip on the Queen Mary for four weeks. This was my first trip home and I was excited – I was going home to Mayo and good fortune was with me.

I remember well my thoughts as I boarded the train in Cork bound for Ballina Station. There'd be no Mother waiting. Perhaps it was this trip that implanted the distinct noise that the wheels of a railcar make while running along the steel rail. It's an echo, and this has always been the source of my daydreaming about the carefree days in Ballymacredmond.

As a lad my aspiration was to drive the train; however as a young adult I doubted this dream. Sometimes the break a person needed in order to fulfill their goal never arrived, and there were plenty still waiting. However, I have to admit that the luck of the Irish was with me, I held the lucky penny, I wished upon the lucky star; I don't know why, but my break had arrived! Upon my return I would begin to serve my internship for four years and finish as an Engineer. It was still hard for me to comprehend all that had occurred during the last four years, and I was grateful to God and The United States of America for these opportunities.

I saw everyone, visited Brogan's Pub, Healy's in Pontoon and attended any dance I could get a lift to. The village was quiet. Immigration had taken its toll. Teasie came home from Scotland and Pat from England and the rest of Bourkes were content. I made my last visit to the cemetery the day before leaving. I knew my mother and father were content and, likewise, so was I. This was not my final farewell; I knew I would return again. My last thoughts boarding the steamship *Corraine* were not of Mayo, but of the ones waiting in Chicago – now I truly felt that I was going home.

The Santa Fe Railway was the oldest fleet of steam engines and the fireman's job was to shovel coal into the burner. In the early 1950's Santa Fe converted to diesel, and the fireman's position, as known, became obsolete. However, the railroad kept the position as a hands-on or apprentice program, which developed into mandatory training for an engineer.

There was one major book to study from and it was broken down into four parts. At the end of each year one portion of the exam was given. These consisted of rules, mechanical setups, steam engines and so forth and then, at the end of the fourth year, a cumulative exam. The rules of the road were the most important. Not only did the Engineer have to know and understand the different gesture and warning signs that the Santa Fe enforced, but also had to be qualified to operate over foreign main tracks of other railroads that converged at Corwith Yards. For example, the N & W is a British owned railroad, which means that the controls and warning signs are located on opposite sides of the tracks.

In railroad yards, accidents are costly as far as time lost. The tracks are held up for investigation, as well as repair and this delays arrivals and departures of boxcars containing livestock and produce. There is a very small margin allowed for error and the penalty can be severe, such as time off without pay or dismissal.

It was mandatory to have a watch with a second hand and each year it had to be checked and calibrated at a specific jewelry store on 63rd street and the receipt handed in at the office. I purchased two pinstriped bib coveralls and never worked in any other clothes. I never wore them to or from work, only at the yards. These bibs were not a mandatory uniform, but I felt it was part of being an Engineer on the railroad. As the years passed these bibs became my trademark, as well as the pipe and tobacco pouch that I carried in the center front pocket.

On March 16, 1952, my first day of employment, the bus dropped me at 39th and Kedzie and I walked toward the entrance referred to as the "fire road," which was the main road leading to Corwith's office building. Be Jesus now, I was nervous and insecure. But I knew that given half a chance I would accomplish what I set out to do: become an engineer. God only knows how many times I sauntered this road, and always from that first day, one hour ahead of starting time. It was more than a half mile and especially in the snow it was tough. Although a car never passed me up, and as the years went by, I'm sure I was in a car as often as I walked the fire road.

There were only a couple of rules that the men followed; you never snitched and always had a deck of cards ready. A railroad man's card game was "rummy." That was it! If you worked on the railroad, you played rummy and, usually there was plenty of time sitting above in the engine waiting for the signal to shove down the track. There always seemed to be a train unloading, and of course this backed everything up in the yard; there was no such thing as rerouting. It was here that a man practiced patience and recognized the fact that "patience is a virtue."

I worked with fine, upstanding men and at that time, there were some old timers known as, Chicken Legs, Rubber Nose, Dirty Balls, Willie Whiskey and Boston Blackie. I worked with Timmons for thirty years and he called me Polish Bourke. You were called by your last name or a nick name, and by God I heard some unusual ones over the years – I couldn't repeat half of them. Was it any wonder that I didn't realize for the longest time that the majority of the men with me were Irish with the names Doolahan, Shannahan, Walsh, Demsey, O'Brien or Mitchell. Before my time, the men hired did not retire. They refused their supplementary pension and continued to work with fifty years of service or more. I am sure I attended more wakes of men still working their forty hours plus than friends who had retired.

I had the opportunity to work with a man born in Germany and actually fought with the German's in World War I. These men had an integrity that was unique from my generation and would not be understood at all in today's world. These old timers loved their jobs; they were real characters and I developed many of the same habits. A few of these men had the ability to use swear words that made their explanation, "poetry in motion."

Ninety-nine percent of the men smoked cigarettes, cigars or chewed tobacco. To my knowledge, I was the only one who carried the pipe. It wasn't very often that I was caught without a "small one," which was a half pint of whiskey in my back pocket. Chicago's winters were cold and damp and it helped to keep the bones warm. I shared many a one with a comrade and he did the same for me.

Before long I realized that hand signals were as important to understand as the English language. You couldn't be color blind, because when the signal lit up "red," well you better stop. Don't forget there were no radios to give directions or send warnings to start or stop. There were flags by day, and the light that burned from red flares gave the signals at night. Flares could burn in increments of five and ten minutes and would not burn out in inclement weather. The lantern that the switchmen carried was run from a battery and is still carried today at night. Previous to the battery, they burned from kerosene oil.

Before long I was studying for my first exam and this would end my first year on the Santa Fe Railway. I recognized the fact that the railroad was in my blood and I knew, without question, that I had found a career where I was happy and felt secure. The camaraderie amongst the men was tight, but it took some time before I was accepted and trusted. The day did come, and it was a good sign, when the name Bourke was replaced by the nickname "Irish."

the garden where the praties grow

Have you ever been in love my boys
Or have you felt the pain?
I'd sooner be in jail myself
Than be in love again
For the girl I love is beautiful
I'd have you all to know
And I met her in the garden
Where the praties grow.

She was just the sort of creature boys
That nature did intend
To walk right through the world, my boys
Without the Grecian bend
Nor did she wear a chignon
I'd have you all to know
And I met her in the garden
Where the praties grow

Says I, "My pretty Kathleen
I'm tired of single life
And if you've no objection,
Sure I'll make you my sweet wife."
She answered me quite modestly
And curtsied very low
"Oh you're welcome to
the garden where the praties grow."

Oh the parents they consented
And we're blessed with children three
Two girls just like their mother
And a boy the image of me.
And now we're going to train them up
The way they ought to be
For to dig out in the garden
Where the praties grow.

Well now, about this time in my life I decided to make the big move, you know, tie the knot. I had roamed around long enough and I knew, without a doubt, that my love for Kitty Morley was not a passing phase. I knew she had feelings for me and she knew my actions were sincere, but we had never sat down and made a commitment to each other. Time has a way of getting away and the hours I worked were crazy at times. It's hard to have a normal relationship. But when I heard the news, I soon put my priorities in order.

I held her in my arms and sang, *Love Thee, Dearest,*

Love thee, dearest, love thee
Yes, by yonder star I swear
Which thro' too oft dim with tears like him,
Like him my truth will shine,
And love thee dearest, love thee
Yes, till death I'm thine.

Leave, thee, dearest, leave thee
No! that star is not more true
When my vows deceive thee
He will wander too
A cloud of night may veil his light
And death may darken mine
But leave thee dearest, leave thee
No! till death I'm thine!

Kitty told me that she was taking a vacation and had booked her return trip home for May 1953, but in my heart I believed she would never return. The thought crossed my mind that she might have an old boyfriend hanging around. To tell the truth, someone had come for a visit not so long before and that was enough to open my eyes and realize she wasn't going to be available forever.

Well, I said, "Let's go back as man and wife."

And, low and behold she answered, "Yes."

We went to Saint Leo's Church to make the arrangements, and on May 16, 1953 at a 10:00 mass, Father Debricks married us. Jim Fitzpatrick stood for me and my nephew, Dick Curtin and Kitty was fortunate enough to have her two sisters as attendants, Mary of course and Della, who had arrived a few weeks earlier. There was a brunch right after the ceremony at the original Beverly Woods Restaurant on Western Avenue. Then, everyone went back to the Curtin's house for a party that lasted well into the night. More friends and family arrived in the evening and we danced, sang and ate till the wee hours of the morning. There was plenty for everyone, as well as the traditional *Irish fruit cake* made with Kitty's mother's recipe:

Cake ingredients

1 pound butter	*½ pound yellow raisins*
1 pound brown sugar (light)	*½ pound almonds*
1 pound flour	*¼ pound cherries*
½ pound currants	*½ pound mixed peel*
½ pound raisins	*6 eggs*
½ glass of brandy	

Beat well butter and sugar and add well-beaten eggs
Very slowly add flour, fruit and brandy (fold in ingredients)

Bake four hours in a low oven 300 to 325 Fahrenheit

1st Topping - Marzipan

3 packages of almonds grounded
½ pound brown sugar
1 egg
½ cup brandy
3 drops of almond extract

Mix together and form a paste. Roll out and press over cooled cake.

2nd Topping - Icing

½ pound powder sugar
2 eggs – white only, whipped
1 ounce of lemon juice

Separate egg yolk from white and whip the white until stiff. Add lemon.
Mix in powdered sugar. Cover entire cake.

We never went to bed that night. The train was leaving early the next morning for New York and we had a long day ahead of us. The hours flew by this time; we had so much to talk and laugh about. The ferry was waiting at the port ready to take us out to our ship, *The Georgia*. It was here that I had my first experience with blatant rudeness from an Englishman. Kitty, Margaret and myself were seated on deck chairs while the children were exploring.

An Englishman approached me saying, "You don't belong here. This is first class!" Well, needless to say, I had to answer him. My first instinct was to haul back and give him a good slap with my fist. I certainly was not going to prove myself by showing a ticket, and we were not going to move. I stood up and looked him square in the eye and said,

"Stand off to the side with me so I can have a word with you."

I don't know if this shocked the son of a bitch or not, but he obliged. Well between gritted teeth I gave him a mouthful of his own rudeness and finally he turned and left with his "tail between his legs." I kept a watchful eye out for him, but never caught sight again. He was only a weak and mouthy man who had too much money and used his power to intimidate the less fortunate. Although as I think back, he didn't look seasick and probably had a better time than I did as my stomach lurched up and down.

We were traveling on the *S.S. Georgia*, a beautiful cruise ship, but I waited too long to book my passage. Kitty and I ended up in separate berths, and this was our honeymoon. It didn't matter. The weather wasn't with us and the storms we hit were terrible. Nearly everyone was seasick. I seldom saw anyone until land was sighted and we disembarked at Belfast City and from there caught the train to Ballina Station.

As Kitty often said, "Small loss," and she was right, we were together and on our way home. We were happy!

It had been eighteen years since my sister Margaret had left home and had not made a trip back yet. "Think about traveling with us," I said one day. It didn't take long for her to make a decision and she booked for three, herself, Donna and Johnny.

I rented a car and headed straight for Ballymacredmond and they were all waiting. What a welcome home and a Céad Míle Fáilte (welcome) for my wife. There, for the first time in many years stood Margaret with John, Dick, Michael, Jim, Bridgie, Nellie, Pat was home from England for a week, Teasie from Scotland and myself. As much as Kitty wanted to get to Redhill, we couldn't leave for two days. Everyone was down to meet the new bride and the hours passed quickly.

There was company at the old house every night and some good old songs were sung, as well as *The Old Turf Fire:*

Oh, the old turf fire
And the hearth swept clean
There is no one so contented
As myself and Paddy Keane
With the baby in the cradle
You can hear her Granny say,
"Won't you go to sleep Álanna,
while I wet your daddy's tay.

Oh the man that I work for now
Of noble blood is he
But sure somehow I'd be tellin' you
We never can agree
He has big towering mansions
He has castles great and tall
But I'd not exchange the roof that crowns
My own thatched cottage hall.

So I've got a little house and land
As neat as you could see,
You'd never meet the likes of them
This side of Lisnaskea
I've no piano in the room
No pictures on the wall
But I'm happy and contented
In my little marble hall.

Oh the old turf fire
What a welcome now it brings
As the cricket chirrups gaily
While the kettle also sings
And we all join in the chorus
With a merry lilting song,
And the kindly neighbors "droppin'in"
To join the happy throng.

Round the old turf fire
Sit the old folk bent with years,
As they watch us trippin' lightly
And they smilin' through their tears
For so sadly they are dreaming
Of their youthful heart's desire
In those dear old days so long ago
Around the old turf fire.

Oh, the old turf fire
And the hearth swept clean
There is no one so contented
As myself and Paddy Keane
With the baby in the cradle
You can hear her Granny say,
"Won't you go to sleep Alanna,
while I wet your daddy's tay.

Finally, we headed for Redhill and Kitty was crying before we turned the car on the last road that would lead to her home. What a welcome home! A mother and a father to have their daughter return from America was really something special. Her father held her in his arms, almost in reverence, and the tears in everyone's eyes were tears of happiness.

I can still remember, as if it were yesterday, Kitty's grandmother grabbing my hand and asking me to move into the light so she could see my face better.

She said, "I heard you were nice looking."

She was all of one hundred years of age with a great sense of humor and still knitting while sitting by the fire. It was during one of our many conversations that she told me about children and the joys and the sadness that they bring. There was something in her eyes that I never forgot. Now as an old man, and after raising my children, I understand. I never lost a child to immigration.

I was fortunate that the Santa Fe granted me a three month leave of absence for my honeymoon. We spent the weeks going back and forth and around the villages and towns of Mayo and seeing the sights in other parts of Ireland. This may appear to some as a very long holiday, but don't forget it took a long time to arrive at your destination and then, traveling even by car wasn't all that easy. Ireland's roads were terrible. It would take several hours to arrive at a destination, whereas today, it might only take one hour.

The weather was lovely. In fact, some days were unusually warm, actually hot for Irish conditions. This made the tar on the main roads bubble, which then caused a puncture in the tire. The car tires were not steel belted. If a tire had a puncture, it was repaired with the same rubber material and glued on similar to our bicycles of today. But what was happening to me, the heat caused the glue to melt and the patches were coming off the tire.

This is no lie. Kitty and I were talking about getting away for a few days on our own and decided to go to County Kerry. We had seven flat tires in one day. When the last one happened, it was late and I knew we were in trouble. All the garages were closed and it was a long walk back to the town we had just passed through.

I was standing beside the car when I spotted the roof of a car, between the hedges, coming down the windy road towards us. A man, a complete stranger, pulled to the side and offered to help. All through life one tends to recall the negative things that a person has done. Well, this man I will never forget, and I have told the story many, many times, but for the life of me now, I can't remember his name, although I bet I'd be able to find his house again.

I said, "I've had seven punctures from Ballina today alone."

With a nod he went to the boot of his car and pulled out his own spare tire. "I'll give you mine if you return it."

I explained that we were on our honeymoon and were on our way to Kerry and with the intention to drive the beautiful and scenic Ring of Kerry. I said, "It will be a few days before we are back this way."

"No rush," He said, "You know where I live," As he pointed to a house up the field.

On our way home to Mayo, Kitty and I stopped at his house to switch. This gentleman had taken the tire to the garage, had the puncture repaired and with a wave and a "good luck" refused money. But, I know I pushed a pound note in his pocket, which more than covered the repair and service. Money could never have repaid his kindness and generosity. That was enough sight seeing. For the remainder of our time in Ireland we stayed where we belonged, with our family and friends.

My sister Nellie was so mad at her husband Paddy McHale. She had just found out that he had pulled a fast one on her, and had no remorse. I could hear him laughing at the door when my brother Jim, Kitty and myself walked in. With the good weather, Paddy had been going to bog every day now for a couple of weeks and, as usual, Nellie made a sandwich for his lunch.

That morning Nellie had said to Paddy, "I've been up the fields a few times this week and I've not seen the auld ass. Is it alright?" She didn't see the donkey everyday, but at some point it would appear.

"Arrahh, the auld ass is fine, just wandering about," Paddy had answered.

Nellie had it in the back of her mind that there was something strange going on, so that morning after Paddy left with his sandwich, she waited a bit and then followed. There was only one road that could be used, and sure enough, Paddy had been walking the road – there was his sandwich stuck between two rocks in the ditch and further up a bit was another sandwich.

Nellie was waiting when Paddy arrived home with a big smile. He knew it was over, as he said, "The proofs in the pudd'n" and he came clean with the story.

While walking the road to the bog with his auld donkey and cart, he met a family visiting in the area. Well the children loved the auld ass and asked if they could sit on him. Paddy, being the nice and obliging man that he was, handed the reigns over and for a good while the children took turns sitting on him. Paddy said that they took all sorts of photographs and then, it was time to go. The little children started to cry and asked their father to please buy the nice donkey.

The father said, "How much?" Paddy gave a fair price and the man paid him on the spot. Well, he decided that there was no point in rushing to the bog now; he may as well go for a few jars.

"Sure Nellie," He said, "We needed a younger ass."

"Willie," she said, "He's above in the pub enjoying the money from the donkey and the turf needs cutting."

Well there wasn't a concern in Paddy McHale's face about the turf as he laughed and said, "If you know so much, why are you telling me?"

But my sister wasn't laughing as much as we were. She was still angry about the gambling incident that was fresh in her mind. Paddy McHale loved the horse races and had come home from the pub with a tip from an auld fellow. He told everyone and collected a good bit of money to place on the horse. So Paddy and Nellie went to the races the next Sunday and the favorite won the race.

The race was over and Nellie hadn't seen Paddy since he went to collect the winnings. However, on the way home she soon found out why.

"Nellie, I played a different horse and it lost."

It silenced Nellie. She didn't know what to say to the blaggard.

"Well," said Nellie to Paddy, "You're taking me out to dinner."

Paddy was seated at the table with the appearance of a man without a care in the world. He leaned over to me and whispered, "Isn't it God that has sent you. Let's get out of here."

"Oh be jessus," Paddy said as they climbed into the car headed for the pub, "I've a hole in the knee of my pants."

Jim said, "Arraaahh, don't worry who'll see it."

Paddy was quick to reply, "Sure I'll put me foot on me knee and no one will see a thing." We went off together, and the craic was mighty that night as we all sang *Love is Teasing*:

> *Oh love is pleasin' and love is teasin'*
> *And love is a pleasure when first love is new*
> *But as it grows older, sure love grows colder*
> *And it fades away like the morning dew.*
> *I left my father, I left my mother*
> *I left all my sisters and brothers too,*

I left all my friends and my own relations,
I left them all for to follow you.
But the sweetest apple is the soonest rotten
And the hottest love is the soonest cold,
And what cannot be cured love, must be endured love,
And now I am bound for Americay.

And love and porter make a young man older
And love and whiskey make him old and grey,
And what cannot be cured love, must be endured love,
And now I am bound for Americay.
I wish, I wish, I wish in vain
I wish I was a maid again,
But a maid again, I ne'er will be
'Til cherries grow on an ivy tree.

While driving back to Redhill one afternoon, we stopped in Irishtown and it is there that I heard the story about the Village of Kilvine, almost deserted now, just a few miles from Redhill. "Kil" means village and vine, it is said was St. Patrick's sister's name and at one time she lived around this area. According to John Hosty, (my son-in-law's brother) who lives with his wife Pauline in the village of Shanballybocht, Kilvine at one time had ninety eight cottages. It was a flourishing community where everyone worked together. He said that the cottages were built right next to each other, with only enough room for the horse or ass to pull the cart.

John remembers well listening to his father, Patrick telling stories about Kilvine and its people and an incident that happened right around 1900. A farmer who was doing well for himself decided to purchase a new rod iron gate. This was really something special; no one had iron gates. He installed it on the main road and hung a sign that said, "Road leading to Kilvine."

Well, the young lads from the area decided to play a prank. During the night they removed the entire gate and installed it in the neighbor's field – upside down. Well there was such uproar that the priest had to be called. Oh, there was terrible trouble! Down to the village the priest comes asking for the names, but no one gave them up. After the gate was returned and installed again, a song was written about the ruckus and it is still remembered today:

The night it was bright
And the moon it shone light
Stood seven young fellows
All in good cheer
Longgriff, short Burke,
young Jennings were there
Says one to the other,
We ought to take down
John McWalter's magnificent gate.
It was a good gate
A strong gate, painted in blue
It was hung on good hinges
And led to the road
To Kilvine.

The young lads were full of devilment and played another prank on an auld man from the village. The lads knew well that he was taking his two pigs to the fair on this particular morning. He awoke early, hitched the ass and cart, loaded his two pigs and left the ass tied to a tree in order to feed before the journey to town. Well now the old man was feeling a bit lost, with nothing to do but twiddle his thumbs together and so he decided to take a quick jaunt to the pub at the end of the road. He needed a bit of sustenance for the long journey.

The lads were watching and it didn't take them long to make the change. They were watching when he returned. Well he rubbed his forehead, then his face, and began to pace and mumble,

"Where the devil is the ass? The cart? And be jeessuss, where the helllll are miiii pigs?"

Up and down, back and forth the old man went from the tree to his door with his two hands in the pockets and mumbling the whole time. His first thought was that the strap had loosened and the ass wandered. Aaahh, he knew this wasn't very likely. The auld ass was lazy. What else could he do but go inside to think about it.

As he lit the old lamp, the auld fellow nearly fell over as he let out a shout,

"Glory be to God the Almighty! How did this happen?" There in the kitchen was the ass, the cart, and the two pigs just as he had left them outside.

No one ever told the names of the culprits. But for sure there were at least three involved to be able to disassemble the cart and then reassemble it in the short time. Well the auld fellow never made it to town, and he spent the rest of day putting things right. Needless to say the story spread like wildfire and no one for a very long time left their ass and cart unattended.

After the mass departure, mostly due to the famine, Kilvine declined quickly. Today there are only three families still living there. The thatched roofs of the old cottages have caved in around the stone walls. In some areas the grass is so high you would never know that the remnants of what was once a home lay beneath. As the wind blows the grass, you can spot a piece of a stone wall here and there. The old people died and their children are in all corners of the world. I heard a good tale or yarn that I've told for many, many years about another auld couple who lived in the country and they had one daughter, Mary. And it goes like this…

> It was coming up to fair day and the wife wanted her husband to sell the calf and bring home the money. So, to make sure that the money got home straight away and not

side tracked into the pub, Mary was told to accompany her father that day.

Up first thing in the morning and off the two went as happy as can be to spend the day in town. Mary was all excited, but she also knew her mission.

"Mary," said the mother, "Now listen, right after the sale and you are sure that your father has the money, ask to go home."
"I will, mammy," said Mary.

Mary had a wonderful day and forgot all about the time. It wasn't until the darkness came that she remembered her promise and ran for her father. They left straight away and had only crossed the narrow bridge when a crowd of bandits halted the cart and demanded their money.

"We have no money," said the auld man, "What I made I spent."
After searching them both, but to no avail, one of the robbers jumped in the cart and they all disappeared.

"Mary, Mary," asked the father in a frightened voice, "Where did you hide the money?
Mary answered, "In my mouth Daddy."
The auld man sighed and said, "Well it's too bad that your mother's not here, we could have saved the ass and cart.

Well laugh! I should say Cathy, everyone laughed except your Mother. But I knew she didn't mind me telling it, or she'd have told me so.

I have another recitation that is just as good about a man who arrived home drunk and just received a good tongue lashing from the wife. All he could do was fall into the bed and sleep it off. But, he didn't sleep too sound; he had a dream and it went like this:

There's a story now told about the great (name)
And his wonderful dream.
Being tired of working he laid down in bed
And amongst many other things
He dreamt he was dead!

To heaven he went straight
And upon arriving up there
He knocked at the gate.
Saint Peter looked out and in a voice loud and clear
Said, "be gone (name)
For we don't want you here."

Well he turned on his heels and away he did go
at the top of his speed to the regions below.
Well, upon arriving down there
he heard Ole Nick say to his imps
"Now look here boys, we're expecting (name)
down here in the morning, but don't let him in
for to me it's quite clear
he's a very bad boy and we don't want him here."
"Oh, Satan my friend, oh please let me in
And I'll write to wife for some silver and gold."
With a snicker and a snort, Old Nick said,
"And here is some sulfur and some matches
Go make a hell for yourself!"

And just at that moment dear (name) awoke
He jumped out of bed
And in a shivering sweat said,
"Oh that dream I shall never forget,
To heaven I won't go
Oh that I know well,
But it's really too bad
To be kick out of hell!"

moonlight in mayo

It was just a year ago today
I left old Erin's Isle
My heart was throbbin' in the soft light
Of my colleen's smile
In all my dreams I seem to hear
Her sweet voice soft and low
I know she's waiting where we said
Goodbye in old Mayo.

For two Irish eyes are shining
And an Irish heart is pining
And when I kissed her and caressed her
In the gloaming long ago
Loving Irish arms will press me
And true Irish love caress me
And sweet Irish lips will bless me
When it's Moonlight in Mayo.

Her Irish eyes like beacons shine
All in the darkest night
I know the sweet love beams below
Will always fill the world with light
The roses of her cheeks will lend
Enchantment to the sea
And when shamrocks wear the dew
I'll wed my sweet colleen.

It was just a year ago today
I left old Erin's Isle
My heart was throbbin' in the soft light
Of my colleen's smile
In all my dreams I seem to hear
Her sweet voice soft and low
I know she's waiting where we said
Goodbye in old Mayo.

The *S.S. United States* completed its maiden voyage and as the anchor dropped in the New York harbor, our honeymoon was also over. Kitty and I stayed in a hotel near the train station and immediately upon arrival, asked to use a public phone. I had taken advantage of the full three month leave and was anxious to get back into a routine. I "marked up" for work right then and there and had to report in twenty four hours. Kitty was ready to go home also. She had had a miscarriage and wasn't feeling well. Although, we soon found out why she wasn't feeling well, she was pregnant again. We were happy!

Our home was a studio apartment on the third floor in Saint Leo Parish, across the hall from Mary Morley. While we were on our honeymoon, Mary was on the lookout for an apartment for us when we returned. Housing was hard to come by at this time due to the war. The country had not caught up with building supplies or the manpower to build the houses. However, within a few months we moved to a two bedroom, apartment just down the street from the Curtins. It wasn't much, but it was our own little haven. Kitty went about getting it cleaned and putting away wedding gifts and buying whatever else we needed. My nephew John Curtin was around fifteen years old at the time, a great worker and willing to help, but full of the devilment. Kitty had asked him to help wash the windows on the outside and he obliged.

Everything was going along quietly, too quiet, so John decided to play a trick. Kitty had gone into the other room, so he quickly ran down the stairs, laid on the concrete sidewalk beneath the opened window, and yelled. She ran to the window that was now wide open, and of course assumed he had lost his balance while sitting on the ledge and fell backwards onto the concrete. Well, Kitty nearly lost her life as she ran down the stairs, only to hear his laughter.

Another good one was when he said, "I'll paint the pantry."

Kitty had arranged it so that on one side there was food storage and the opposite side there were dishes for decoration, she would stand the saucers behind the cups leaning against the wall.

"I'm finished," said Johnny and left before Kitty could say more than a thank you. Later that day when she took the plates out for dinner, didn't she see what he did. The "sketherroach" had painted around all the plates that were leaning against the wall. How many years ago did this happen and I'm still laughing. Johnny came another day and, without a bother, repainted everything. It was all good fun and brought me good memories.

It was around this time that I received a letter from my brother Pat.

It said, "I'll come to America, if you'll have me." Well of course I'd have him. I never forgot how he took care of me in Scotland. Pat was ready to try his luck in Chicago. Construction work was slow and I had spoken with him about coming to Chicago while on our honeymoon. Kitty invited him to come live with us. He wouldn't have his own room, but where we lived, he would live. Pat was in his late forties now and I knew he needed a home, more than a room to sleep in; he needed family. His lifestyle was rough in England, living alone, moving from one job to the next, and too much idle time in the pubs or the racetracks.

Pat wasn't here yet when another letter arrived from my brother Jim also saying he wanted to cross the pond to America. Jim had heard, "A person finds money thrown in the streets." I don't know who he got this information from, and I never saw dollars growing on trees either. He soon understood, a man worked for his money and did not throw it in the streets.

I didn't realize it until many, many years later that Pat's connection to London was more than just a job or being closer to his native homeland. He had fallen in love with a young girl during the war. However, as many love stories of that time, it ended abruptly with her untimely death.

An air-raid had occurred in London and everyone was in the dark, scrambling for shelter wherever possible. Pat heard the ambulance sirens and he knew his love was driving one of them. He continued to listen and, suddenly, there were more bombs and more bombs. He found out later that her ambulance was hit directly and the occupants killed immediately. She didn't have a chance. He lost the only girl he ever loved and made a promise to her soul that night that he would remain faithful.

Pat always wanted me to sing *The Mountains of Mourne*.

Oh Megan, this London's a wonderful sight,
With people here working by day and by night.
They don't sow potatoes nor barley or wheat
But there's gangs of them diggin' for gold in the street.
At least when I asked them, that's what I was told,
So I just took a hand at this diggin' for gold,
But for all that I found there, I might as well be
Where the Mountains of Mourne sweep down to the sea.

I believe that when writing a wish you expressed
As to how the fine ladies in London were dressed.
Well if you believe me, when asked to a ball
Faith they don't wear a top to their dresses at all
Oh I've seen them myself and you could not in truth
Say if they were bound for a ball or a bath
Don't be starting them fashions now, Megan macree
Where the Mountains of Mourne sweep down to the sea.

You remember young Peter O'Loughlin of course
Well now he is here at the head of the Force.
I met him today, I was crossing the Strand
And he stopped the whole street with one wave of his hand
And there we stood talking of days that are gone
While the whole population of London looked on
But for all these great powers he's wishful, like me
To be back where the dark Mourne sweeps down to the sea.

There's beautiful girls here – oh never you mind
With beautiful shapes nature never designed.
And lovely complexions all roses and creams
But O'Loughlin remarked with regard to the same
That if at those roses you venture to sip
The colors might all come away on your lip
So I'll wait for the wild rose that's waiting for me
Where the Mountains of Mourne sweep down to the sea.

Now there were five Bourkes residing in Chicago. Mary and Pat
hadn't seen each other since she left home and her only memory of Jim
was in the cradle. It was a shame; they were complete strangers. But

we weren't the only sisters and brothers that were separated at early ages due to immigration during these years. It was a great reunion!

Pat hadn't changed; he couldn't be bothered with the dances or any Irish social. On his night off, Pat could be found sitting on a familiar bar stool at a neighborhood tavern sipping his cold beer, and every so often, a short one, or as most people called it, a shot of whiskey. He would take the shot glass filled with V.O. or Canadian Club and drop the whole lot into the stein of beer, and drink it down. This was referred to as "boilermakers."

Sundays were different. Pat would be up early for the fry of bacon and eggs and then to mass in Saint Sabina Church. There was a newsstand at 79th and Loomis where he would buy the daily scratch sheet listing all the races, the horses and their jockeys, and then, hop on the bus to watch the trotters at Hawthorne. When that season finished, he followed the jockeys to Sportsman's Park where sometimes he'd win and sometimes he'd lose. As much as we talk about the curse of drink, gambling is another terrible vice and it took all Pat worked for week after week.

Before we were married one year, I had passed my second exam and Kitty was due with our oldest child, Margaret Mary, who my niece Donna nicknamed Peggy. Sure we didn't know what to do; she weighed 5 pounds 2 ounces at birth and was as tiny of a living creature as we had ever laid eyes on. Pat, Jim and myself often thought she would never survive. We would all arrive home from work and go into the room and pick her up. Kitty would be ready to kill us. We'd wake the baby, she'd begin to cry, and then hand her over.

Peggy wouldn't suck the bottle. She looked so small and I suppose she didn't have the strength, which gradually weakened her causing dehydration. We called the doctor and he came right away to the apartment. There wasn't a thing he could do. All he said was keep trying to make her suck the bottle and left. All night long Kitty was up and down with her. She'd take a small drop here and there, but not enough to make a difference. It was in the middle of the night that the word popped into my mind "Guinness."

I remember well the old women talking in Ireland about the good nourishment in Guinness's Stout; full of vitamins and iron. I went to the liquor store and bought four bottles and let me tell you, this was a big chunk of change from my paycheck. We put an ounce of stout with an ounce of milk, warmed it on the stove, and be jessuusss, Peggy sucked down the two ounces and thrived from then on. She was baptized within a few weeks and my brother Pat and Kitty's sister Mary were Godparents. The doctor came one more time to check on her and as it happened I was home. I told him about my cure and he said, "The old ways are not always the wrong ways."

Well we thought that we were a little smarter the following year. Kitty knew the feelings now of pregnancy and had made arrangements to call my sister Margaret's house for a ride as soon as it was time. I was on the night shift and around midnight Kitty knew she had to go to the hospital. She phoned Connie Curtin who had just bought a new car. It was a good thing Margaret went with or Connie would have gone into a panic - didn't they get caught by a train. Thank God they arrived at the hospital before Catherine Marie arrived, but just barely. Cathy was born in the elevator of Little Company of Mary Hospital in Evergreen Park and was all of ten pounds. She was healthy and a good baby.

My brother Jim "stood" for Cathy at her baptism, which meant he was the Godfather and Kitty's sister Della, the Godmother. He was only here for about two years and never really settled. Jim knew everyone and everyone knew Jim in every tavern and social event that was around from the day he landed in Chicago. Although, I always knew he would end up back in Mayo, which he did shortly after the christening, I was thankful that he made the trip that time. Now he knew what city life was like in Chicago and so there were no regrets as he boarded the plane with a one-way ticket to his home.

The city of Chicago was expanding and modernizing and with that the old must leave and new comes in. The "hod" carriers were no longer needed. Long before the computers, machines were taking jobs away from the working man. Now a machine could lift the bricks onto a platform rather than from a man's back. Pat worked on the last building in Chicago that set pylons with the hod carriers.

Chicago was, and still is, a great city for unions. These unions were organized and run by men who fought for the rights of the working man; a fair wage for a fair day's work. During the late 1950's I found that inflation was up, but the wages remained much the same. It was hard to save money, or to have a budget, and then raise a family in a decent way. I suppose it hasn't changed much over the years. Modern equipment is wonderful, but it also minimized the number of jobs for the working man who can do nothing else. When a profession becomes obsolete, it had and still has a devastating effect on our economy.

However, the union leaders found a way to combine the Hod Carriers with the labor's union and within a short period of time, all the men were back working. Still today there is a worry about medical coverage and pension plans. I have a great respect for our unions and those who represent workers who are not able to stand up for themselves. I learned this a long time ago, that there is strength in numbers and belonging to a union gives a man or woman's job security.

By the late fifties I had witnessed many life-altering inventions and I still say electricity has been the most significant invention for mankind's advancement. The creation of "aspirin" was huge, and then the radio. The radio brought not only news from around the world, but also music and talk shows. It was in 1951 that Jack Hagerty, an Irish-American started the radio show *The Irish Hour* from radio station WPNA 1490 on the A.M. dial. You could hear traditional Irish music and songs, current news about the "auld sod" and every social event that was of interest to the Irish immigrant. Every Saturday morning from 9:00 until 11:00 A.M., if a radio was to be had, the Irish Hour was playing.

Jack Hagerty announced his program without pay every week until his death in 1980. He made this program a non-for-profit radio program, and asked only from those who asked to solicit their cause on the program – not to make a profit from their advertisement. Still today, Jack Hagerty's children have continued his legacy with the Saturday morning Irish Hour that brings news and activities in and around the Chicago land area for the Irish community. For all the years, Jack Hagerty closed his program with a sign-off that his children continue to use today after more than fifty years:

"Say a little prayer for me and my family and a peaceful and united Ireland."

We'd get all the news about any benefits or deaths. It's a fact that we enjoyed going to wakes; not for pleasure, but to see all our friends. I won't deny that I spent longer in the tavern at the corner of the funeral home than I did at the wake. Also, benefits were a source of entertainment during my time. A committee would be setup, a Saturday night booked with music and plenty of drink, sandwiches and homemade bread. It was all voluntary. A donation was accepted at the door and everyone had a great time, as well as helped the family in need.

I'm not exactly sure of this, but I believe that the Irish community was probably the first ethnic group to offer this to comrades in financial trouble. There was no such thing as disability insurance, and since most men worked in the construction field, there were accidents and too often, no medical insurance. Medicine had come a long way, but still men and women were dying from influenza, tuberculosis, infections, etc. and their children had to be cared for and this was a monetary means of helping.

Paddy Concannon was born in Ballyhaunis, County Mayo and aired another program during these early years also from WPNA. I'm not exactly sure why, but the program didn't come in very clear in our house; there was static. I know that the station was a good distance from our house on Bishop Street, so I'm sure this had an affect on the reception. But it always frustrated Kitty and when Paddy was over for the dinner, which he often was, she complained. He'd shake his head and tell her each time that it had nothing to do with him. She couldn't believe this and insisted that he speak to someone, and being a smart man, he agreed to put in the complaint again the following Saturday.

I remember well when Paddy arrived with a Christmas package wrapped with a bow just as he received it from WPNA, and handed it to Kitty. It was a portable radio and she was thrilled. Every year Paddy was given a radio from the station and every year he gave it away to some family. After twenty five years as an announcer for his Irish Hour Program, the station gave him a package wrapped in fancy gold paper, which he brought to the house and gave to our oldest son, Richard Patrick.

Dick was sure it was a transistor radio with an antenna, and actually so was Paddy and that was why he didn't open it. Well, Dick was so disappointed when he saw a gold mantel clock in the box. Kitty wanted to return it, but all Paddy said was, "What will I do with it? Keep it and remember me."

Slánte, fad caoil agus bás in eireann.

Good health, long life, and may you die in Ireland.

BLACKBIRD

I am a young maiden, and my story is sad
For once I was courted by a brave sailor lad.
He courted me strongly by night and by day
But now my dear sailor is gone far away.

If I was a blackbird, I'd whistle and sing
And I'd follow the ship that my true love sails in.
And on the top riggings, I'd there build my nest,
And I'd pillow my head on his lily white breast.

He promised to take me to Donnybrook Fair
To buy me a red ribbon to bind up my hair.
And when he'd return from the ocean so wide
He'd take me and make me his own loving bride.

If I was a blackbird, I'd whistle and sing
And I'd follow the ship that my true love sails in.
And on the top riggings, I'd there build my nest
And I'd pillow my head on his lily white breast.

His parents they slight me and will not agree
That I and my sailor married should be.
But when he comes home I will greet him with joy
And I'll take to my bosom my dear sailor boy.

If I was a blackbird, I'd whistle and sing,
And I'd follow the ship that my true love sails in.
And on the top riggings, I'd there build my nest,
And I'd pillow my head on his lily white breast.

In the spring of 1956 a letter arrived from my cousin and childhood friend, Father John Flynn stating that he would be stopping in Chicago en route from Japan to Ireland. He had been in the missions for eight years now and this was his first trip home. After leaving Currabaggan School, Father Johnny received a five year day-scholarship (which meant he was not a boarder) to Saint Muredach's College in Ballina. This was quite an accomplishment for a poor farmer's son in the west of Ireland at this time in Irish history, and could only mean one thing; Father Johnny Flynn had intellectual intelligence.

Father Johnny was fourteen years of age when he began his secondary education, cycling to and from school each day. The Flynn's lived about four miles from the school. Becoming a priest had crossed his mind, but nothing definite was said. He realized that upon graduation there would be other avenues of employment available other than becoming a priest. However, the unshakable Catholic faith that was instilled in him from his parents as a child was strong and held merit when he announced his decision.

But, it wasn't that easy. If you wanted to be a priest in Ireland you had to attend Saint Patrick's College located in Maynooth, County Kildare, which was the major seminary in Ireland for the education of priests for the Dioceses of Ireland. Tuition fees were high and had to be paid by his parents. There was no question about it, the funds were not available. His father made a small wage, as well as the fact that Father Johnny was the oldest of thirteen. There was only one approach that he could take in order to be a priest - join the foreign mission and his educational fees were waived.

While in high school Father Jack Byrne, a Columban Father from the headquarters of Maynooth Mission to China, visited the college occasionally and spoke to students about the need for missionaries in foreign countries. It was here that the seed was planted and at the age of eighteen, my friend was accepted at Saint Columban College Dalgan Park in Naven, County Meath in September, 1941. However, Father suffered with asthma from childhood, and this was the reason he missed so many days at Currabaggan. He was accepted to Dalgan Park on the condition that the asthma would not be an issue or problem, and if it was, he would have to find another avenue of employment. I am convinced that there was divine intervention since Father never had a problem with the asthma during his seven years of study that followed. Upon his ordination on December 19, 1947, Father was appointed to the Philippine Islands in the fall of 1948 and worked with university students in Manila.

However, after eighteen months Father had to leave because of severe asthma problems, which was due to the weather. He fought for as long as he could, but the body could take no more, so under medical advice, Father was sent to Japan where there was a more temperate climate and never had a problem again. Here Father worked for the next ten years and was then transferred to the Fiji Islands in the South Pacific for the remaining fifteen years of his foreign missionary tenure.

I remember well seeing Father Johnny exit the plane at Midway Airport in Chicago. He was as thin as a rail and wearing sandals. You see men wearing them in public now, but in 1956 you wouldn't see a man in the city of Chicago wearing sandals, let alone at the airport. I found out later, the sandals were not due to lack of funds; it was the culture where he lived and the weather. I was so happy to see him and the feeling was mutual. He stayed with Kitty and me in 1956 and every seven years after that en route back home to Ireland. Upon his arrival, a date was chosen immediately for a party and everyone came to see him. Often Father mentioned the generosity of the people he met in Chicago and how much he appreciated their kindness. He was always so content and happy with his vocation, but also longed for his family and Mayo.

After retiring from the foreign missions, Father Johnny was stationed in the United Sates in the state of California. Here he was assigned for five years, with another priest, to preach in the dioceses of southern California, Arizona, Texas and New Mexico requesting financial support and the need for missionaries. Father's parents were now old and his mother was continuously asking him to return to be closer to them during their final days.

In 1977, Bishop Thomas McDonnel, who was then the Bishop of Killala Diocese, invited Father Johnny to work as a priest in his own native dioceses. Father was appointed to the parish of Bangor Erris in northern Mayo on the Owenmore River, and there he spent the following eighteen years. Father Johnny's family renovated his parent's home where they lived and died, and upon his retirement at the age of seventy five, he returned and resides quite happily.

As we sit and talk today, Father Johnny tells me that his years in the mission were wonderful and if he had to do it all over again, he would not change one day. Prior to working in the missions, he believed that there was only one "color" of Catholicism, which had to be green and Irish.

I asked Father Johnny, "Would you change anything?"

He answered emphatically, "If I were starting life now, I would do the same thing. My life was very fulfilling, happy; I loved the mission and in particular the Fijian people. It was because of their quiet charm and demure temperament that I found true job satisfaction."

My friend, Father Johnny Flynn brought something to my family that cannot be purchased with money. He brought our faith into our humble home. Whenever he would visit, mass was offered in our house daily and all my children were there. And now they have masses in their houses with their children attending and participating as servers and lectors. I feel that we have been blessed with this honor.

In June of 1957 our son Richard was born. Another year flew by quickly and in August of 1958 our third daughter was born. I asked Kitty if I could name this little girl and she said yes. No one knew why she was named JoAnn and not named after one of her ancestors. Well, I'll tell everyone now. On our return voyage, after our honeymoon, there was a movie star on board the ship named JoAnn. She was an entertainer and I thought she was beautiful and I liked the name.

Our two-room apartment was as close to a nursery as anyone had ever seen, but we managed. It was hard on Kitty, but she never complained. Sometimes I would do the wash early in the morning and hang the diapers on the line that ran the length of our back porch. She did everything else that had to be done to run a household, and did it efficiently.

We were saving to buy a house, but we needed a certain amount of accessible cash in case of an emergency. However, there was one thing she would not skimp on and that was buying vitamins for the children. It was very important to her that the children remain healthy, and of course she was right. If the children got sick, a doctor's bill far exceeded the cost of vitamins. It was agreed that we would give up one night out every other week to pay for the vitamins. As the family grew our social life dwindled, and we only attended necessary functions as wakes, weddings, benefits, and so forth.

Kitty and I bought our first home, a Chicago bungalow, at 82nd and Bishop, a 2 bedroom, one bathroom, and a den that was converted into a third bedroom for my brother Pat. Now we had a home. Kitty didn't let the children go far. It was her greatest fear that something would happen, such as a bad fall that would cause broken bones or a cut so bad that stitches were needed. So the only way to prevent this was to keep the children in their own backyard.

Kitty got an awful scare shortly after Billy was born. No matter how Kitty tried to protect the children and watch that they didn't get into mischief, there were always things going on. However this incident gave Kitty gray hair. We weren't in the house long when either Cathy or Dick found matches and started to light them in the bedroom. Of course an article of clothing caught fire and they couldn't put it out, so quickly decided to throw the burning cloth down the basement stairs and close the door. Well, at the bottom of the stairs was another pile of clothes for the wash. Thank God she was able to put it out with the hose from the wash basin and no one was hurt.

Of course they were in trouble and I'm sure she gave them a couple of taps on the bare legs and they were sent to the bedroom. From what I was told, Dick and Cathy were very upset and so decided to run away. It wasn't until dinner that she realized they were gone. The neighbors were out and finally she had to call the police. It was close to an hour later when a neighbor spotted the two, sound asleep, in the corner of our backyard. We had a small plastic pool that was pushed up against the garage and the two went in behind it - but not without some comforts. They brought a loaf of bread, knife and a jar of peanut butter and had made sandwiches. But they also took a pillow, and after eating, fell sound asleep and didn't hear anyone calling. What a fright!

On my day off, and if the weather permitted, I would go to the park with the pram or buggy. Kitty always kept the baby and I'd take the others. I'd stop and buy a quart size bottle of beer and sit down under a tree and enjoy the moment. It seems like yesterday that Dick was in the buggy and Peggy and Cathy racing around picking dandelions to bring home to their mother. These memories are few since I worked as many hours as I could and, whenever possible, picked up side work for cash with a plumbing contractor from the neighborhood.

Three years after moving into our home all four children, Peggy, Cathy, Dick, and Jo Ann had the mumps. It was May 7, 1961 when Kitty felt the labor pains, and again in the middle of the night. There was no one we could ask to come over to stay with four sick children. Everything happened fast; thank God I was home. All I could do was phone for a taxi and explain that it was an emergency, which it was.

It seemed like an eternity, but really it was only minutes when the driver arrived and we got Kitty settled into the back seat. I can still remember kissing her goodbye and her squeezing my hand. Della arrived early the next morning and let me go to the hospital, but it was all over. Kitty was holding our second son, my namesake, and the two were well. I was exhausted from the worry of it all. I often said that I would rather dig a hole fifty feet deep than go through that again. Of course Kitty's reply would be, "Sure, wouldn't anyone think you had the baby!"

These were the baby boom years and there were plenty of children walking to and from Saint Sabina's School. They all traveled together, which was great protection. Peggy was the only one that I remember ever getting sick at school. I was on nights and Billy was just a baby. I walked to the school and when I saw how sick she was, I had to call a taxi to take us home. The little girl had the flu and had vomited all over herself.

Many a night after the children were put to bed, Kitty and I would study. There was always an exam coming up and she would go over the questions with me. One exam in particular I found very hard. I had to identify every part on the diesel engine. I received a hundred percent and if Kitty took the exam beside me, she would have received the same.

The months continued to pass quickly and before we knew it another year was gone. Due to the children, our life became somewhat of a routine. We attended mass at Saint Sabina Church, and our children attended Saint Sabina Grade School. Peggy and Cathy were old enough to go to the school's gym to roller skate on a Saturday. There were social events constantly going on in this parish. However, it was nearly a mile walk to and from the school and, in those days, everyone went home for lunch. So, about seven years later we decided to move to Little Flower Parish, about two miles west.

It was a five minute walk from our home on Bishop Street to Ashland Avenue and there was Lyons' Tavern, which Jim and Hannah now owned, and a few blocks south, John Hackett's Tavern. When I walked into Hackett's I knew the man behind the bar looked familiar. Well, be jeessuss, it took a couple of minutes for us both to register our faces from a memory long ago, and sure enough, didn't we travel together on the train from New York to Chicago when we arrived. It's a small world and as the years passed, it became smaller.

About three city blocks north of our home was where one could find Hanley's House of Happiness. And that was where we found – laughter and good fun. Yes, it was a tavern, but there were plenty of Irish and Irish Americans who never put a drink to their mouths, but visited Hanley's for the atmosphere. Oh the memories I had there with Jack and Kathleen Hanley, both gone for years now, God rest them.

Sunday was a day of rest for the Irish. Often after mass I would stop for a beer on my way home. The kids loved to go and get a bag of chips and a coke. Everyone would give the girls change to play the jute box or to play the shuffle board. This was a treat. The Hanley's insisted that everyone went home for their dinner and the bar was closed from 4:00 until 6:00 P.M. and reopened again in time to prepare for the Irish Hour that broadcasted with Martin Fahey from 8:00 until 9:00 P.M.

Peggy and Cathy loved to go to the Irish Hour. Bringing the children to these events is why the Irish culture has remained so strong in Chicago. Our children knew the Irish music, songs and stories from a young age, and now, have taught them to their children. It was all amateur performances at the Irish Hour and anyone that was able to sing was welcome to come forward and take the microphone.

I remember well seeing three, four, or perhaps five men sitting on the folding chairs above on the small stage with their accordions, fiddles and other instruments entertaining with plenty of music. The Irish step dancers performed every week, the dance floor was always full, and this party continued on well after midnight. I'm sure there were many a sore head on Monday mornings. However, missing work because of alcohol was unacceptable then, and today. There was a saying, "If you are going to hang with the big dogs, you can't piss like a pup."

through the eyes of an irishman

When I was a boy 'round about three
I remember my grandfather saying to me
He said, "Learn to appreciate all that you see
For one day it'll mean so much more to you."
Well without realizing the words he did say
"Sure it started me seeing things a different way,"
Just like the colors of the sun going down in the bay
It was a sight I'll never forget.

And we'll all meet tonight every child, woman and man
For we know in our heart that we'll always be part
Of a proud and wonderful land.
Yes, we'll all meet tonight
And we'll sing as loud as we can
Of an island so green that can only
Be seen through the eyes of an Irishman.

Oh the days of my youth I spent searching around
And I couldn't believe all the beauty I found
Just like the flowers and trees growing up
From the ground full of color and so full of life.
Well at twenty four years that's when I started to roam
But it didn't take much to remind me of home
And I think of all the places and people I've known
That I may never see again.

I was as predictable as I was reliable. Anyone working my shift knew I'd be at the end of the fire road at least one hour before starting time ready for a game of cards. It was against every rule and regulation to gamble on the premises of the Santa Fe Railroad. The railroad police, referred to as "gumshoes" would take your name and you would be fired; that was the penalty. But, everyone was careful and looked out for each other. Even when the trainmaster entered the locker room, he respected the men's privacy and would yell, "Trainmaster coming in," before opening the door, which gave us time to stick the cards in our pockets. There weren't too many switchmen that didn't know how to run my engine; I made damn sure he could. How do you think I got so good at playing rummy?

I learned a good lesson early in my career about gambling. There were six of us in the locker room this particular afternoon and, as human nature leads us, we were careless; no one was on lookout. In walks the gumshoe and takes all our names down. I won't deny that I was scared. This offense could not be taken lightly. However, there was one fellow in the group that didn't seem too concerned. I had heard that he was connected to the syndicate, but never paid any attention to it. Well, when I heard him say, "I'll take care of this!" I had a suspicion that I knew how, and I won't deny, I hoped it was true. The next thing I heard was that a contract was put on this gumshoe. Needless to say, the investigation was canceled and the gumshoe transferred further down the line. Those were different times.

In the beginning I took an awful teasing from the guys about my lunch. I carried a dinner rather than a lunch. It was neatly packed in a brown paper bag consisting of a piece of meat, such as a steak or pork chops, two slices of toasted bread wrapped separately, a sliced onion, carrot, and pickled beets. Kitty always made sure I had a couple of pieces of homemade raisin bread with jam. If I had to work overtime, this would keep me until I got home. I'd put the meat on the old hot water tanks above in the engine and it would be good and warm when it was time to eat. Later when the electric sidewall heaters were installed, that's where you'd find the brown bag. It never entered into my mind to go to a restaurant and buy food; not when I had better at home and didn't have to pay for it.

The 1960's brought many changes to the United States and to the Santa Fe Railroad's Corwith Yard. One major addition was the hiring of African Americans. There were no African Americans working in Corwith Yard when I was hired. Fowler was one of the first hired and I was fortunate to call this young man my friend.

During the first few weeks, Fowler was working steady with me and, as I said the name calling was part of the railroad's culture. Well, I would hear Fowler and other African Americans calling each other "nigger." I didn't realize that it was not acceptable for me to say this, but to tell you the truth, I thought nothing of it.

I really didn't know that he didn't like it when I called him that name until one day he stopped, looked me in the eye and said, "Stop calling me nigger."

Shocked at his request, I answered immediately, "What, I'm not as good as the others!"

He could tell I was sincere and that he had taken me completely off guard. I wasn't calling him this name in a disrespectful way, although I never said it again. It came to my mind that Fowler had been dealing with prejudice men his whole life, and I'm sure some were Irish, even though the Irish were looked down upon for many, many years. From that day on, we were friends. Under my fine tutelage he soon perfected the game of rummy and many a pint of whiskey we shared during the cold winter nights. Fowler took good care of me until my retirement. In fact, Fowler's wife, who was a nurse, picked me up many a night standing at the bus stop and dropped me at the fire road.

Thirty five years I worked at Corwith and had one bad accident, and it was not my fault. It occurred at 47th and Archer in 1972. The collision put my engine over the viaduct. Can you imagine seeing the engine, pulling a full freight train, dangling over the bridge onto a main thoroughfare? I remember like yesterday seeing the engine coming for me, and without a doubt, I knew I had to jump. I hit the guardrail and broke seven ribs, not to mention all the other bumps and bruises. My fireman, who was training with me at the time, didn't make it completely away from the engine and shattered his leg and heel. It was just luck on my part; I went out one side of the engine and he went the other side. After an investigation it was discovered that the oncoming train missed the switch and we literally had a head-on collision.

Everyone kept asking if I was hurt, and at the time, I didn't think so. The train master said he would drive me home and I accepted. We took a detour to 81st and Ashland and stopped for a good stiff or strong, drink at Jim Lyons' tavern. Before leaving, he put a $10.00 bill on the bar, and so, I was good for the day. By the time I arrived home, my side had turned purple, but I felt great, no pain at all, and was singing Eileen Álannah for them all. Kitty knew better and called a taxi and we went to the hospital. After a couple of hours, let me tell you, I was suffering from the accident and from the drink.

No one could understand why I didn't sue the Santa Fe for money. I never sued anyone in my life and I wasn't going to, and that was my final word on the subject. It was an accident and I truly believed that the money would bring no luck. It was an accident. The Santa Fe Railroad paid me for the six weeks I was off recuperating and that was good enough. I thought that was fair. I said to my son, Dick, "How can I sue the company that is paying me?"

I watched Neil Armstrong, walk on the moon and saw jets soar into the heavens. Kitty wanted an automatic washer and then the machine that would automatically dry the clothes. We were watching colored television and taking colored photographs. Man was so intelligent, and yet another war was coming. Vietnam was on the news now and, as the saying goes, "I could smell the dirt behind it." I wasn't too wrong either. The conflict was never named, but men were sent by the hundreds and then thousands, and again as in previous wars, too many were hurt and too many died.

This was a time that changed the way men and women once thought, or at least, believed was the right way. We all crowded around the television to watch the Beetles perform on the Ed Sullivan Show and a new era of music and free love evolved. The men wore long hair and side burns and I could see more legs than ever imagined with the miniskirt.

I remember well a story told to me by Jack Chambers when his son Tom wanted to borrow the car to take Cathy on date. He said, "Tom, get a haircut and you can have the car!"

Tom threw back the words, "Jesus Christ had long hair."

"Well," Jack said, "If you want to look like Jesus Christ, you can ride an ass."

The Second Vatican Council took place, which had me looking face to face with the priest on the altar who was saying mass. Latin was gone and masses were in English. The best change of all was when the nuns replaced their old habits with a more modern dress. My God they had to be hot in the summer, and I'm sure not warm enough in the winter. I often thought that it was penance for those women to wear such outfits. Their veils would be wet with sweat in the summer, and no air conditioning or fans. In the winter I'd watch the wind blow their black cloaks and veils as they trudged through the snow.

Over the years I have read countless headlines in the newspapers, and I wonder today, if it is just my imagination or are we still talking about the same deficits, health issues, funding for education, murderers and swindlers. Again, on the news our soldiers are in the Middle East fighting another war. I do wonder what is being done to help the military men and women who are returning with physical or mental problems. How are they coping with everyday life or adapting to a so-called normal life?

It took fifty-two years before my friend Mike Fitzpatrick received his American citizenship papers. This was accomplished only through the persistence and faith of his sister Mary (Mae) Fitzpatrick Doody and her extended family. Prior to the passing of a recent Bill in Congress, a soldier only became an American citizen if he/she survived during their term serving in the armed forces. Now, however, if an immigrant is killed while enlisted, they will automatically receive citizenship. Isn't that the way it should be. This soldier has died for our country in the name of democracy, and is entitled to their rightful place in American history and whatever benefits are available.

As far back as I can remember, there has been talk about hard times and bad luck, but really, these were the best years of my life. I had my family around me and my health. What more could a man want? I was able to get up for work in the morning and I had a job to go to, and received a fare wage as well. Sometimes a person has to take a step back and really look at what he or she has and ask, "What do I really need?" Now, of course I wanted more for my children, but more importantly, I want them to be true to their father's name and be willing to work hard for what they wanted.

I would say, "No one will give you anything free, nor should you expect it. You must work for it." It's sound advice. Once a person has to work to pay for something, then it is appreciated. I am great at giving this advice now, but believe me I got caught up in the long hours at work and the drink.

There really was an Irish fellowship in Chicago that strengthened during the years between 1948 and 1952. We knew how to play, but more importantly, the vast majority of the Irish formed a strong bond of allegiance to each other in this wonderful country called the United States of America. I don't know if I will ever be able to explain or describe the camaraderie that was found amongst us. Our Irish culture that has so often been described with humor and laughter, as well as quick to shed a tear when sad, will never be lost. We have instilled this into our children, not by speaking, but actions through faith, family, and friends.

I have been fortunate enough to have made seventeen trips over the years to my native County Mayo. I had a drink in the pub where John Wayne and Maureen O'Hara filmed *The Quiet Man* and I stood in Ashford Castle and had a drink at the bar. Several years ago John's grandson, Gerry Duffy, a railroad Engineer, took me for a ride in his train from Ballina Station to Dublin City and back again. I never would have thought or even conceived the notion that I would have experienced these things.

Two years ago when I made a trip back with Peggy and Cathy, I was told that Mount Falcon Castle had been sold and the owners were Catholic.

"Well I'll be damned," I said, "The Knox Family must be turning in their graves."

I wanted to see the castle, but the scaffolding was all around the building and the inside was also being renovated. I believe it is now opened as a hotel, and from what I hear, it is lovely. I hadn't seen the castle in nearly seventy years. Think of the changes that have happened in Ireland since then. Hopefulness is indestructible. It has revealed itself through hundreds of years from despair, to anticipation, to the Ireland we see today.

I was blessed with my parents, my sisters and brothers, my wife and children, wonderful friends, and now my grandchildren are around me, as well as great-grandchildren. All the other worries throughout my life have been, as Kitty often told me, "a small loss." I have had many, many more happy days than sad ones and I have always appreciated the gift of life. However, when Kitty died, a part of me died as well. My religion says that when I die, I will meet all those who have gone before me. I am not afraid, and when the time comes, I'll have a smile on my face and I'll reach for the hands that held my hand through life.

an irish lullaby

Over in Killarney
Many years ago
My mother sang a song to me
In tones so sweet and low.
Just a simple little ditty
In her good old Irish way
And I'd give the world if she could sing
That song to me this day.

Too-ra-loo ra-loo-ra
Too-ra-loo-ra-li
Too-ra-loo-ra-loo-ra
Hush now don't you cry!
Too-ra-loo-ra-loo-ra
Too-ra-loo-ra-li
Too-ra-loo-ra-loo-ra
That's an Irish lullaby

Oft in dreams I wonder
To that little cot again
I feel her arms a-huggin' me
As when she held me then.
And I hear her voice a-hummin'
To me as in days of yore
When she used to rock me fast asleep
Outside the cabin door.

It was January, 2006 and our Chicago winter was not severe – not the way I remembered winters as a child or young woman going downtown to work. It has been said that El Niño created a weather change, but also global warming has impacted our Midwestern state dramatically. We have a few dreary, wintry, cold and snowy days, but before you know it, the sun is out, the streets are dry and the air feels crispy cold. It was on a day like this that my brother agreed to go with Dad.

"Dick," Dad shouted from the kitchen, "Take me for my license."

Dick was stretched out in his bed watching television, but with Dad's request he sat up slowly, stretched and rubbed his hand across his mouth, and squeezing his eyes shut he admitted, Dad wasn't giving up. He was so stubborn and adamant about renewing his driver's license. So what if it expired!

Well, Dick thought, "It's now or never." This topic had been argued many times during the past month and it had gnawed in Dick's mind daily. He knew that not allowing Dad to renew his driver's license would make an impact on his idea of independence, but it would be safer for him, and God knows, everyone else. He shouldn't be driving; he was too old. Well, talking and explaining obviously hadn't worked, so it was on to Plan B.

"Dad," Dick said, "They're not going to pass you. Why go through all this."

"We'll see. Drive me over." He says in a soft voice looking down.

There was only one way to end this. Dad had to go through the test and then be told, by an instructor, that he failed. It would be better for his self-esteem not to have to go though this, but there was no reasoning with him. Actually, Dick decided that this would work out to his benefit; the instructor would be the bad guy.

"Let's go now before I have second thoughts and I get cold feet," said Dick.

"Up yours," Dad answers with a grin and was out the door and in the car – on the passenger's side.

"Dad, drive so you are more relaxed!"

"What the sh… are you talking about? Aaarrahh, I don't have a nervous bone in my body. I've been driving for years. I can teach these young fellows how to drive."

Oh my God! This wasn't good. "Dad", Dick asked, "Did you have any drink?"

He gives that quick tilt of his head and looked straight in my eyes, "Not a drop!"

All that went through my mind was the word *bullshit*. But if he had something it wasn't much and it was a good while ago. We got in line and started the procedure. About an hour later we were standing in the area where the instructor goes in the car with Dad.

A man approached who was as short as he was wide and asked a few questions. He specifically asked Dick, "About how much driving does your father do on a daily basis?"

Dad was standing there when Dick answered "He goes to church and my sister's house a couple of blocks away."

"All right," he said, "Let's go to the car."

I gave the keys to Dad and with a nod of encouragement, they left. Four or five cars pulled out at the same time, all with senior citizens and they all pulled back into the parking lot within a half hour. One, then another and another, but no sign of Dad. Dick began pacing and that silent dread of what might have happened was creeping into his mind. And then, the silver Buick appeared and turned slowly, and continued to crawl to the stop sign. The instructor got out, no smile, with a pallid color and emphatically stated, "He sucks! He cut off a cement truck! He's terrible, terrible!"

What made my brother laugh and all of us was that Dad continued to blame the cement truck and said, "I had the right of way!" and "The truck saw me!" Well, as it happens the instructor agreed to pass him, but with the understanding that he drove only in the neighborhood.

Dick said, somewhat relieved, "Come on, let's go home," and as he held the door for Dad to go through, Dad turned back for his last hurrah and shouted "You fat f…!" There was a grin on his face from ear to ear and the renewed license in his hand.

Dad hadn't left the neighborhood in several years or surpassed twenty-five miles per hour. None of this had to do with driving; it was a matter of pride. He put his license into his wallet and walked around to the passenger's side very pleased with himself.

Dad never drove the car with his new license, but every so often he would turn the key in the cold weather. Early that summer, he gave it to his granddaughter Colleen to use for work and school.

That summer Tom and I moved to a home that had an extra bedroom and fewer stairs. I told Dad that the room was for him, but he was having a hard time settling. When he stayed he would get confused and go into the wrong bedroom, up instead of down and so forth. I left him alone one morning for about a half hour and when I returned, he had never moved from the chair. He was afraid of getting lost. I noticed in the mornings he would stay in bed longer, and I finally realized what was going on; he wasn't sure where he was at and was waiting for some noise or familiar voices. I left lights on and doors opened, but from dusk until early morning, Dad was restless.

We had a wonderful Christmas and celebrated Dad's birthday on New Years Day, 2007. Our family is growing and Dad loved being around his grand and great-grandchildren. It is the children that really make holidays enjoyable and meaningful. Now with the holidays gone, life for all of us took on a normal pattern, and we watched the winter turn to spring. This was good for Dad and now he would sit outside, smoke his pipe and walk around a little more to strengthen his legs. That was what we wanted and expected, just like every other spring that we could remember, but this time it wasn't happening.

The doctor said that he probably was having mini-strokes. It was early June and he had been with me for four days and, I knew he was failing. He didn't want to be alone, but he wanted to go home, so arrangements were made. It seemed like it happened over night. I had to take his hand and walk with him to the door. He stopped me that morning and said, "Cathy, old age has caught up with me. I know I'm dying." I told him he was talking nonsense and he would be around for a long time. But, as I pulled out of the driveway my heart was breaking, because I knew that this would be my father's last visit.

We all decided that it was best for Dad to stay in his own home. He did much better with his familiar surroundings. And so, the weeks went by and we realized that Dad was not going to get better. He would never be as strong and lively as he once was and he needed to be cared for day and night. He went from his bedroom to the living room to the kitchen and back to bed.

For more than two years Dad and I have been talking and reminiscing about his childhood memories. I had a feeling that I pulled everything from him that he could recount and, again we talked about putting all this information into print. I told him that it was going to be a book. I can still remember that night. He was really happy about this idea. However, I warned him not to say anything to anyone until I finished, because if I didn't, there would be no pressure.

Well, my son Kevin drove him home that night and when he returned he said, "Mom, you're writing a book?"

I had a stupid look on my face and it took ten seconds before it registered. I asked, "Did Grandpa say that?"

Kevin explained that he had walked ahead of Grandpa to open the car door and as he got into the seat, he said, "Kevin, did you hear your mother is writing a book about me?"

Now I was committed!

Dad wanted this book to be ready for Saint Patrick's Day of 2007, but what he didn't anticipate, or I, was that he would not be well. There was a gradual change, nothing too drastic that made any of us concerned, but as I look back now I suppose the signs were there. He slept later, took more naps, ate less, and started to tell one story and finish it with another. But still, I attributed this all to aging, and it was okay. Peggy made the doctor's appointments and followed up with everything possible to make Dad comfortable, and he was. By midsummer of 2007 Dad was diagnosed with dementia, however, this disease has a mind of its own. There is no way to tell how a person will succumb.

I remember asking many times, "Do you have any pain?"

And, always he answered, "Just in my legs - besides that, not an ache or a pain."

I never said the word dementia in front of Dad, nor did any of my sisters and brothers, but he knew exactly what was happening. He told Peggy that he wasn't remembering the way he used to. She told him not to worry, that she would remember for both of them. He hated being dependent and many times he apologized for being so troublesome. Sometimes, I prayed that the dementia would make him forget immediately what was going on around him. It was early August now and he was noticeably weaker, but still able to eat in the kitchen, but his movements were very slow. His gait was worse, but he could still call us by name.

One of the moods that a person with dementia usually feels, at some point during the illness, is agitation. When Dad went into this phase, my sister JoAnn brought a compact disk with a variety of familiar Irish ballads. Several of them are in this book. She put the music on next to his bed and, I am not lying, it was better than any sedative. He sang himself to sleep and woke up many times singing that same song. For five weeks the same disk played over and over again. We all began to memorize the words to the songs.

Dad had been sleeping for two days so the doctor stopped the medicine for agitation. Once he was more alert, he would adjust his medication. We all took turns staying with him, but for some reason I decided to take a ride over on Friday evening about 7:00. My sister Peggy was there and we sat and talked for an hour. JoAnn had told us that Dad was praying in Gaelic all morning, first the Our Father and then the Hail Mary, over and over. His voice was strong and we really thought that he would snap out of this comatose state at any moment. Before leaving, I remember standing in his bedroom doorway; staring at him in the hospital bed, so sound asleep. He was snoring, not loud, just that even, methodical in and out breathing that I had listened to many times. I regret not sitting with him or talking to him. All I did was whisper, "See you in the morning, Dad."

When the phone rang around 9:00 on Saturday morning and I heard the tears in Peggy's voice, I cannot express the sadness that I felt. Dad would say, "Isn't this life – one must live in order to die." There was no struggle; he was at peace. Dad had lived a good, healthy and long life. There were no regrets, and I know he had no regrets because I asked, and he told me so. All those hours that I sat with him gave me the opportunity to meet a man that otherwise would have died with so many secrets about my family and his beloved Parish of Knockmore, near the town of Ballina in the County of Mayo.

Bill Bourke was just a boy from home who had great faith and prayed everyday. He loved his wife and family, and I discovered without question that no words are necessary where there is unconditional love. He was a proud Irishman who appreciated the opportunities that were offered to him in the United States of America, and never took them for granted.

Once Dad said, "Cathy, stay with it!" Did he mean stay with finishing this book or just life? I suppose it is all one in the same. As I write these last few lines, I can hardly believe that he is gone and won't be here to see this book in print. I'm wrong. He is with me now, and always!

Printed in the United States
137432LV00003B/1/P